REFERENCE MANUAL FOR

Stenographers and Typists

RUTH E. GAVIN

City College of San Francisco
San Francisco, California

E. LILLIAN HUTCHINSON

Coauthor, *Business English and Communication,
Second Edition—Words, Fourth Edition*

THIRD EDITION

GREGG PUBLISHING DIVISION

McGraw-Hill Book Company, Inc.

New York   Chicago   Dallas   San Francisco   Toronto   London

Published by Gregg Publishing Division

McGraw-Hill Book Company, Inc.
Printed in the United States of America

About this manual

This manual has been designed for ready reference and use by persons engaged in any one of many different pursuits—as students or as workers. For example, it is designed for the stenographer who transcribes dictation in an office, as well as for the student who is preparing to do this kind of work; for the typist who types manuscripts, reports, and other materials, and for the student who is learning to do so; for the advertising copywriter who types his own copy; for the author who types the manuscripts of his books or articles—in short, for anyone who works with words, and principally through the medium of the typewriter. Such students and workers will find in these pages answers to many of the puzzling questions that constantly arise in the endeavor to turn out acceptable typescripts and mailable letters.

The importance to a stenographer or a typist of being able to produce an acceptable typescript quickly on the first writing is dramatically proved by the results of recent surveys showing that over $5,000,000 is spent daily in the United States on business correspondence and that the average cost of a letter is approximately $1.80. The rewriting of letters or reports to achieve acceptable copies is not only costly to the employer in time and stationery but most discouraging to the stenographer or the typist.

The first two sections of the manual, "Efficiency in Taking Dictation and in Transcribing" and "Getting the Most Out of Your Typewriter," summarize the "know-how" that efficient stenographers possess as part of their technical skill. Those who require a more complete treatment of the topics are referred to basic texts on transcription and typewriting.

In the sections that deal with the details of punctuation, capitalization, use of figures, word division, and abbreviations, the aim has been to select, from the multitude of problems that *might* arise, those that are encountered again and again. Where authorities differ—and they do differ—the style favored in standard business practice has been selected. A separate section has been provided for the guidance of those wishing to know the preferred social forms.

Many offices have their own style rules. Stenographers in such offices should, of course, adhere to these rules rather than to the ones presented here.

The sections on "Helps for the Puzzled Speller" and "Your Grammar Is Showing" present practical tips for "licking" typical spelling and grammar "puzzlers." The rules are not intended to supplant the dictionary and the English grammar that should be a part of the desk equipment of every stenographer and typist.

The exercises at the close of the manual may be used either as a self-testing device or by the teacher who uses this manual as a class text.

To all the inquiring, earnest students whose reiterated questions have been the inspiration for this book, the authors express their gratitude.

RUTH E. GAVIN
E. LILLIAN HUTCHINSON

Contents

SECTION 1

Efficiency in taking dictation and in transcribing

PEN AND PENCILS

1   Even though you use a pen, have several well-sharpened pencils at hand for an emergency. (Notes written in ink are more legible.)

NOTEBOOK

2   Start each day with the *date* written in longhand; for example, *Nov. 10, 19—*. Many stenographers write the date in the lower left corner of the page for ease in reference.

3   Cancel notes (with a diagonal line) as each letter is transcribed.

4   Check the notebook at the end of each day to be sure you have transcribed all notes.

5   Keep a rubber band around the notebook (at last page used) to avoid thumbing pages already transcribed.

6   Use a distinctive mark (perhaps a line) to indicate the end of each letter dictated.

7   Number each letter.

8   Use letters or figures (encircled) to indicate changes or insertions in notes. For instance: Place an encircled Ⓐ at the point in the notes where an insertion or a change is to be made. Key the insertion or change in the same way. When, in transcribing, you reach the Ⓐ, refer to the notes also marked Ⓐ at the end of the letter. If the dictator is accustomed to making many changes during dictation, keep one side of the notebook page free for these changes.

9   Be efficient in turning notebook pages. One method is to keep both hands on the notebook, using the left hand to keep the book steady and the left thumb to move the page gradually upward as the bottom of the page is approached.

10   Use longhand in your notes to write:
  a) The name of the addressee, unless it is familiar to you, to be sure of the correct spelling; for example, *ec welford.*
  b) Street names if you are not sure of the spelling.
  c) Any doubtful words, trade names, or other unusual words.

11   Underscore in your notes as follows:
  a) Use one line under words or groups of words that are to be underscored in the transcribed letter. (Such words would appear in italics in printed material.)
  b) Use two lines under words or groups of words that are to be typed in all capital letters.

c) Use three lines to indicate that the words are to be typed in all capital letters and underscored.

12   Make provisions for special instructions from the dictator.

a) Special instructions referring to the letter just dictated should be written above the notes for that letter and marked in a distinctive manner. Leave a few lines vacant between letters for such notes.

b) Telegrams or letters that are to be transcribed first should be marked "Rush." Turn back the corner of each page containing such items (or use paper clips), so that you can quickly find these items when you start to transcribe.

c) Always check for special instructions before starting to transcribe a letter. Never trust your memory for "little details," such as "Transcribe this first," "Send a copy to our New York office," "Make 2 extra carbons," "Send special delivery," "Check that address," and similar instructions.

INTERRUPTING DICTATOR

13   Do not interrupt the dictator unless he is so far ahead of you that you are losing the meaning of the dictation.

14   If you are in doubt about a word or a sentence, check with the dictator *after* he has finished dictating. Read back the sentence, indicating the point in question.

TYPEWRITER

15   A typewriter may be:

a) *Pica or elite.* If a great deal of your work is with Government forms, elite type must be used. Also, most business offices prefer elite type.

b) *Manual or electric.* Electric typewriters are particularly useful to make multiple carbons, to prepare many masters for duplicating, or to do a job necessitating almost continuous typing.

TRANSCRIBING

16   Always transcribe directly from your notes. Make at least one carbon copy of all correspondence. (See also ¶ 136.) Develop the ability to read ahead as you transcribe in order to foresee special problems, such as: *(a)* errors in grammar, *(b)* incomplete sentences, *(c)* words or sentences that do not seem to make sense, *(d)* corrections and insertions.

17   Question any words, spellings, figures, or other details about which you are not sure *before* typing, not afterward.

18   Proofread your letter before removing it from the machine. This does not mean simply "scanning" or "looking over" the letter. Proofreading means reading the material *word for word;* both for accuracy and for thought content. If you merely "look over" the copy, you are likely to miss word substitutions, such as *than* for *that* or *now* for *not,* or you may miss simple omissions.

A helpful device in proofreading is to use the paper bail as a guide. Turn the paper back to the top; and then, as you turn it slowly forward, read each line carefully—checking against your notes—as the line appears above the paper bail.

SUBMITTING YOUR WORK

19 Submit clean copy—without smudges, finger prints, or obvious erasures.

20 When the letters are ready for the dictator's signature, place the letters and the enclosures, if any, under the flaps of the envelopes, with the address side of the envelopes on top.

a) If a carbon copy is to be sent to someone, place this copy, with its correctly addressed envelope, below the typed letter.

b) Attach the file copies (carbon copies) to the original (incoming) correspondence and place these in a separate pile.

c) If the dictator is not at his desk when you present the letters for his signature, place them on his desk either face downward or enclosed in a folder.

YOUR DICTIONARY

Form the habit of consulting your dictionary frequently, for a reliable, up-to-date dictionary is a comprehensive reference work. Several reliable ones are listed on page 162. The following suggestions will help you use yours efficiently.

21 *Introductory section.* Study the introductory section carefully for an explanation of the meanings of the marks, abbreviations, and symbols used in *your* dictionary.

22 *Spelling.* When two spellings are given for a word, as *catalogue, catalog,* choose the first, or preferred, one. If the two forms are listed separately, choose the form that is accompanied by the various definitions of the word.

23 *Past tense.* When the past tense of a verb *is not given,* this means that the past tense is formed by adding *-d* or *-ed;* as *force, forced; profit, profited.* When the past tense is formed in some other way, it *is given;* as *acquit, acquitted; pay, paid.*

24 *Plurals.* When the plural form of a noun *is not given,* this means that it is necessary to add only *-s* or *-es;* as *hat, hats; sash, sashes.* (See also ¶¶ 468, 469.) When the plural is formed in some other way, it *is given;* as *company, companies; man, men; half, halves.*

25 *Prefixes.* Under commonly used prefixes, such as *un-, non-, out-,* or *over-,* there are often lists of many of the words compounded with this prefix. Generally these words do not require definitions, and so each word is not given a separate entry elsewhere.

26 *Word division.* A word can be divided only between syllables.

a) A syllable is either a single letter or a group of letters that, taken together, form one sound.

b) Every syllable must contain at least one vowel. *In' de pen' dent,* for example, contains four syllables, each of which contains one vowel. A single vowel may constitute a syllable, as in *sen' a tor.*

c) Dictionaries indicate by an accent mark the syllables most emphasized in pronunciation (*fi · nan' cial*). Long words usually contain two accents, the primary and the secondary accents (*fun' da · men' tal*). If possible, divide after an accented syllable.

d) In the Merriam Webster's Dictionary:

(1) The end of a syllable is indicated either by a centered period, as in *com · mand,* or by an accent, as in *com' ma.* In longer words, both

centered periods and accents are used, as in *com·mem' o·rate;* but both marks never appear together at the same point.

(2) Hyphenated words contain heavy-faced hyphens; as *double-faced, would-be.*

(3) Compound words written as one solid word appear with a centered period between the words; as *let' ter·head.*

(4) Compound words written as two or more separate words appear with a space between the words; as *floor lead' er.* (Compare with *floor·walk' er.*)

27 *Pronunciation.* Words are respelled and especially marked with diacritical and accent marks; as *in·dite' (ĭn·dīt'), heir (âr).* When two forms are given, the first one is generally the preferred one; as *à·dŭlt', ăd' ŭlt.*

28 *Definitions.* In some dictionaries, definitions are listed according to the historical development of the word; other dictionaries give current meanings first. Many words have several definitions. Reading any illustrative sentences given will help you determine whether you have chosen the correct word.

29 In your dictionary you will also find:

a) The principal parts of irregular verbs; as *drive, drove, driven.*

b) The comparative and superlative forms of some adjectives; as *bad, worse, worst; happy, happier, happiest.*

c) The cases of pronouns; as *who, whose* (possessive), *whom* (objective).

d) Levels of usage; as *nob* (Slang), *nohow* (Dial.).

e) Synonyms (words that have very nearly the same meaning) and often antonyms (words having the opposite meaning).

f) The parts of speech in which words are generally used.

g) Foreign words and phrases.

h) The spelling of geographical names and names of prominent people.

i) A list of abbreviations (see ¶ 433).

Note: In some dictionaries items *g, h,* and *i* appear in separate lists at the back of the book; in other dictionaries they appear in the main alphabet.

SECTION 2

Getting the most out of your typewriter

CARE OF THE TYPEWRITER

30 Daily care.

a) Dust both the exterior of the typewriter and the desk underneath it.

b) Brush out any eraser particles with a long-handled dusting brush.

    c) Brush the type keys with a type brush.

    d) Keep the carriage centered when the machine is not in use.

    e) Cover the machine at night and whenever it is not in use.

31   Weekly care.

    a) Clean the type (unless carbon ribbon is used, making this unnecessary). If liquid cleaner is used, apply sparingly; then brush the keys thoroughly.

    b) Clean the paper cylinder (platen) only when it becomes glossy; use denatured alcohol, carbon tetrachloride, or a liquid cleaner intended for that purpose. Never rub the cylinder dry.

32   Before changing a ribbon, study carefully the threading and movement of the old ribbon if you are not familiar with the particular make of machine you are using.

MAKING CORRECTIONS

33   Crowding. There are two methods of typing a word that contains one more letter than the erased word. For example, to type *that* for *may:*

    a) The backspace method

        (1) Move the carriage to the usual position of *t* (same position as *m*).

        (2) Depress the backspacer halfway; hold it in that position and type *t*.

        (3) Depress the backspacer halfway; hold it in that position and type *h;* and so on.

    b) The space-bar method

        (1) Move the carriage to the space preceding the correction spot.

        (2) Hold the space bar down and type *t*.

        (3) Release the space bar.

        (4) Hold the space bar down and type *h;* and so on.

Note: If your machine is electric, neither of these methods can be used. Instead, brace your left hand against the frame of the machine, at the side; and press your finger tips against the end of the carriage to move it part of a space.

34   Spreading. There are two methods of typing a word that is one letter shorter than the erased word. For example, to type *the* for *when:*

    a) The backspace method

        (1) Move the carriage to the position of *w*.

        (2) Space once, depress the backspacer halfway, and strike *t*.

        (3) Space once, depress the backspacer halfway, strike *h;* and so on.

    b) The space-bar method

        (1) Move the carriage to the space preceding the correction spot and space once.

        (2) Hold the space bar down and type *t*.

        (3) Release the space bar.

        (4) Hold the space bar down and type *h;* and so on.

Note: If your machine is electric, see ¶ 33 *Note.*

35   Erasing.

    a) You will need the following tools:

        (1) A typewriter (ink) eraser for original copy.

        (2) A soft eraser for carbon copies and for removing excess ink on original copies if the paper is of an inexpensive grade.

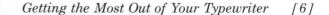

(3) An erasing shield; also a small, stiff card or metal erasing guard for erasing on carbons.

(4) An emery board or a piece of sandpaper.

b) Move the carriage to the extreme right or left, depending on the side of the page on which you wish to erase, so that the eraser waste will fall on the table and not into the machine. Use the margin-release key and the carriage-release lever, holding both down at the same time.

c) Roll the paper forward before starting to erase.

d) Hold the paper firmly by pressing it against the roller with your finger tips. (Be sure your hands are clean. Never place your fingers on the typed material.)

e) Use a clean eraser; otherwise, the paper will be smudged. Keep the eraser clean by rubbing it on an emery board or a piece of sandpaper.

f) Do not dig in or press on the paper when erasing; but erase lightly at first, using a "digging-lifting" stroke that is light and swift and goes in only one direction. *Never dampen the eraser.*

Hint: To improve your erasing techniques, experiment with the quality of paper you are using. Find out which way the grain of the paper runs and erase with the grain. Erasing against the grain roughens the paper. Also experiment with the type of eraser to be used. Some types of paper require an eraser with less abrasive material than others.

g) Before typing a correction, blow or brush the eraser particles off the paper. Smooth the paper with thumb or fingernail if the paper is roughened.

h) In turning the paper back to type the correction, use the line reset (ratchet release) rather than the variable line spacer. This will prevent original and carbon copies from slipping.

i) If you are erasing *carbon copies,* place a card or metal guard between the carbon sheet and the particular copy you are erasing. Use a soft eraser for your carbon copy. A typewriter eraser that has been used on the carbon copy is thereafter too dirty to use satisfactorily on the original.

j) In typing corrections, use a light stroke (retype with a still lighter stroke if necessary), so as to blend the erased word into the rest of the copy. On an electric machine, reduce the pressure dial to zero before typing the correction; be sure to return the dial to its normal position before resuming the regular typing.

k) If an erasure is necessary very near the bottom of the page, roll the paper back and erase from the bottom end. This will prevent the paper from slipping. If, as you erase, the carbon copies slip a little out of alignment, wait until you have completed the page to make the correction. Then re-insert each page separately and correct. Engaging the line reset (ratchet release) helps to avoid slippage of a carbon pack.

l) To correct carbon copies after they have been removed from the machine, replace each copy in the machine separately. A carbon correction (rather than a ribbon correction) may be made by placing a small piece of carbon paper over the spot where the correction should be typed.

36 Reinserting paper.

a) Using the aligning scale in front of the cylinder, vertically align the base of the word to be corrected with the top edge of the aligning scale. Use your variable line spacer or line reset (ratchet release) for this operation.

b) Using the paper release, very carefully move the paper to the left or the right until you have an *i* or an *l* or a *period* in alignment with one of the white marks on the aligning scale. Recheck the vertical alignment and readjust if necessary.

c) Test your placement with a *very* light stroke. (*Hint:* Turn the ribbon to "Stencil" in order to avoid showing the ribbon imprint, or test over a piece of cellophane.)

d) Use a light stroke in typing in the correction.

PREPARING CARBON COPIES

37 Assembling the carbon pack.

a) Be sure the *glossy* side of the carbon paper is placed against the paper on which the copy is to be made. (The pack will contain one more sheet of typing paper than of carbon.)

b) Pick up the pack loosely by the sides and tap the left and top edges lightly on the desk until the sheets are even. (See also ¶ 61.)

38 Inserting the carbon pack into the machine.

a) As you place the carbon pack on the paper rest behind the cylinder, be sure the glossy side of the carbon paper is toward you.

b) After insertion, be certain that the face of the letterhead and the dull side of the carbon paper are toward you.

c) Before starting to type, momentarily operate the paper-release lever, to release the tension and flatten the papers. This will prevent "treeing" of carbons.

d) You may have difficulty in inserting a number of carbon copies in the machine. Try inserting the carbon pack (if it does not contain more than four or five carbons) with the paper-release lever down. A thicker carbon pack should be guided into the machine by using a sheet of paper or an envelope as described in (1) and (2) below.

(1) Insert a piece of paper halfway into the machine, so that the top and bottom halves are about equal behind the cylinder. Then, with the paper-release lever depressed, insert the carbon pack between the cylinder and the sheet of paper. Roll forward and remove the sheet of paper.

(2) Place the entering edge of the carbon pack under the flap of a large envelope. With the paper-release lever depressed, insert the pack into the machine far enough so that the envelope may be removed in front of the cylinder. Whichever method you use, be sure that the pack is straight in the machine.

(3) To avoid slippage of a large carbon pack, engage the line reset (ratchet release) when inserting the pack into the machine. This device is also helpful when turning carbons back to make corrections, as well as when inserting stencils, ditto masters, etc., into the machine.

39   The use of carbon paper that has had the upper left and lower right corners cut off diagonally will help in separating carbons from typed sheets quickly. After removing the carbon pack from the typewriter, grasp the left corner of the pack between the thumb and finger of the left hand and shake out the carbons. Also, carbons that extend below the typed sheets can be pulled out easily with the right hand.

TYPING CARDS AND POSTAL CARDS

40   Use card holders to keep cards in position. Adjust paper-bail rolls against the card if it is necessary to write to the bottom of the card.

41   In typing on stiff or smooth cards, use the cylinder knob instead of the carriage-return lever to insure even line spacing. Sometimes it is necessary to hold the card with one hand as you turn the cylinder knob.

42   Government postal cards measure 5½ by 3¼ inches. When the message is typed the long way of the card, the typed line should not be longer than 4½ inches (45 pica strokes; 54 elite strokes). There are 20 line spaces to a card. To allow for margins, use only 16 of the writing lines. Also:

a) Plan the message so that a margin of at least ½ inch will appear on each side.

b) Type the current date in the upper right corner on the message side of the card. The return address may be typed above the date or it may be typed in the upper left corner on the address side of the card.

Note: For addressing cards, follow the same procedure as for addressing envelopes. (See ¶ 167.)

c) On the message side of the card, omit the name and address of the person to whom the card is being sent.

d) If the message is long, the salutation and the complimentary closing may be omitted.

Note: For the chain feeding of cards, use the same method as in the chain feeding of envelopes. (See ¶175.)

DUPLICATING

43   Plan the positioning of the copy carefully. If necessary, type a first draft on paper the same size as that to be used for the printed material, using the same margins.

44   Prepare the typewriter by cleaning the faces of the keys thoroughly. If cleaning fluid is used, be sure that the keys are completely dry before starting to type. Keep keys clean with a stiff-bristled brush.

45   As you finish each paragraph, proofread it carefully, checking, word for word, with your copy. (See ¶¶ 18, 50.)

TYPING STENCILS

46   Move the ribbon lever on your typewriter to *stencil* position.

47   Compare the typed copy and the stencil to determine:

a) On what line to start writing on the stencil. The numbers down the side of the stencil are a guide to the lines.

b) At what point or points on the scale at the top of the stencil to start writing.

48   Place the stencil in the typewriter.

    a) Insert the cushion sheet smoothly between the stencil and the backing sheet. Do not use a cushion sheet that is torn or badly worn.

    b) Hold the stencil pack at the bottom as you make the insertion, to keep the cushion sheet from slipping. If the stencil does not feed in easily, depress the paper release briefly. Be sure the stencil is not wrinkled.

    c) Straighten the stencil in the typewriter.

49   Begin to type the stencil. Type with an even touch at a rate a little slower than you ordinarily use. Punctuation marks and *o, e,* and *c* should be struck with a lighter touch; *w* and *m* and capital letters, with a heavier touch. If you are using an electric typewriter, you may wish to lessen the pressure by setting the pressure dial at a lower figure; it is not necessary to alter your normal touch when typing on an electric machine.

50   On a major stencil project you may wish to make a carbon copy of what is typed on each stencil, to use in final proofreading or as a reference pending the duplicating of the material. To make such copies, place a piece of paper and a carbon sheet between the backing sheet and the cylinder.

51   To make corrections:

    a) Roll the stencil forward a line or two.

    b) Smooth the surface of the error to close perforations in the stencil. If a burnisher is not supplied with the correction fluid, a smooth paper clip may be used for this purpose.

    c) Apply a *thin* coating of correction fluid. Replace the cover of the bottle of fluid at once.

    d) Type the correction with a slightly lighter stroke than you normally use, so that corrected words will not appear darker than the rest of the copy.

52   To avoid wrinkling a stencil as it is turned back in the machine, hold the lower edges of the three sheets securely together and roll the stencil back slowly, with the line reset (ratchet release) released.

53   The first time that you use a new type of stencil, be sure to read *carefully* the directions that accompany the package of stencils.

TYPING MASTERS FOR DIRECT-PROCESS OR FLUID DUPLICATING

54   Remove the protecting sheet that is inside the master set (the white master paper and its attached, colored carbon sheet).

55   Insert the master set, open end first, so that the white master paper faces you, backed up by the carbon side of the carbon paper. As you type on the master paper, the carbon prints on the reverse side of the white paper. If you desire additional copies or especially clear copies, insert a stiff backing sheet behind the master set.

56   Leave the ribbon in the regular position. Type with a very sharp touch. If using an electric machine, reduce the pressure two or three points.

57   To correct an error of a few letters, turn up the paper; bend the master toward you; using a single-edged razor or desk knife, *lightly* scrape off the carbon of the error; place a slip of fresh carbon at the point of correction; type the correction right over the error; and remove the carbon slip. To correct a longer error, retype the line correctly in an unused part of the master; cut out both the correct and incorrect lines; and tape the correct line into the position originally filled by the incorrect line.

58   To display some portions of the material in color, place a sheet of colored duplicating carbon between the white master paper and the carbon sheet before typing the part of the material that is to be so displayed.

SECTION 3

Details that mark the acceptable letter

Note: The rules in this section apply to business correspondence. See ¶ 149 for variations common in social correspondence.

STATIONERY

In the business office, stenographers are ordinarily provided with the following stationery for correspondence work.

59   Letterheads and envelopes. The standard sizes of stationery, with the number and dimensions of the envelope appropriate to each size, are:

	Size of letterhead	Envelope No.	Approximate size of envelope
Standard	8½ by 11	6¾ or	3⅝ by 6½
		10	4⅛ by 9½
Half sheets	8½ by 5½	6¾	3⅝ by 6½
Baronial	5½ by 8½	5⅜	4⅝ by 5¹⁵⁄₁₆
Monarch	7¼ by 10½	7	3⅞ by 7½

The half sheets are used for very short letters; the Baronial and Monarch, for personal and professional letters.

60   Sheets for interoffice correspondence. (See illustration on page 29.)

61   Carbons.

a) Carbon paper is obtainable in different weights (standard, medium, light) and finishes (hard to soft). The selection made usually depends on the number of carbon copies desired. (See also ¶¶ 37, 38.)

Copies	Weight	Finish
1–4	Standard	Hard
5–8	Medium	Hard
9–20	Light	Medium

Hard-finish carbon produces cleaner copies and does not smear.

b) Ready-made, snap-out carbon packs are used in many offices today. They are available from stationers and may be purchased with any number of sheets, each sheet of typing paper in a different color if so desired. These packs alternate sheets of typing paper and carbon paper, which are fastened together at the bottom. After a job is typed, the carbon sheets are detached by a sharp tug on the bottom of the packet and thrown away. When such packs are used for correspondence, the company letterhead is used for the original copy.

DATE

62 Never abbreviate the name of the month.

63 Use figures for the day of the month and the year; as *January 15, 1961.*

64 Never use the styles *2/12/61, 2-12-61,* or *'61,* even in informal memorandums. The dates represented by these styles are easily confused.

65 When the *name* of the month precedes the day, do *not* use *th, st,* or *d* after the figure. Write *September 15.*

66 In the *body of the letter,* when the *day* precedes the name of the month or when the day stands alone, include *th, st,* or *d* or spell out the day in words. (See also ¶ 453.)

> I have just received your card of the 24th.
> By the fourth of March we expect to have complete information.

67 In Army and Navy correspondence and in correspondence received from foreign countries, the day precedes the name of the month; as *21 June 1961.*

68 No period follows the date line, except when the full style of punctuation is used. (See Letter Style 6.)

69 Note the correct use of the comma in these variations:

> June, 19—   June 5, 19—
> Your letter of June 5, 19—, was received today.
> (*But:* Your letter of June 5 was received today.)

70 Dates in a sequence are written:

> June 10–22   1956–1960

(See also ¶¶ 422, 423.)

71 In the most commonly used letter form, the blocked (see Letter Styles 1 and 3), the date line may be placed as follows:

a) Three lines below the letterhead or on line 15, *whichever* is *lower* on the page, with the line ending at the right margin.

b) Centered under the letterhead. (See Letter Style 2.)

c) At any point that results in an attractive alignment with some part of the letterhead.

72 In full-blocked letters, the date line starts at the left margin. (See Letter Style 4.)

73 When a letterhead is not used, place the address of the writer above the date line.

> 753 Lombard Street
> Oakland 2, California
> December 10, 19—

INSIDE ADDRESS

74 The inside address of a business letter should consist of at least three lines. If a street address is not used, place the name of the city or town on the second line and the name of the state on the third line.

75 *"Personal"* or *"Confidential."* If a writer desires to indicate that a letter is of a confidential nature, *Personal* or *Confidential* is typed three spaces above the inside address and is underscored. (See also ¶ 169.)

NAMES AND TITLES OF PERSONS

76 Verify the spelling and the initials of every personal name you type, by consulting the original correspondence, the files, mailing lists, directories, or, finally, the dictator.

a) Typical of common variations are:

Clark and Clarke	McDonald, MacDonald, Macdonald
Stuart and Stewart	Hutchinson, Hutchison, Hutcheson

b) Do not abbreviate a personal name unless the owner so signs it himself; for example, write *Charles,* not *Chas.* Some short names, however, as *Fred, Sam, Ben,* are often full names, not abbreviations. Follow the owner's preference.

c) For names that begin with such prefixes and particles as *O', Mc, de, la, van,* and so on:

(1) Always capitalize the *O'* in Irish names; as *O'Neill.*

(2) Always capitalize *Mc* and the letter that follows the prefix; as *McCarthy.* Also capitalize *Mac,* but follow the owner's style for writing the remainder of the name; as *MacIntosh, Macfadden.*

(3) Do *not* capitalize the *d', da, de, della, di, du, la, le, van, von* of foreign names when a given name or a title precedes the surname; as *René de Michele, Angelo della Rocca, Duc d'Orleans, Madame de Pompadour, Karl von Behr.*
Caution: Always check the spelling of names with prefixes and particles, because the owners sometimes prefer a style other than the general one given in (3); as *Reginald De Koven, Paul de Kruif, Hendrik Van Loon.*

(4) Capitalize these elements when the surname stands alone; as *De Michele, Von Behr.*

(5) When names containing prefixes occur in all-capitalized lines, capitalize the entire prefix if it is disjoined, but capitalize only the initial letter if the prefix is joined; for example, *VON BEHR, McGRAW.*

Note: No space follows the prefixes *O', Mc, Mac,* and *d';* a single space follows the other prefixes.

77 Spell out a person's given name rather than use an initial for that name (for example, write *Howard S. Logan* rather than *H. S. Logan*) unless the owner signs only with the initials. Also, if a person uses his first initial and spells out his second name, follow his preference; as *W. Vincent Wilson.* However, if a person has adopted an initial that does not represent a name, no period should follow the initial; as *Harry S Truman.*

78 Use a *title* before the name of every person to whom you write. If the person has no special title, such as *Professor, Doctor, Honorable,* then use *Mr., Mrs.,* or *Miss.* (See also ¶ 434.)

   a) Always place a period after *Mr., Mrs.,* and *Messrs.* (plural of *Mr.*), but not after *Miss, Misses,* or *Mesdames,* which are not abbreviations.

   b) If there is nothing to indicate whether a woman is *Miss* or *Mrs.,* use the title *Miss.*

   Note: N.O.M.A. (the National Office Management Association) recommends the use of *Ms.* in such cases.

   c) A small boy is addressed as *Master.*

   d) Long titles, such as *Lieutenant, Governor, Commander, Superintendent,* may or may not be abbreviated in the inside address. In informal correspondence, technical matter, or tabulations, the usual practice is to abbreviate. In formal correspondence and where only a few titles are mentioned, the titles should be spelled out. If in doubt, spell out.

   e) In legal correspondence, *Esq.* (abbreviation for *Esquire*) usually follows the name of a lawyer. No other title, such as *Mr.* or *Dr.,* should precede the name if *Esq.* follows it.

79 When *Jr., Sr., Esq.,* and the abbreviations of religious orders (as *S. J.*) or of academic degrees (as *Ph. D.*) follow a name, a comma separates the abbreviation from the name.

   Note: When these abbreviations occur in sentences, a comma should also follow the abbreviation. (See ¶ 234.)

80 Do not use two titles meaning the same thing, one before and one after the name. *Dr. Herbert Booth, LL.D.,* for example, is incorrect because both *Dr.* and the *D* in *LL.D.* are abbreviations for *doctor.*

81 The wife of a man who holds a title—*Dr.,* for example—is addressed thus: *Mrs. Thomas West* (not: *Mrs. Dr. West*).

82 The honorary titles *Reverend* and *Honorable:*

   a) Are preferably spelled out in formal use, as in invitations and announcements, with *The* preceding the title; as *The Honorable John S. Clinton; The Reverend Howard Crane.*

   b) Are usually abbreviated to *Rev.* and *Hon.* in business correspondence.

   c) Should always be followed by either a given name or a title; as *Hon. James Lee; Rev. Mr. Page.*

83 In letters to business persons and to executives of organizations, include if possible the business or executive title that shows the person's official connection with the firm or organization.

Mr. Henry T. Burke, President	Mr. William Dudley
Miss Mary Lee, Vocational Director	Chairman of the Board of Directors

   Note: In inside addresses and on envelopes, these titles are capitalized if they follow the name. (See also ¶¶ 531, 532.) See ¶¶ 352, 353 for their use in sentences.

84 Make an effort to have the lines of the inside address equal in length.

   a) If the addressee's name is shorter than the firm name, type his title on the line with his name. (See illustration on page 14.)

> Mr. Merrill Statler, President
> Lyon & Caylor Van and Storage Company
> Center and Vallejo Streets
> San Bernardino, California

b) If the firm name is short, type the addressee's title on the second line, preceding the firm name.

> Mr. William R. Longsworth
> Treasurer, Atlas Supply, Inc.
> 1478 16th Street
> Chicago 14, Illinois

c) Type the addressee's title on a line by itself, depending on the length of the title, the length of the addressee's name, or the length of the firm name. An unusually long title may be broken and carried over to the second line, indented two spaces.

> Mr. Ralph P. Williams
> Director of Personnel
> Robinson & Young, Ltd.
> 50 York Street
> Toronto 1, Ontario
> Canada

> Mr. Harry R. Fitzgerald
> Vice-President and General Manager
>   in Charge of Sales
> Lawrence, Steton & Sons, Inc.
> 782 North First Street, E.
> Seattle 3, Washington

Note: Whenever an addressee's name and his title, or his title and the firm name, appear on the same line, separate the items by a comma. (See examples in *a* and *b*.)

NAMES OF FIRMS

85 Check the spelling of every firm name you write; also the style of punctuation and abbreviation used. The letterhead of incoming correspondence is the best source for this information. Here are a few actual variations.

> Macy's, New York
> The Macey Company
> Libbey Glass Manufacturing Company
> Libby, McNeill & Libby, Inc.
> Remington Rand Inc.

> Standard Motor Co. Ltd.
> Chas. H. Bohn & Co.
> Ebasco Services Incorporated
> The MG Car Company Limited

86 If the official form cannot be ascertained from incoming correspondence or some other source:

a) In general, use the ampersand (the & sign) in company names, particularly when the name consists of the names of persons.

> Ellis & Wilson
> Curtis & Hall, Inc.

> Messrs. Regin & Brown
> *But:* Acme Lead and Tin Company

b) Write *Inc.* for *Incorporated* and *Ltd.* for *Limited* and precede each abbreviation by a comma.
   Note: In a sentence, also place a comma after the abbreviation. (See ¶¶ 235, 509.)

c) Spell out *Company* and *Corporation* unless the firm name is very long, in which case these words may be abbreviated to *Co.* and *Corp.,* respectively.

87 Capitalize the word *The* if it is part of the company name; otherwise, the word should not be capitalized.

88 When the name of an organization contains a noun in the possessive:

a) The apostrophe is usually dropped in plural forms unless such names end in irregular plurals.

Teachers College	Veterans Bureau
American Bankers Association	The Children's Shop
Farmers Investment Company	Businessmen's Association

b) Singular names usually retain the apostrophe. (See also ¶¶ 492–509.)

Harper's Bazaar   Woman's Home Companion

89 It may be necessary in unusually long company names to carry over part of the name to a second line, indenting two spaces. (See Letter Style 2.)

STREET ADDRESSES

90 Always write house, building, apartment, room, or rural-route numbers in figures. Do not use either the abbreviation *No.* or # before such figures.

700 Market Street	900–920 Grant Street	P.O. Box 789
R.D. (or R.F.D.) 5	Room 1601	1840 Ross Building

Exception: For clarity, the word *One,* rather than the figure *1,* is used in house numbers; as *One Park Avenue.*

91 In street names, do not abbreviate such words as *Street* and *Avenue* unless it is necessary for reasons of space on an envelope or in a list. When abbreviation is necessary, however, the following forms are correct.

Alley	Al.	Heights	Hts.	Road	Rd.
Avenue	Ave.	Lane	La.	South	S.
Between	bet.	Near	nr.	Square	Sq.
Boulevard	Blvd.	North	N.	Street	St.
Court	Ct.	Opposite	opp.	Terrace	Ter.
Drive	Dr.	Park	Pk.	West	W.
East	E.	Place	Pl.		

92 Numbered street names are written as follows:

a) Spell out names that consist of numbers through ten.

177 Second Avenue   1128 East Fifth Street

b) Use figures for names over ten.

27 East 22d Street   144 65th Street (*or* 144 – 65th Street)

Note: The practice of omitting *th, st, d* from street names is growing because of the increased readability of this style on envelopes.

➤ **See** ¶ 425 for style of writing large house numbers.

93 When *North, South, East, West, Northeast, Southwest,* and so on appear in street names, spell the words out.

230 East 48th Street

94 Initials representing sections of a city should be written:

1895 North 179th Street, S. W.

95 When *and* appears in a street address, the word is spelled out.

Tenth and Market Streets

CITY, COUNTY, STATE, PROVINCE, AND COUNTRY

96 Type the name of the state or province on the same line with the name of the city unless there is no street-address line. Place a comma between the name of the city and the state if the names appear on the same line. (See Letter Styles 1–8.)

		The Ellis Company
Webster & Small, Inc.	Paulson & Green	Norton
38 Sansome Street	Centerville	Essex County
San Francisco 1, California	California	Vermont

97 Never abbreviate the name of a city or a town. Write *Chicago,* not *Chic.; Los Angeles,* not *L. A.*

98 Never write *City* in place of the full name of a city or town.

99 Never abbreviate the words *Fort, Mount, Point,* and *Port* when these words are part of a city or town name.

Fort Dodge   Mount Vernon   Point Pleasant   Port Huron

In the names of American cities, however, *Saint* is usually abbreviated; as *St. Paul, St. Louis.*

100 Write postal zone numbers in arabic figures immediately after the name of the city; as *Columbus 10, Ohio.* No comma should separate the figure from the city.

101 Do not abbreviate *County* to *Co.,* which is easily confused with the abbreviation for *Company.*

102 Spell out names of states and provinces. (But write *Washington, D.C.*)

103 However, if space requires it on envelopes and in lists, names of states and provinces may be abbreviated as follows:

Alabama	Ala.	Mississippi	Miss.	Virginia	Va.
Arizona	Ariz.	Missouri	Mo.	Washington	Wash.
Arkansas	Ark.	Montana	Mont.	West Virginia	W. Va.
California	Calif.	Nebraska	Nebr.	Wisconsin	Wis.
Colorado	Colo.	Nevada	Nev.	Wyoming	Wyo.
Connecticut	Conn.	New Hampshire	N. H.		
Delaware	Del.	New Jersey	N. J.	**CANADIAN PROVINCES**	
District of	D. C.	New Mexico	N. Mex.		
Columbia		New York	N. Y.	Alberta	Alta.
Florida	Fla.	North Carolina	N. C.	British Columbia	B. C.
Georgia	Ga.	North Dakota	N. Dak.	Manitoba	Man.
Illinois	Ill.	Oklahoma	Okla.	New Brunswick	N. B.
Indiana	Ind.	Oregon	Ore.	Newfoundland	Nfld.
Kansas	Kans.	Pennsylvania	Pa.	Nova Scotia	N. S.
Kentucky	Ky.	Rhode Island	R. I.	Ontario	Ont.
Louisiana	La.	South Carolina	S. C.	Prince Edward	P. E. I.
Maryland	Md.	South Dakota	S. Dak.	Island	
Massachusetts	Mass.	Tennessee	Tenn.	Quebec	Que.; P. Q.
Michigan	Mich.	Texas	Tex.	Saskatchewan	Sask.
Minnesota	Minn.	Vermont	Vt.		

Never abbreviate *Idaho, Iowa, Maine, Ohio, Utah, Alaska, Hawaii.*
Note: In sentences, names of states and provinces should always be spelled out.

the Green Mountains of Vermont   the gentleman from Indiana

104   Always spell out names of countries, with the one exception of *U. S. S. R.* (*Union of Soviet Socialist Republics*).

> *Note:* U. S. A. stands for *Union of South Africa* and *United States Army* as well as *United States of America.*

SALUTATION

105   Always start the salutation at the left margin and follow it by a colon, except when open punctuation is used. (See Letter Style 7.)

106   Double space above and below the salutation.

107   Abbreviate only the titles *Mr., Mrs.,* and *Messrs.* in salutations. All other titles, such as *Professor, Doctor, Captain,* should be written out.

108   Capitalize the first word and any noun or title in a salutation.

Dear Sir:	Right Reverend and dear Sir:
My dear Mr. Brand:	Dear Father Brown:
Dear Doctor Sinclair:	Your Excellency:

109   The following are the approved forms of salutation.

> *Note:* The salutation is omitted in the Simplified form of letter. (See Letter Style 8.)

> To a business organization (even one consisting of a single name, as *John Wanamaker*): *Gentlemen*
> To an organization composed entirely of women: *Mesdames* or *Ladies*
> To two men: *My dear Messrs. Thomas and Woolsey* or *Gentlemen*
> To a woman and a man: *My dear Miss Allen and Mr. Kent*
> To two women:
>
> > Married: *My dear Mesdames Brown and White*
> > Unmarried: *My dear Misses Green and Black*
> > Sisters: *My dear Misses Simpson*
>
> To persons:
> > Least formal: *Dear Mr. Jones* (preferred to *Dear Sir*)   *Dear Miss Jones*
> > More formal: *My dear Professor Olson*   *My dear Mrs.* (or *Miss*) *Hood*
> > *Note:* Never write just *Dear Miss;* always include the surname.
> > Formal and impersonal: *Dear Sir*   *Dear Madam*
> > Very formal—for letters to government officials, etc.: *Sir, Madam*

(See also Section 17.)

BODY OF THE LETTER

110   Begin the body of the letter a double space below the salutation.

111   In the blocked and full-blocked letter (see Letter Styles 1, 3, and 4), each paragraph starts at the left margin. If paragraphs are indented, indent five (seldom more than ten) spaces. Always indent paragraphs in a double-spaced letter.

112   Ordinarily, use single spacing, except for very short letters, and double space between paragraphs.

> For spacing before and after all punctuation marks, see ¶¶ 347, 348.

ATTENTION AND SUBJECT LINES

113   The Attention line, which is considered part of the inside address, should be typed two spaces *below the inside address.* It may start at the left margin, be indented the same as the paragraphs, or be centered in the page width. It may be in all capital letters, all underscored, or only *Attention* underscored. Preferably *Attention* should not be abbreviated. Neither *of* nor a colon is necessary after the word. (See also Letter Style 2.) Two common arrangements are shown here.

```
Webster & Thane                 Webster & Thane
1760 Shattuck Avenue            1760 Shattuck Avenue
Berkeley 3, California          Berkeley 3, California

Attention of Mr. Ellery         ATTENTION SALES MANAGER

Gentlemen:                      Gentlemen:
```

114   Since the purpose of an Attention line is to direct the letter to a particular person in the company, the inclusion of this line does not change the salutation. The letter is *addressed* to the firm; therefore, the salutation must be *Gentlemen.*

115   *Mr., Miss,* or some other title, as *Professor,* should precede a name in an Attention line.

116   The Subject line, which is considered part of the body of the letter, should be typed two spaces *below the salutation.* It may start at the left margin, be indented the same as the paragraphs, or be centered in the page width. It may be in all capital letters, or it may be underscored with only the principal words capitalized. Sometimes *Subject:* or *In re:* (used in legal correspondence) precedes the actual subject. In the first of the following illustrations the subject line might read: "Subject: Morgan Lease" or "In re: Morgan Lease" or "File No. 28796" (the company file number for the Morgan lease). (See also Letter Style 3a.)

```
Ellis & Logan, Inc.             Ellis & Logan, Inc.
1450 Market Street              1450 Market Street
San Francisco 8, California     San Francisco 8, California

Gentlemen:                      Gentlemen:

      MORGAN LEASE              Introductory Offer to New
                                         Subscribers
```

PARAGRAPHING

117   Watch for subdivisions of thought as you are taking dictation, and paragraph accordingly. Some dictators indicate paragraph breaks as they dictate.

118   If possible, do not make a paragraph more than eight or ten lines long.

119   Avoid dividing the letter into a great many very short (two- or three-line) paragraphs.

120   The first and the last paragraph of a letter are often short.

121   Enumerated (or lettered) statements are better displayed by paragraphing than by running them in one paragraph. (See Letter Style 3a.)
   ➤ **See** ¶¶ 276–314 on *quotations in the body of the letter.*

COMPLIMENTARY CLOSING

122 Capitalize only the first word of the complimentary closing and place a comma at the end of the line, except when open punctuation is used. (See Letter Style 7.)

123 Start the complimentary closing near the center of the page, two spaces below the body of the letter, unless the full-blocked or square-blocked style (see Letter Styles 4, 5, and 8) is used, in which case the line starts at the left margin.

124 The dictator often dictates the complimentary closing desired. The most frequently used closings are:

a) Formal

Yours truly,   Yours very truly,   Very truly yours,

b) More personal in tone

Sincerely yours,   Very sincerely yours,
Yours sincerely,   Yours very sincerely,
Cordially yours,   Very cordially yours,

c) In asking for a favor or in writing to a superior

Respectfully yours,   Very respectfully yours,
Yours respectfully,   Yours very respectfully,

d) If the dictator prefers to replace a complimentary closing with an informal closing phrase, such as *Best regards* or *Thanking you for your interest,* the phrase is typed in the complimentary-closing position and is followed by a comma. Or if both the complimentary closing and the phrase are used, the phrase starts at the paragraph margin and is followed by a comma, the complimentary closing being typed as usual.

e) In business letters, *yours* is always included in the complimentary closing.

Note: No complimentary closing is used in the Simplified form of letter. (See Letter Style 8.)

SIGNATURE

125 If the *firm name* is part of the signature, double space after the complimentary closing and start typing the firm name in all capitals under the first letter of the complimentary closing.

In the indented form (see Letter Style 6), however, the firm name, if used, would be indented five spaces from the start of the complimentary closing.

126 Four spaces below the firm-name line, type the name and the title or official position of the person dictating the letter. More space may be left if the handwritten signature will be large. If the title is short, place it after the name; otherwise, on the line that follows.

Note: If the firm name is not included in the signature, type the name and the title of the dictator four spaces below the complimentary close. (See also Letter Style 3b.)

Yours very truly,

LINCOLN CONSTRUCTION COMPANY, INC.

(4 spaces)

George A. Norton, Manager

Yours very truly,

(4 spaces)

Robert M. Mead, M.D.

Yours very truly,

(4 spaces)

Herbert S. Walsh
Director of Industrial Research

127   Never type *Mr.* in the signature line.

128   The following are the correct forms for signatures of women.

  a) An *unmarried woman* may write *Miss,* enclosed in parentheses, in her *pen-written* signature. Or she may include it, *not* in parentheses, in the *typed* signature. If no title is given in the signature, *Miss* is implied.

(Miss) Constance Booth   or   *Constance Booth*

Miss Constance Booth

  b) A *married woman* may write *Mrs.* in parentheses before her *pen-written* signature.

(Mrs.) Nancy Eaton

Her *typed* signature may be in one of three forms.

  (1) She may wish to be addressed by her given first name, plus her married last name. She then includes *Mrs.,* but not in parentheses, before her *typed* signature.

  (2) Or she may wish to be addressed by her maiden name, plus her married last name. This style is frequently adopted by professional women.

  (3) Or she may wish to be addressed by her husband's Christian name or initials.

(1)	(2)	(3)
Nancy Eaton	*Nancy Ross Eaton*	*Nancy Eaton*
Mrs. Nancy Eaton	Mrs. Nancy Ross Eaton	Mrs. John A. Eaton

c) A *widow* may follow any one of the styles shown in *b*. Socially, she selects style *b* (3).

d) A *divorcee* may adopt one of three styles of signature.

    (1) She may sign her own given and maiden name and her divorced husband's last name.

    (2) Or she may combine her maiden name and her divorced name.

(1)   (2)

Elsie Hoyt Prince   *Elsie Hoyt Prince*

Mrs. Elsie Hoyt Prince   Mrs. Hoyt Prince

    (3) If she has resumed her maiden name, she may use either of the styles shown in rule *a.*

129 A secretary who signs mail for her employer uses the following style.

Dorothy Cook

Secretary to Mr. Benedict

130 If the person who signs for another is not actually the secretary, this form is used:

Mabel Phillips

For Mr. Benedict

IDENTIFICATION DATA (reference initials)

131 Identification or reference initials identify the dictator and the transcriber. Since the initials fix responsibility, they are an important company record. The form used is often a matter of company style. Some common arrangements are:

ABG:D   LDHSr:DD   MFF:CCR   JDeL:C   B. D. Dixon:RP   lba

The dictator's initials, if used, always precede the transcriber's. Some companies use only the transcriber's initials if the dictator's name is typed in the signature line. (See Letter Style 2.) If the dictator's name is not typed in the signature line, and especially if the handwritten signature is illegible, it is advisable to type the name in full in the identification data.

132 The identification data should be typed at the left margin, four spaces below the complimentary closing (or firm name) or on the same line as the title of the signer. The data may be written one or two lines below the official title of the signer. (See also ¶ 163.)

Exception: In the square-blocked letter form, the identification data appear at the right margin. (See Letter Style 5.)

133 When a letter has been composed by the typist, her initials only are used as the identification data.

134 No identification data are included in personal letters.

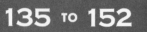
ENCLOSURE AND CARBON-COPY NOTATIONS

135   Enclosures are indicated by the word *Enclosure* (or the abbreviation *Enc.* or *Encl.*) written one or two lines below the identification data. An "attached" paper is classed as an enclosure. If there is more than one enclosure, indicate the number. These forms are typical:

```
Enclosures      Encs. 4      Encl.      Enclosure—Check
```

Note: Some dictators and offices prefer the spelling *inclose* (abbreviated *Inc.* or *Incl.*).

136   When carbon copies are sent to certain persons, that fact is indicated just below the identification-data line. The title *Mr.* (or *Miss, Mrs.,* etc.) usually precedes the name. (See also Letter Style 2.)

```
cc to Miss Robinson     CC:  Mr. A. C. Case, B & G Company, Inc.
CC:  JST                cc Atlas Company, Chicago
```

If several persons are to receive carbon copies, the names should be listed either according to the person's rank or, if there is no difference in rank, alphabetically.

Sometimes the dictator prefers not to indicate on the letter that a carbon copy is being sent to some person. In such cases, the information is not typed on the original letter but on the file carbon copy, and on other carbon copies if required, usually at the top left corner. Such copies, often called *blind copies*, are identified by *bcc;* thus: *bcc Mr. Case.*

137   If a letter is to be sent by registered mail, by certified mail, by airmail, by special delivery, or by messenger, the information should be typed either below the date line or below the identification data. (See Letter Style 4.) In many offices, when a letter is sent by air, the notation *Airmail* is typed only on the file copy below the identification data. This information serves as an office record.

POSTSCRIPTS

138   Postscripts are important and must stand out. Start the postscript at least a double space below the carbon copy notation (or whatever is the last line at the left).

139   A postscript usually starts at the left margin (or at the paragraph indention if paragraphs are indented) with the initials *P. S.* or *PS*, although some dictators do not consider these indications necessary. (*See* Letter Style 3b.)

TWO-PAGE LETTERS

140   Use plain paper of the same quality as the letterhead, but never a letterhead, for the second page of a long letter.

141   Use the same left and right margins that you used on the first page.

142   Start the heading on the second sheet 1 inch (six line spaces) from the top edge, and leave two or three spaces between the heading and the first line of the continued letter.

143   The name of the addressee, *Page 2* or *2*, and the date constitute the heading. The forms shown on page 23 are acceptable.

Mrs. L. R. Austin   2   September 30, 19—

Mrs. L. R. Austin
Page 2
September 30, 19—

144 Never carry over fewer than three lines to the second page. Leave at least two lines of a new paragraph at the foot of the first page; likewise, see that the first paragraph carried to the second page has at least two lines at the top of the second page.

145 Never hyphenate the last word at the foot of the first page.

146 Wherever possible, without crowding the letter, use but one page; but leave at least a 1-inch margin at the foot.

147 If the letter runs to a third page, leave the same margin at the foot of the second page that you did at the bottom of the first page.

INTEROFFICE CORRESPONDENCE

148 The style of interoffice correspondence differs in certain details from that of ordinary business correspondence. (See illustration on page 29.)

SOCIAL CORRESPONDENCE

149 The style of social correspondence differs from that of business correspondence in the following details.

a) In the heading, which may either appear on the stationery or be written, a house number may be spelled out; as *Two Pleasant Road.* (See also ¶ 73.)

b) The salutation may be very informal and may be followed by a comma.

c) Any appropriate complimentary closing may be used. The word *Yours* may be omitted entirely, or the closing may consist only of *Yours.*

d) No identification initials are used.

e) Numbers are frequently spelled in words; for example:

(1) Days of the month (and even a year, in formal invitations); as *October twelfth.*

(2) Numbers representing measurements, as *five miles.*

(3) Amounts of money; as *ten dollars.*

(4) Numbers over 100, however, are usually written in figures.

(5) Spelled-out fractions are ordinarily not hyphenated; as *a majority of two thirds.*

f) The correct forms for invitations and announcements may be found in a standard book of etiquette.

LETTER STYLES

150 The *blocked* and the *semiblocked,* both also known as the *modified block* (see Letter Styles 1, 2, and 3), are the most commonly used business-letter forms. Note that the paragraphs are indented in the semiblocked form.

151 The *indented* (see Letter Style 6) style is conservative in tone and is not used so extensively as the blocked form.

152 The *full-blocked,* or *extreme block* (see Letter Style 4), is not an artistic letter form; but it saves time.

(*Text continues on page 29.*)

QUINN TRAVEL SERVICES, Inc.

10 OCEAN ROAD
SALEM 2, OREGON

CABLE ADDRESS: QUITRAS
Telephone: GReen 3-0909

October 14, 19--

Mr. Lee R. Kline, Manager
Griffin & Hartley, Inc.
5879 K Street
Sacramento 2, California

Dear Mr. Kline:

The blocked form is the letter style most frequently used in business.

The date often ends even with the right margin. Use the backspacer to determine the point at which to start writing. The date, however, may be centered
or may be placed at any point that results in an attractive alignment with
some part of the printed letterhead.

The inside address, the paragraphs, and the identification data are blocked
at the left margin.

In standard punctuation, no punctuation is used after the date or any line
in the inside address, except after a line that ends with an abbreviation;
for example, "Inc." A colon is placed after the salutation and a comma
after the complimentary closing.

Start the complimentary closing at the center of the paper. If a company
name is used, type it in all capital letters two spaces below the complimentary closing.

A typed signature or title is blocked four spaces below the company name or
the complimentary closing if no company name is used. The dictator's title
may be typed on the same line with his name. However, if his title is long,
such as "General Manager" or "Supervisor, Media Merchandising Activities,"
it could be typed on the line below his name; or it could be broken and
carried over to the second line.

The word "Enclosures" in the identification data shows that additional papers
are being enclosed in the envelope.

Very sincerely yours,

QUINN TRAVEL SERVICES, INC.

Charles A. Gordon, Head
Adjustment Department

CAG:REM
Enclosures

Letter Style 1. *Blocked (also known as "modified block"), with enclosures notation. Punctuation is standard (also known as "mixed").*

Note: The body of each of the letter styles illustrated describes the features of
that particular form.

Hartley Sales Corporation

146 PALM GROVE AVENUE   *HOUSTON 6, TEXAS*

SERVING THE GULF STATES

September 17, 19--

The Glenn Phillips Industrial
    Fabricating & Processing Company
1853 Third Avenue, S. W.
New Orleans 6, Louisiana

Attention Mr. Graham

Gentlemen:

The semiblocked form is like the blocked form except that in the semiblocked form the paragraphs are indented five or more spaces.

The date may be centered as shown here, started at the center of the page, typed so that it ends even with the right margin, or placed at any point that results in an attractive alignment with some portion of the letterhead.

A long company name, like the one shown here, may be divided. The part carried over to the second line should be indented two spaces.

The Attention line may be written as here — that is, centered two lines below the inside address and underscored — or it could be started at the left margin. It also could be written in full capital letters and not underscored. It is not necessary to use either a colon or "of" in the Attention line.

A letter having an Attention line is addressed to a firm; therefore, the salutation must be "Gentlemen."

Some companies use only the typist's initials in the identification data, as shown here, if the dictator's name is included in the signature line.

The notation "cc" indicates that a carbon copy is being sent to one or more persons. The notation may also include the company name and address. (See also ¶ 136.)

Sincerely yours,

HARTLEY SALES CORPORATION

R. C. Perry

R. C. Perry, Sales Manager

obf
Enc. 4
cc: Mr. Lewis
      Miss Ellis

Letter Style 2. *Semiblocked (also known as "modified block with indented paragraphs"), with Attention line, enclosure notation, and carbon-copy notation. Punctuation is standard (also known as "mixed").*

Minnehaha Supply Corporation

249 JOLIET AVENUE SOUTH · MINNEAPOLIS 3, MINNESOTA

H. P. BENET
President
A. D. MORRISON
Vice-President
F. A. GRAUSON
Secretary & Treasurer

November 18, 19--

Mr. Jonathan R. MacKenzie
President, Engle & Carr, Ltd.
1089 Commonwealth Avenue
Edmonton, Alberta
Canada

Dear Mr. MacKenzie:

                    Subject: Quoted Matter, Tabulations, and Enumerations

The Subject line in this letter is centered two spaces below the salutation.
It could, however, be written at the left margin; or it could be typed in full
capital letters and not underscored. The word "Subject" is often omitted.

This letter also illustrates various methods of handling quoted matter, tabulations, numbered paragraphs, or other material that the writer desires to have
stand out from the body of the letter. Always double space before and after
such material.

To quote from a recent article in a secretarial magazine:

            When a quotation will occupy more than three lines, give
            it special display (use a shorter line length than
            that used for the remainder of the material) and type it
            single spaced, instead of using quotation marks.

If quotation marks are used, however, it is not necessary to indent the margins
(see ¶ 281b).

To set off listed items or tabulated material, indent the left and right margins
equally and single space such material. (See also Par. 622-645.)

	1960	1961
Gross income.............	$340,977	$368,972
Expenses and taxes.......	280,009	292,472
Net income...............	$ 60,968	$ 76,500

Points may be brought out more forcibly by indenting an equal number of spaces
from the left and right margins and numbering the paragraphs.

            1. Your profit will increase 10 per cent.
            2. Your deliveries will be made promptly.

These methods can be applied in various ways to bring material to the reader's
attention quickly and artistically.

Letter Style 3a. *First page of a two-page letter, blocked style (also known as "modified block"), with Subject line, quoted matter, tabulations, and enumerations. Punctuation is standard (also known as "mixed").*

Mr. Jonathan R. MacKenzie
Page 2
November 18, 19--

Letters over 300 words in length usually require two pages, particularly when typed on a pica-type machine. The right, left, and bottom margins on the first page should be balanced. The heading of the second page starts six line spaces (1 inch) from the top and consists of the name of the addressee, "Page 2," and the date. The letter continues two or three spaces below. (See also ¶¶ 144, 145.)

Tabulations, quoted material, and enumerations in the body of the letter affect the working out of the letter-placement rules in Par 161. It is often necessary to adjust the marginal stops for a longer line of writing and very often to raise the letter on the page.

Start the complimentary closing, the firm name, and the signature near the center of the paper.

When the signer's typed signature and title are both long, type the title on the line below his name, so that it will not extend into the right margin. It may, however, end even with the right margin.

A postscript is typed at least two spaces below the identification data. The dictator's initials may be typed below the postscript.

                              Very sincerely yours,

                              Franklin B. Collingsworth

                              Franklin B. Collingsworth
                              General Merchandising Manager
                              in Charge of Sales

FBC:RE
Enclosure--Check

P. S. The dictator's title in this letter is such a long one that it is necessary to break it and carry part of it over to the next line.

Letter Style 3b. *Second page of a two-page letter, with "Page 2" heading, three-line dictator's typed signature and title, enclosure notation, and a postscript.*

FRANK FERRIS FARMS

29316 VALLEY ROAD   ≋   *BALTIMORE 16, MARYLAND*

Finest Fresh Produce

February 2, 19--

Mr. Lloyd R. McConnell, Jr.
Director of Personnel
The Province Corporation
Market and Sansome Streets
San Francisco 9, California

Dear Lloyd:

In the full-blocked letter, every line begins at the left
margin. A full-blocked letter is never double spaced.

If a company name is part of the signature, it should be
typed in all capital letters two spaces below the complimentary closing. If a company name is not used, the
signature line is typed four spaces below the complimentary
closing.

Note the form of the identification data. Other accepted
forms could, of course, be used with this letter style.

When letters are sent by other than regular mail, the
method used is indicated in small letters below the identification data or the enclosure notation; for example,
"Registered," "Special Delivery," etc. This information
could be typed in full capital letters and underscored
two spaces below the date line.

Sincerely yours,

FRANK FERRIS FARMS

Service Office

Louis Allen/sun
Registered Mail

Letter Style 4. *Full-blocked (also known as "extreme block"), with dictator's name in identification data and registered-mail notation. Punctuation is standard (also known as "mixed").*

Interoffice Memo

To: Lawrence R. Jensen   **Date:** January 17, 19--

From: Robert C. Nelson

Subject: Memo Form

Interoffice memos are used for correspondence between individuals, departments, and branch offices of the same firm. The forms contain printed headings, against which pertinent data are typed. The sheets vary in color and quality of paper from the regular stationery.

The left marginal stop should be set even with the printed headings and the right margin made the same width as the left.

If the dictator's name appears in the "From" line, his initials are typed a few spaces below the body of the memo. If only the dictator's title appears in the "From" line, his name is typed a few spaces below the body of the memo.

Reference initials and enclosure notations are used as in other letters, although it is permissible to use only the typist's initials in the identification data.

R. C. N.

CS

An interoffice memorandum.

153   The *hanging-indented,* with inverted paragraphs (see Letter Style 7), is used chiefly in advertising or topical letters.

154   The *Simplified* letter format (see Letter Style 8) is recommended by the National Office Management Association as an important step toward improving business correspondence.

155   Double spacing is often used for very short letters. If the indented style is used, the inside address can also be double spaced. If the blocked form is used, the inside address should be single spaced.

PUNCTUATION OF LETTER STYLES

The various parts of a letter (except the body) may be punctuated according to the three methods described here. The rules that apply to the body of the letter are given in Section 5.

156   Standard (mixed) punctuation (see Letter Styles 1–5). This is the most commonly used style. End punctuation marks are not used (outside the body of the letter) except after the salutation and the complimentary closing, unless a line ends with an abbreviation.

157   Full (close) punctuation (see Letter Style 6). The date line, each inside-address line, the salutation, and the complimentary closing end with punctuation.

(*Text continues on page 32.*)

Clifton & Clifton, Inc.

CROCKER BANK BUILDING · 710 MONTGOMERY STREET · SAN FRANCISCO 4

June 7, 19--

Osborne, Clay & Black
568 Fifth Avenue
New York 10, New York

Gentlemen:

ATTENTION: ACCOUNTING DEPARTMENT

File No. 469-24

The square-blocked letter form is an interesting new letter style
that permits many more words to the page than any other letter
style.

A 50- or 60-space line should be used. The letter is started
about halfway between the points where the date and the inside
address would be in any other letter style.

The date is positioned on the same line with the name of the
addressee and ends even with the right margin.

An Attention or a Subject line could be centered as here, or
either could be written at the left margin.

The closing lines are started at the left margin. The company
name could be typed in all capitals a double space below the
complimentary closing. The reference initials and even with the
right margin. They could be written as here, or the dictator's
initials could be omitted.

Cordially yours,

George R. Noyes

George R. Noyes, Editor
CLIFTON SALES MONTHLY

GRN:RBM
2 Enc.

Letter Style 5. *Square-blocked, with Attention line, Subject line,
two-line dictator's typed signature, and reference initials and enclosure notation at right. Punctuation is standard (also known as
"mixed").*

MAYER-SEMPLE COMPANY, Inc.

1410 WEST PHELAN STREET
PITTSBURGH 3, PENNSYLVANIA
Cable address: MAYPLECO
TABUR 5 5570

January 19, 19--.

My dear Senator:

This letter illustrates the indented letter style, as well as the
semipersonal, formal, or official letter style.

The date could be placed as here, centered, or end even with the right
margin. Each line of the inside address, after the first one, is indented
five spaces. The paragraphs are indented five or more spaces.

In full punctuation, the date line, each line of the inside address,
the salutation, and the complimentary closing end with punctuation marks.
Standard punctuation (see Style 1) would also be acceptable with this letter
style.

The distinguishing feature of the semipersonal or formal letter style is
the writing of the inside address two to five spaces below the body of the
letter. This style is often used in diplomatic correspondence; in letters
addressed to Federal, state, or municipal officials; and in personal letters
written by executives and professional men.

Some authorities make a distinction between the semipersonal and the
formal style. In both cases, the address is written below the body of the
letter; but the blocked form (see Style 1) is used for the semipersonal and
the indented form for the formal style. The salutation "Sir" and the complimentary closing "Respectfully" are used in the most formal letters.

The complimentary closing starts at the center. The firm name, typed
signature, or typed title is indented five spaces. The identification data
and enclosure notations, if any, are typed two lines below the inside address.

In an ordinary business letter--not a semipersonal or a formal letter--
written in the indented style, the inside address would be typed in its usual
place above the salutation. The identification data and any necessary
enclosure notations should also be included.

Sincerely yours,

Lawrence R. MacKnight

Lawrence R. MacKnight.

The Honorable John S. Randolph,
United States Senate,
Washington 25, D. C.

Letter Style 6. *Indented, with inside address at foot to make letter
formal. Address could also be in usual position. Punctuation is full
(also known as "close").*

Gila River Industries

▲ Grand Avenue and 18th Street · Phoenix 5, Arizona

September 17, 19--

Mr. K. Stanley Watson
Executive Vice-President
and Head Geologist
The Butte Copper Company, Inc.
375 Madison Avenue
New York 14, New York

Dear Mr. Watson

The hanging-indented form is most commonly used in advertising letters or letters containing a number of different topics that should be set off from one another.

In open punctuation, no punctuation is used at the end of any line outside the body of the letter, except a line ending with an abbreviation. Either standard or full punctuation could also be used with this letter style.

The first line of each paragraph is typed even with the left margin, but succeeding lines in each paragraph are indented five or more spaces.

After typing the inside address, the salutation, and the first line of the letter, move in the left margin stop to govern the remaining lines in the paragraph.

For the first line of succeeding paragraphs, set a tabular stop at the desired starting point. Use the margin-release key to return the carriage. Depress the tabular key. The carriage will then be in the correct position so that you may start typing the first line.

The identification data are placed even with the left margin. The dictator of this letter did not use a typed signature, but his name is written in full in the identification data.

Cordially yours

Charles S. Casper

Charles S. Casper
Secretary-Treasurer
and Senior Economic Analyst

CFS

Letter Style 7. *Hanging-indented (also known as "inverted paragraph"), with dictator's name on separate line in reference position. Punctuation is open.*

Fiske Inc.

5312 BRUNSWICK DRIVE
ATLANTA 2, GEORGIA

May 29, 19--

Businessmen's Association
2981 Lincoln-Liberty Building
Philadelphia 7, Pennsylvania

THE SIMPLIFIED LETTER

This letter form has been recommended by the National Office Management Association as an important step in improving business correspondence.

Each line begins at the left margin. The formal salutation is omitted.

The subject is typed in capital letters at least three spaces below the address. The body of the letter starts three spaces below the Subject line.

Questions, listings, or similar items in the body of the letter may be indented five spaces from the left margin, except when preceded by a number or letter.

Notice the following points:

1 Location of date
2 The subject
3 Periods omitted after numbers in outlines
4 Typed signature

The complimentary closing is omitted, and the signer's name is typed in capitals four or five spaces below the end of the letter.

The initials of the typist are blocked at the left margin, two spaces below the signature. Enclosures are indicated below the initials. The names or the initials of individuals receiving carbon copies are typed at the left margin, below the initials and enclosures.

Nelson A. Rollins

NELSON L. ROLLINS

lc

Letter Style 8. *The Simplified letter of the National Office Management Association (a modification of Letter Style 4, full-blocked), with Subject line but no salutation, complimentary closing, nor dictator's initials. Punctuation is open.*

158 Open punctuation (see Letter Styles 7 and 8). No punctuation is used at the end of any line outside the body of the letter unless that line ends with an abbreviation.

LETTER-PLACEMENT GUIDE

159 Typewriter spaces to the inch.

a) *Pica* (large) type normally measures 10 spaces to the inch.

b) *Elite* (small) type normally measures 12 spaces to the inch.

c) Lines are usually spaced 6 to the inch.

d) Thus, a page 8½ inches wide and 11 inches long will contain 66 type-written lines and will measure 85 pica spaces or 102 elite spaces cross-wise.

160 The letter-placement guide on page 33 is offered as an aid to better placement. It is to be used as a *guide* only and is not to be followed unconditionally.

161 Type the date three lines below the letterhead or on line 15, *whichever is lower* on the page.

a) Such details as paragraphing, tabulations, enumerations, Subject and Attention lines affect the working out of this guide. The typist, therefore, must learn to modify the guide to meet varying conditions.

b) Use two pages for a letter over 300 words. Leave six to eight blank lines at the bottom of the first page. (See also Letter Style 3b.)

c) For placement of a double-spaced letter, double the number of words in the letter body.

Note: To set the margin stops for the length of the line indicated—

(1) Find the center of your paper. (See ¶ 164.)

(2) Set the left margin stop half the desired line length to the left of the center; then add to that point the full length of the line desired and set the right margin stop. An example:

	Pica	Elite
Length of line desired.	60	60
Centering point.	43	50
Less half of desired line (½ of 60).	—30	—30
Set left margin stop at.	13	20
Add length of desired line.	60	60
Set right margin stop at.	73	80

(3) Most typists prefer to add five additional spaces in the right margin. This extra space provides greater leeway in returning the carriage as soon as possible after hearing the bell and eliminates frequent use of the margin-release key.

162 Many offices have adopted the timesaving device of using the same line length for all letters under 300 words in length.

a) The date is typed either on line 15 or three spaces below the letter-head.

b) A 50-space (pica) or a 60-space (elite) line is used. A tabular key is set for the paragraph indention. A tabular key is set at the center for the date and for the complimentary close.

c) The inside address is started:

(1) On line 18 or 19 for a long letter (under 300 words).

Letter-Placement Guide

Words in Body	Length of Line in		Lines Down from Date	Length of Letter
	Inches	*Spaces*		
Up to 100	4″	Pica 40 Elite 50*	8	(Short)
100–200	5″	Pica 50 Elite 60	6	(Average)
Over 200	6″	Pica 60 Elite 70*	4	(Long)
Over 300	6″	Pica 60 Elite 70*	4	(Two-page)

*Rounded off.

    (2) On line 22 or 23 for a medium-length letter (under 200 words).

    (3) On line 26 or 27 for a short letter (under 100 words).

  d) If the letter is between a short- and a medium-length one or a medium-length and a long one, more spaces or fewer spaces are allowed, as the case may be, between the date and the inside address. (See also techniques for adapting the length of a letter, ¶ 163.)

163   Techniques for adapting the length of a letter.

  a) To make a letter shorter by altering the placement:

    (1) Raise the date.

    (2) Reduce the lines between the date and the inside address.

    (3) Reduce by one line the lines allowed for the signature.

    (4) Omit the company name, if permitted.

    (5) Raise the identification data to the signature line.

    (6) Use half a space between the paragraphs and between the body of the letter and the complimentary close.

  b) To make a letter longer by altering the placement:

    (1) Increase the number of lines between the date and the inside address.

    (2) Use 1½ lines before and after the salutation, between the paragraphs, between the body and the complimentary close, and between the complimentary close and the company name.

    (3) Allow six lines for the signature.

    (4) Lower the identification data.

    (5) Place the signer's name and title on separate lines.

    (6) Allow additional space before the identification data.

Note: All the above techniques may be used, if necessary, or any combination of them that is needed to condense or to expand a letter.

164   Center your paper in the machine. To find the center:

  a) Pick a centering point (50, 45, or 40) on the carriage-position scale. Set the carriage at that scale point.

  b) Fold a piece of paper evenly lengthwise and insert it in the machine. Then loosen the paper and slide it right or left until the fold appears at the center of the V-shaped printing point.

c) Set the paper guide at the left edge of the paper. *Note* exactly where you have now set the paper guide and always check to see that it is in that position before you begin to type.

d) Use that centering point to compute marginal-stop placement (see ¶ 161) and to center various parts of the letter, such as the date and the Attention or Subject lines.

e) On some typewriters the scales are arranged so that *0* appears in the middle of the carriage, with the scale points marked off evenly right and left from the *0* center.

f) The distinction between pica and elite type:

(1) Pica (large) type (10 spaces to an inch) • • • • • • • • • •
Elite (small) type (12 spaces to an inch) • • • • • • • • • • • •

(2) If you do not know whether your machine has *pica* or *elite* type, type a series of periods and compare them with the ones above. To use the letter-placement guide accurately, you must know whether you are typing with *pica* or *elite* type.

ADDRESSING ENVELOPES

165   The address may be blocked (see below) or indented (see page 35). No. address should consist of fewer than three lines.

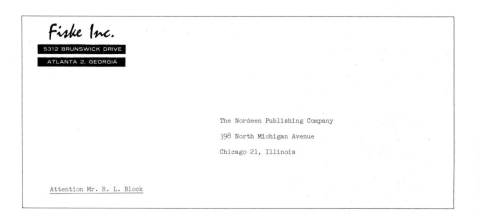

INTERNATIONAL SUPPLY COMPANY, Inc.

463 North LaSalle Street   /   Chicago 2, Illinois

REGISTERED

Mr. Lloyd R. Reardon, Treasurer
Blake, Walsh & Taylor Company, Inc.
101 Beale Street
San Francisco 6, California

Personal

At the left, a small *business envelope with a single-spaced, four-line address and two special notations. Below, a* large *business envelope with a double-spaced, three-line address and an Attention line.*

Fiske Inc.

5312 BRUNSWICK DRIVE
ATLANTA 2, GEORGIA

The Nordeen Publishing Company

398 North Michigan Avenue

Chicago 21, Illinois

Attention Mr. R. L. Block

JUDD-KANE, INC.

1410 GLENARM STREET • DENVER 2, COLORADO

Mr. Lloyd R. Sommerville
Manager, Sales Department
Lewis & Erickson Products, Inc.
598 East 77th Street
Los Angeles 8, California

PLEASE FORWARD

Above, a large *business
envelope with a single-
spaced, four-line address
and a special notation. To
the right, a* small *business
envelope with a double-
spaced, indented, three-
line address.*

Madison Business Council

120 Monona Avenue ▪ Madison 2, Wisconsin

Mr. R. L. Landers

Guerneville

California

166 Use double spacing when an address consists of three lines; single spacing
when it consists of more than three lines.

167 *Small* business envelope (No. 6¾, measuring 6½ by 3⅝ inches). (For illustration, see above.) Start the address on line 12, five or six spaces to the
left of center (at approximately 26 on pica scale, 33 on elite scale), when
the envelope is inserted at *0* on the scale.

168 *Large* business envelope (No. 10, measuring 9½ by 4⅛ inches). (For illustration, see above.) Start the address on line 14, five or six spaces to the
left of center (at approximately 43 on pica scale, 52 on elite scale), when
the envelope is inserted at *0* on the scale.
Caution: If the first line of the address is long or the lines of the address
are being indented, it may be necessary to start the first line more than
five or six spaces to the left of center.

169 *Special notations and return address*
Place any special information (*Attention, Care of,* or *Personal*) in the lower
left corner. Place an *Airmail, Special Delivery,* or *Registered* notation below the point where the stamp will be placed, approximately nine or ten
spaces below the top edge of the envelope.

170 If no return address is printed on the envelope, type the sender's name
and address in the upper left corner.

FOLDING AND INSERTING LETTERS

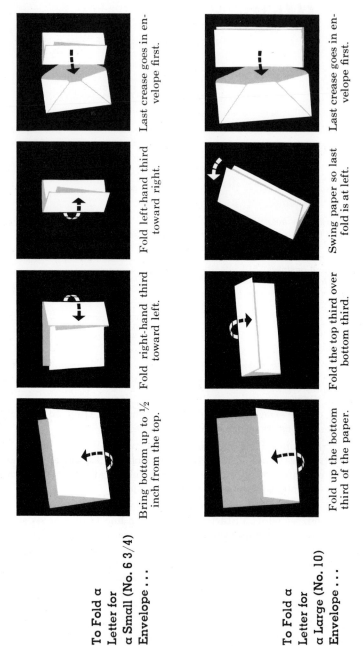

To Fold a Letter for a Small (No. 6 3/4) Envelope . . .

Bring bottom up to ½ inch from the top.

Fold right-hand third toward left.

Fold left-hand third toward right.

Last crease goes in envelope first.

To Fold a Letter for a Large (No. 10) Envelope . . .

Fold up the bottom third of the paper.

Fold the top third over bottom third.

Swing paper so last fold is at left.

Last crease goes in envelope first.

FOLDING AND INSERTING LETTERS

171   Always check for enclosures before folding letters.

172   To fold a letter for insertion into a *small* business envelope (page 36):

   a) Fold from the lower edge of the letter. Leave a ½-inch margin at top.

   b) Fold from right to left. Make the fold a little less than one-third the width of the sheet.

   c) Fold from left to right. Leave a ½-inch margin at the right.

   d) Insert the left creased edge into the envelope. This will leave the ½-inch margin near the envelope flap.

173   To fold a letter for insertion into a *large* business envelope (page 36):

   a) Fold from the lower edge of the letter. Make the fold about one-third the length of the sheet.

   b) Fold down from the top. Leave a ½-inch margin at the first fold.

   c) Insert the second fold into the envelope. This will leave the ½-inch margin near the envelope flap.

174   To fold a letter for insertion into a *window* envelope:

   a) Fold from the lower edge of the letter. Make the fold one-third the length of the sheet.

   b) Fold the upper edge of the letter *back* to the first fold so that the letterhead and the inside address will be on the outside.

   c) Insert the letter with the letterhead and the address toward the *front* of the envelope.

175   There are two methods of chain feeding envelopes.

   a) Back-of-cylinder method: Insert envelope halfway. Insert second envelope, placing it between first envelope and paper rest. Drawing first envelope into position draws second into halfway position. When first is addressed, insert third envelope as you did second. A quick twirl removes one envelope and draws next into position for addressing.

   b) Front-feed method: Make chain from front of cylinder by inserting new envelope between top of first and cylinder and by then "backing out" addressed envelope.

Courtesy Remington Rand

Chain feeding of envelopes by (a) *the back-of-cylinder method.*

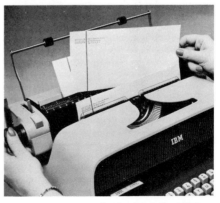

Courtesy International Business Machines Corporation

Chain feeding of envelopes by (b) *the front-feed method.*

SECTION 4

"Send a wire, please"

Note: The details regarding the sending, counting, and charging for telegrams, cablegrams, and radiograms change from time to time. Your local telegraph agency always has the latest information.

DOMESTIC SERVICES

176   *Telegram.* A full-rate fast service taking precedence over all other services. Accepted at any hour and transmitted immediately. Delivered by telephone or messenger. Charge based on a minimum of fifteen words, with a slight additional charge for extra words.

177   *Day letter.* A deferred service for longer messages. Transmitted during lulls in sending of regular messages, but delay is seldom more than one or two hours. Time-zone differences must be taken into consideration; for example, if the message is sent to a zone where the time is ahead of that of the sending zone, the message may be received too late for delivery the same day. In such a case, the message should be sent by night letter

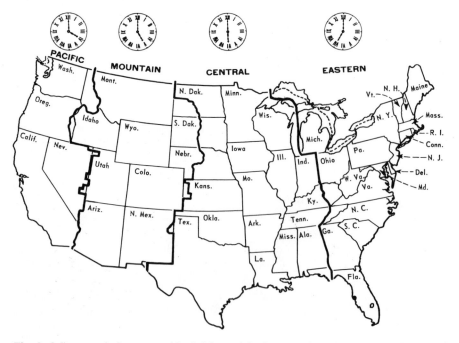

The dark lines mark the geographic divisions of the four standard time zones in the United States. The clocks show the differences in time from zone to zone.

instead. Based on a minimum of fifty words, with a slight additional charge for extra words.

178 *Night letter.* The most economical service. Messages accepted up to 2 a.m. for delivery any time before noon the following morning. Also based on a minimum of fifty words.

MESSAGES TO FOREIGN COUNTRIES

Used for messages to all foreign countries except Mexico and Canada.

179 *Full-rate cablegram or radiogram.* Fastest service. Minimum charge for five words. Plain language, code, or cipher may be used. *Code* language, used for economy, consists of real or artificial words of not more than five letters. Some concerns have private codes; there are also several commercial codes. *Cipher,* unlike code, is designed for secrecy. It consists of groups of figures or words having a secret meaning.

180 *Cable letter or letter telegram.* A slower service. Messages delivered the day after they are accepted, except in a few countries where they are delivered the morning of the second day after filing. Neither code nor cipher accepted.

181 *Typing*

a) Make at least one carbon copy of every telegram or cablegram. In some offices a confirmation copy is sent to the addressee and another to the bookkeeping department, in which case two additional carbons are needed.

b) Double space all messages. Either all capitals or the usual typewritten style is acceptable.

c) Date every message.

d) Omit salutation and complimentary closing.

e) Be sure the address is correct.

f) Use standard punctuation marks in telegrams. (See also ¶ 182*a* [5].)

g) Type the signature.

h) Type the dictator's and the stenographer's initials for reference purposes. These are not transmitted.

i) If the message is to be charged, write the sender's name under *Charge to the account of.* If the sender has no account, type his address in the lower left corner. If a telegram is to be sent collect, type *COLLECT* under *Pd. or Coll.*

j) In the box in the upper left corner, mark with an *X* the class of service desired. On cable letters type *LT* above the address. Messages will be sent full rate unless otherwise designated.

COUNTING

182 The charge for telegrams and cablegrams is based on the number of chargeable words, but the method of computing words differs.

a) Telegrams

(1) The address and the signature are transmitted free. A business signature may include both the company name and an employee's name.

(2) Each dictionary word is counted as one word regardless of length, but artificial words are counted at the rate of one word for each five letters.

DOMESTIC SERVICE	$			INTERNATIONAL SERVICE
Check the class of service desired; otherwise this message will be sent as a fast telegram		**WESTERN UNION**		Check the class of service desired; otherwise the message will be sent at the full rate
TELEGRAM X	S			FULL RATE
DAY LETTER	E	**TELEGRAM** 1206 (3-55)		LETTER TELEGRAM
NIGHT LETTER		W. P. MARSHALL, PRESIDENT		SHORE-SHIP

NO. WDS.-CL. OF SVC.	PD. OR COLL.	CASH NO.	CHARGE TO THE ACCOUNT OF	TIME FILED
			Elite Specialty Shop	

Send the following message, subject to the terms on back hereof, which are hereby agreed to

Omaha, Nebraska

February 18, 19--

Supreme Manufacturing Company

6495 Prairie Avenue

Chicago, Illinois

Wire best price 20 dozen #83, also earliest shipping date.

Elite Specialty Shop

BW:AL

A full-rate telegram.

Courtesy The Western Union Telegraph Company

(3) Each initial is counted as a word unless the letters are written together. *R. C. Adams* would be counted as three words, *RC Adams* as two.

(4) Common abbreviations typed together with or without periods are counted as one word; for example, *a.m.* or *am; f.o.b.* or *fob.* Contractions are counted as separate words and should not be used.

(5) Regular punctuation marks (period, comma, colon, semicolon, question mark, apostrophe, parentheses, dash, and quotation marks) are transmitted without charge. Therefore, such words as *Stop* and *Quote,* which are counted as one word each, should not be used.

(6) Groups of figures, letters, and other characters are counted at the rate of one word for each five figures or letters; thus #8159 (five characters) is counted as one word; $750.50 (six characters, decimal being punctuation), as two words.

b) Foreign messages

(1) Each word in the address and signature is charged for. Therefore, firms doing much foreign business usually have one-word registered addresses.

(2) Each dictionary word is counted at the rate of fifteen letters to a word. Code or cipher language (in full-rate messages only) is counted at the rate of five characters to a word.

(3) Each punctuation mark counts as one word.

(4) Figures or groups of figures are counted at the rate of five figures to a word. Any punctuation included in a group of figures is counted as one member of the group, not as a separate word.

SECTION 5

Punctuation pointers

The various marks of punctuation are the mechanical means for making the meaning of a sentence easily understood. They indicate the proper relationship of the words, phrases, and clauses composing the sentence. The ability to punctuate correctly is extremely important in transcribing business correspondence, which must be unmistakably clear.

Because punctuation is based on the grammatical construction of the sentence, some grammatical terms are used in the following rules. Consult the Glossary at the end of this Manual for any that are unfamiliar to you.

TYPEWRITER SPACING

For spacing before and after all punctuation marks, see ¶¶ 347, 348.

→ *The Period*

END OF SENTENCE

183   Place a period after a sentence that makes a statement or issues a command.

> The news in your letter of June 5 pleases us very much.
> Be sure to follow up this inquiry.

184   Also, place periods after condensed expressions that represent complete statements or commands. In letters, these condensed expressions frequently occur as answers to questions or as transitional phrases.

> Yes, by all means.
> Now, to answer your closing question.

Important Note: Sentences of this type are not to be confused with fragments of complete sentences, which are sometimes incorrectly transcribed as separate sentences.

> If it is satisfactory to you, we can fill the order in imitation leather. (*Not:* If it is satisfactory to you. We can fill the order in imitation leather.)
> The shipment arrived yesterday, after we had waited for it for six weeks. (*Not:* The shipment arrived yesterday. After we had waited for it for six weeks.)

185   Many requests are phrased in the form of a question out of courtesy. Although such sentences are technically questions, they are actually requests. Follow such sentences by periods.
Hint: A courteous request calls for action; a true question calls for an actual answer. The courtesy sentences often begin with *will* or *may.*

> May we have a copy of your fall price list.
> Will you please send us copies of your references.

186 Place a period after an indirect question. (See ¶ 193.)

FOLLOWING ABBREVIATIONS

187 Periods follow abbreviations. Detailed rules governing abbreviations are given in ¶¶ 429–454.

IN DECIMALS

188 The period is used to separate whole numbers from decimal fractions; as *33.33%; $5.50.* (No space before or after decimal points.)

IN OUTLINES

189 Place a period after a number or a letter that indicates a division in an outline, unless the number or letter is enclosed in parentheses. (For illustration, see ¶ 321.)

FOR EMPHASIS

190 Three spaced-out periods are often used, especially in advertising material, for emphasis or to display individual items.

> The Inn at the End of the Road ... where you may enjoy the epicure's choicest offerings ... by reservation only ... closed Tuesdays.
> Where can you match these services—
> ... Free ticket delivery
> ... Flight insurance
> ... On-time departures

➤ **See** ¶ 287 for use of periods to *indicate omissions;* ¶ 305 for periods *with quotation marks;* ¶¶ 322, 323 for periods *with parentheses.*

A FEW DO NOT'S

191 Do not use the period:

a) After roman numerals; as *Volume I, King George VI of England.* *Exception:* Roman numerals attached to items in an outline. (See ¶ 321.)

b) After display headings, titles of tables, charts, etc., unless they are run-in headings followed by reading matter. These rules are illustrated by the headings that occur throughout this text.

c) After items in a list. (See illustration in ¶ 190.)

d) After a letter used instead of a name to designate a person or a thing; as *Miss A, Class B, Grade C,* and so on.

e) After a contraction. (See ¶ 430.)

➤ *The Question Mark*

TO INDICATE QUESTIONS

192 Use the question mark after a *direct* question.

> When can we begin sampling this cereal?
> In which cabinet are the pencils, erasers, paper clips, etc.?

Note: Sales and advertising material often contains sentences that intentionally raise questions in a prospective customer's mind.

> Why not see your dealer today?

193   Do *not* use a question mark after an *indirect* question.

> The publicity manager asked when we could begin sampling this cereal.
> I was asked whether they still doubted his ability.

194   A request or a suggestion phrased in the form of a question, out of courtesy, does not require a question mark. (See ¶ 185.)

195   Also, a sentence may be phrased as a statement, whereas its purpose is to ask a question. (Such sentences are indicated by a raising of the voice.) Follow such sentences by a question mark.

> They still doubt his ability?

QUESTIONS WITHIN SENTENCES

196   Insert a comma before a short direct question that follows a statement.

> You will come, won't you?   I can count on you, can't I?

197   An independent question within a sentence should start with a capital and be preceded by a comma.

> We come now to the question, What profit do we expect? (*But:* What profit do we expect? is the question.)

198   When a sentence contains a series of brief queries, place the question mark after each query; but do not capitalize each one. A series of complete sentences, however, should be capitalized.

> Can you estimate the cost of the roofing? the tile work? the painting?
>
> Consider the following points: Is the plan adequate? Is it financially feasible? Is it popular?

TO EXPRESS DOUBT

199   The question mark, enclosed in parentheses, is used to express doubt or uncertainty.

> He was graduated from Oberlin in 1942 (?).

Caution: Avoid overuse of this device to indicate comments that are intended to be humorous.

> *Not necessary:* His concise (?) report covered ten pages.

➤ **See** ¶¶ 306, 307 for question marks *with quotation marks;* ¶¶ 324, 325 for question marks *with parentheses.*

➤ *The Exclamation Point*

Use the exclamation point sparingly in business correspondence. It is an explosive mark. A safe rule to follow is to insert it only when the dictator dictates it.

Note: The exclamation point is made by typing the apostrophe, backspacing, and typing the period. On some machines, it is not necessary to backspace if the space bar is held down while both characters are typed. Some machines bear the exclamation point as standard equipment.

TO SHOW STRONG EMOTION

200   The chief use for the exclamation point in business correspondence is in advertising matter and sales correspondence, to indicate enthusiastic claims.

> Making way for fall stocks! Dresses, jackets, coats up to 50 per cent off!

201   Expressions that show great emotion, deep feeling, surprise, command, sarcasm, or amusement are followed by exclamation points.

> The possibility of another accident is horrible! (Deep feeling.)
> It can't be true! (Surprise.)
> Stop all work on the Lowell contract at once! (Command.)
> How have the mighty fallen! (Sarcasm.)
> Here's a good story! (Amusement.)

Note: Another method of indicating surprise, sarcasm, or disbelief is to enclose the exclamation point in parentheses directly following some word within the sentence. This device should not be overdone, however.

> Did you see that ad of a sale of genuine (!) Alaska-seal coats for $250?

202   A single intense word may be followed by an exclamation point. The sentence that follows it is punctuated as usual.

> Wait! We can't pass that mistake.

203   When intense words are repeated for emphasis, an exclamation point follows each repetition.

> Hush! Hush! Don't let our competitors hear this.

204   When exclamations are mild, a comma or a period is usually used.

> Well, well, so we've come to the end of that story.
> No. There's no use in vain regrets.

OH AND O

205   The exclamation *oh* may be followed by either a comma or an exclamation point, depending on the emphasis required. It is capitalized only when it starts a sentence. The capitalized *O,* the sign of direct address, is seldom used in business.

> Oh! That is real joy!   But, oh, how clever!

➤ **See** ¶¶ 308, 309 for the exclamation point with *quotation marks;* ¶¶ 324, 325 for the exclamation point *with parentheses.*

➤ *The Comma*

Of all punctuation marks, the comma is the most frequently used—and therefore misused.

Important: Don't punctuate by ear. The fact that you would normally pause at a certain point when reading or speaking is no reason for placing a punctuation mark at that particular point. (See also ¶¶ 240–243.)

COMPOUND SENTENCES

206 A comma should precede the conjunctions *and, or, nor, but,* or *for* when these conjunctions separate the *principal clauses* of a *compound sentence.*

> The critic reviewed the book, *and* our questions were answered.
> I attended the conference this year, *but* I shall not attend next year.
> We must leave early, *for* we have a long trip ahead.
> Please send your remittance at once, *or* we shall be obliged to put your account in the hands of our attorneys for collection.
> The material in this dress is not the right color, *nor* is it the quality ordered.
> Not only must the secretary be a rapid typist, *but* she must also be accurate. (*But:* The secretary must be not only an accurate typist *but* also a rapid one.)

Exception: When a sentence starts with a dependent clause that applies to *both* co-ordinate clauses of a compound sentence, no comma (or semicolon) separates the co-ordinate clauses. Reason: A comma or a semicolon would seem to make the dependent clause apply only to the first co-ordinate clause.

> If you wish to become an executive, you must understand accounting and you must know your product. (You must understand accounting if you wish to become an executive. You must know your product if you wish to become an executive.

Note: If the clauses of a compound sentence are very short, the comma may be omitted before the conjunction.

> *We build* and *they destroy.*

207 Do not confuse a true compound sentence with a sentence having a *compound predicate.*

a) A compound sentence contains at least two clauses, each clause containing a subject and a predicate. (See ¶ 206.)

> *He was graduated* in May with honors, and *he was fortunate* in obtaining a position at once.

b) A sentence may contain one subject with two or more predicates connected by a conjunction. In such sentences, no comma separates the predicates.

> The critic *reviewed* the book *and answered* questions.
> He *was graduated* in May *and began work* for a bank in June.
> Mr. Adams not only *criticized* the report *but* also *recommended* that it be revised.

208 Likewise, do not separate the compound subjects of a sentence, the compound objects of a preposition, nor other compound constructions by a comma.

> *The letters in the tray and those in these folders* are all to be filed. (Compound subject.)
> He may enter the Graduate School of Business at *Stanford* or *Harvard.* (Compound object of preposition *at.*)

209 Do not use a comma between independent clauses that are not joined by a conjunction. This error of punctuation is known as a "comma splice" or a "run-on sentence." Use a semicolon, or start a new sentence.

> Mark "rush" letters with an X in your notes; transcribe these first.
> *Or:* Mark "rush" letters with an X in your notes. Transcribe these first.

DEPENDENT (subordinate) CLAUSES

210 *After, although, as, because, if, since, unless, when,* and *while* are among the more frequent words used to introduce dependent clauses. (See ¶ 212 for a longer list.) A dependent clause that *precedes* a main clause is followed by a comma.

> *Before we can make a decision,* we must have all the facts.
> *Until the survey is completed,* the Board of Directors can take no action.
> *If, however, they had been more conservative in their investments,* the company would have been financially sound.
> *When Mr. Brown calls,* I shall ask for an explanation.

211 The method of punctuating a subordinate clause that *follows* the main clause depends on whether the subordinate clause is restrictive (essential) or nonrestrictive (nonessential). These two types of clauses *look* very much alike and are introduced by the same words, but they differ in meaning—and that smallest mark of internal punctuation, the comma, by its presence or its absence shows the meaning.

a) A *restrictive,* or *essential,* clause is necessary to the meaning of the sentence. It points out what person or what thing is meant. Because it *cannot be omitted,* commas are *not* used to set it off.

> Only political leaders *who are responsive to the wishes of their constituents* are supporting the bill. (Tells which political leaders.)
> The woman *who lives next door* is leaving tomorrow. (Tells which woman.)
> Green's book *that describes his trip to South America* sold a million copies. (Tells which book.)
> Give me a ring *when you get back.* (Tells when.)
> This applies to everyone *who works in the plant.* (Tells which persons.)

b) A *nonrestrictive,* or *nonessential,* clause is descriptive or explanatory. It *can be omitted* without changing the meaning of the sentence, and it *should be set off by commas.*

> Radio commentators, *who are often criticized by their listeners,* help mold public opinion. (Refers to all radio commentators.)
> He stopped in Chicago to see his father, *who is an eminent lawyer.* (Simply adds information about the father.)
> Mrs. Turner, *who lives next door,* is leaving tomorrow. (Mrs. Turner is leaving tomorrow.)
> Green's first book, *which sold a million copies,* is now out of print. (Green's first book is now out of print.)
> Give me a ring tomorrow morning, *when I shall have the information for you.* (Give me a ring tomorrow morning.)

Caution: If an *interrupting* subordinate clause requires a comma after the clause, a balancing comma *must* precede the clause. If the interrupting clause is essential to the meaning of the sentence, however, no commas are needed. If *that* occurs in a sentence of this type, be sure that the first comma *follows* the word *that.*

> Please tell Mr. Jensen that, *although we shall be inconvenienced,* we will attend the meeting. (Nonessential.)
> Doctors will tell you that *when a child is tired and pale* the cause is lack of nutritious food. (Essential.)

212 The words most frequently used to introduce dependent clauses were mentioned in ¶ 210. The list that follows includes still other words and phrases so used. For most of these expressions, two sentences are given— one containing a restrictive clause and one a nonrestrictive clause. In a few cases, only one type of clause is possible. If you cannot decide whether a clause that you may be transcribing is restrictive or nonrestrictive (and therefore whether commas are required or not), compare it with the illustrative sentences containing the word in your sentence.

After. Restrictive: The telegram came *after you left last evening.*
Nonrestrictive: The telegram came this morning, *after the decision had been made.*
All of which. Always nonrestrictive: The rumors, *all of which were unfounded,* brought about the defeat of the candidate.
Although and *Though.* Always nonrestrictive: She bought a new dress for the party, *although I do not believe she will wear it.* (A clause of concession.)
As. Restrictive: The results of the mailing are *as you prophesied they would be.*
Nonrestrictive: The results of the mailing are disappointing, *as you prophesied they would be.*
As . . . as. Always restrictive: He talked *as* well over the radio *as* he did at our meeting.
As if and *As though.* Restrictive: The man walked *as if* (or *as though*) *he were in a hurry.*
Nonrestrictive: The man walked fast, *as if* (or *as though*) *he were in a hurry.*
As soon as. Restrictive: We will fill your order *as soon as we receive stock.*
Nonrestrictive: We shall be able to fill your order next week, *as soon as we receive stock.*
At, By, For, In, and *To which.* Restrictive: I went to the floor *to which I had been directed.*
Nonrestrictive: I went to the tenth floor, *to which I had been directed.*
Because. Restrictive: He left *because he had another appointment.*
Nonrestrictive: This report must be on his desk tonight, *because he is leaving tomorrow.*
Before. Restrictive: The shipment was sent *before your letter was received.*
Nonrestrictive: The shipment was sent on Tuesday, *before your letter was received.*
For. Always nonrestrictive: He read the book, *for he was interested in psychology.* (Clause of reason.)
If. Restrictive: Let us hear from you *if you are interested.*
Nonrestrictive: She promised to write from Toronto, *if I remember correctly.* (Clause added loosely.)
In order that. Restrictive or nonrestrictive, depending on closeness of relation. Restrictive: She spoke clearly *in order that all might hear.*
Nonrestrictive: It will be necessary for all to be on hand promptly, *in order that the exercises may begin as scheduled.*
In order to. Always restrictive: We must have fifteen members present *in order to have a quorum.*

No matter. Always nonrestrictive: The order cannot be ready by Monday, *no matter what the manager says.*

None of which. Always nonrestrictive: We received five boxes of candy for Christmas, *none of which have been opened.*

None of whom. Used of persons and always nonrestrictive: We interviewed ten applicants, *none of whom were satisfactory.*

Since. Restrictive: We have taken no applications *since we received your instructions.*

Nonrestrictive: We are taking no more applications, *since our lists are now closed.* (Clause of reason.)

So . . . as. Always restrictive: The second dress was not *so* well made *as* the first one.

So that. Restrictive or nonrestrictive, depending on closeness of relation.
Restrictive: I studied *so that I would pass the test.*
Nonrestrictive: The store was closed, *so that I could not buy the dress.*

So . . . that. Always restrictive: The man was *so* tired *that* he could not finish the job.

Some of whom. Used of persons and always nonrestrictive: The agency has sent us five applicants, *some of whom seem promising.*

Than. Always restrictive: The employees were more disturbed by the rumor *than they cared to admit.*

That. Used in referring to things; also to persons when a class or type is meant. Preferred to *which* in introducing restrictive clauses: This is the house *that he owns today.* He is the candidate *that I prefer.* (See also ¶ 586 *a* and *b.*)

Though. See *Although.*

Unless. Restrictive: The item will be discontinued *unless customers begin to show an interest in it.*

Nonrestrictive: I shall start transferring the files, *unless you have other work for me.* (Loosely, as an afterthought.)

When. Restrictive: The company will accept bids *when Mr. Polk returns from his vacation.*

Nonrestrictive: The company will accept bids next week, *when Mr. Polk returns from his vacation.*

Where. Restrictive: Please tell me *where you put the paste.*
Nonrestrictive: It is on the top shelf, *where it always is.*

Whereas. Always nonrestrictive: The figures for last year include rural areas only, *whereas those for this year include large cities as well.* (Clause of contrast.)

Which. Used in referring to animals, things, and ideas. Preferred to *that* for nonrestrictive clauses: The bay, *which was full of small sailing craft,* was very rough.

While. Restrictive: The workers struck *while negotiations were still being carried on.* (*While* meaning "during that time," restrictive.)

Nonrestrictive: The workers at the Union Company struck, *while those at the Powers Company remained at work.* (*While* meaning "but," nonrestrictive.)

Who. Refers to persons. Restrictive: All students *who are members of the Student Council* will be excused at two o'clock today.

Nonrestrictive: John Smith, *who is a member of the Student Council,* will be excused at two o'clock today.

Whom. Refers to persons. Restrictive: This package is for the friend *whom I am visiting.*

Nonrestrictive: This package is for my cousin Amy, *whom I am visiting.*

Whose. Restrictive: The prize will be awarded to the student *whose essay shows the most originality.*

Nonrestrictive: Eunice, *whose story showed the most originality,* won the prize.

PARTICIPIAL, INFINITIVE, AND PREPOSITIONAL PHRASES

213 When a participial, an infinitive, or a prepositional phrase *precedes* the main clause:

a) An *introductory participial phrase* is followed by a comma. (See Glossary for treatment of participles.)

> *Speaking in a loud voice,* the chairman called the meeting to order.
> *Pleased by the unusual service,* the woman has become a steady customer.
> *Having made the correction,* I no longer worried.

Note: Do not mistake a gerundial phrase that is the subject of a sentence for a participial phrase.

> *Speaking before a large audience* always frightens me.

b) An *introductory infinitive phrase* is followed by a comma unless the phrase is the subject of the sentence. Infinitive phrases are recognized by the introductory word *to.*

> *To obtain the best results from the camera,* follow these directions.
> *To have displayed the goods more effectively,* he should have consulted a lighting specialist.
> *To have displayed the goods more effectively* would have been an expensive project. (Subject.)

c) An *introductory prepositional phrase* may or may not be followed by a comma, depending on its length.

> *On Monday morning* the mail is always late. (Short phrase.)
> *In response to the many requests of our customers,* we are opening a suburban branch. (Long phrase.)

214 The punctuation of a participial, an infinitive, or a prepositional phrase that *follows* the main clause depends on whether the phrase is restrictive or nonrestrictive.

a) A *restrictive* participial, infinitive, or prepositional phrase is necessary to the meaning of the sentence and cannot be omitted. Therefore, commas are *not* used to set it off.

> All the women *joining in the boycott* were housewives. (Participial.)
> The comments *printed in italics* are most important. (Participial.)
> I sold all my stocks *after having read the news.* (Participial.)
> It is a pleasure *to recommend Miss Brown.* (Infinitive.)
> He was supposed *to have arrived yesterday.* (Infinitive.)
> The copy *with the signatures* should be retained. (Prepositional.)

b) A *nonrestrictive* participial, infinitive, or prepositional phrase *can be omitted* without changing the meaning of the sentence. Therefore, such phrases *should be enclosed* in commas. (*Note:* Infinitive phrases are seldom nonrestrictive.)

> The organization, *realizing the need for publicity,* appropriated $5,000. (Participial.)
> The instructions, *given in the simplest terms,* can be followed without further explanation. (Participial.)

(*Continued on page 50.*)

I'm very tired tonight, *having arisen at six this morning.* (Participial.)

This collar needs interlining, *to mention only one defect.* (Infinitive.)

We are opening a branch, *in response to the many requests of our customers,* at the corner of Broad and Pine Streets. (Prepositional.)

Caution: The caution that applies to the punctuation of *interrupting* clauses (see *Caution* in ¶ 211) also applies to the punctuation of interrupting phrases.

It occurred to me that, *as an operator of trucks,* you might be interested in the claims that are made for these tires.

INTRODUCTORY, PARENTHETIC, OR TRANSITIONAL EXPRESSIONS

215 A word or a short phrase or a short clause that is used parenthetically (that is, a word, a phrase, or a clause that is not necessary to the grammatical completeness of the thought of the sentence) should be set off by commas. Some of the words, phrases, and clauses most frequently used in this way are:

accordingly	for instance	meanwhile	personally
actually	for the time being	moreover	respectively
after all	fortunately	namely	say
again	further	naturally	secondly
also	hence	nevertheless	so
apparently	however	next	still
as a matter of fact	if any	notwithstanding	strictly speaking
as a rule	in addition	now	that is to say
as it happened	in any case	obviously	then
as you know	in fact	of course	theoretically
at any rate	in other words	of necessity	therefore
better yet	in short	on the contrary	thus
consequently	in the first place	on the other hand	to begin with
finally	in turn	originally	to say the least
first	inclusive	otherwise	too
for example	indeed	perhaps	without doubt

a) Use one comma if the word or phrase occurs at the beginning or end of a sentence.

However, we began our investigation at once.

We have considered this step before, *as a matter of fact.*

In any case, we eagerly look forward to reading the report.

b) Use two commas if the word or phrase occurs within a sentence.

It is generally understood, *however,* that he will accept the position.

Current exports to Europe, *for example,* are mainly grain and coal.

You, *too,* will be pleased with the materials used in our products.

c) If a word or a phrase used parenthetically does not interrupt the thought of the sentence, the commas may be omitted.

He was *perhaps* unaware of the situation.

Your plan *therefore* seems feasible.

Mr. Jarrett, who *also* handles our line, should be consulted.

216 When such introductory words or parenthetical terms are used as *plain adverbs* rather than as connectives, no commas should be used.

(*Continued on page 51.*)

However staunch a party member he is, he refuses to sign the petition.
Obviously moved by his reception, the toastmaster gave an excellent speech.
That report is *too* long.

SERIES

217 When the last member of a series of three or more items is preceded by *and, or,* or *nor,* place a comma before the conjunction as well as between the other items.

> Study the rules for the use of the comma, the semicolon, and the colon.
> They did not go to the museum, to the aquarium, nor to the zoo.
> They hiked to the summit, ate their lunch, rested for an hour, and were home by nightfall.
> The critics agreed that the book was well written, that the facts were accurate, and that the conclusions were sound.

218 *Do not,* however, use a comma before the & sign in a company name.

> The machine is manufactured by Ames, Wright & Company.

219 When *etc.* (abbreviation of *et cetera,* meaning "and so forth") closes a series, a comma both precedes and follows the abbreviation (unless, of course, the abbreviation falls at the end of a sentence).

> The sale of suits, coats, hats, *etc.,* will start tomorrow.
> At nine o'clock tomorrow we shall start our sale of suits, coats, hats, *etc.*

220 Do not insert a comma *after* the last item in a series unless the sentence structure demands a comma at that point.

> January 15, March 3, and May 20 are the dates of the three letters.
> January 15, March 3, and May 20, 1961, are the dates of the three letters. (The comma following the year is one of the pair that sets off the year. See ¶ 69.)

221 When *and, or,* or *nor* is repeated with each item of a series, do not separate the items by commas.

> Invitations are being sent to parents and alumnae and faculty.

222 Also, if a series consists of two items only, do not separate the items by a comma.

> I can reach the office quickly either by bus or by subway.

> ➤ **See** ¶ 247 for the use of the *semicolon in a series.*

ADJECTIVES

223 When two or more consecutive adjectives modify the same noun, separate the adjectives by commas. But do *not* place a comma after the final adjective.

> The employer referred to him as a *quiet, efficient* worker. (A worker that is quiet and efficient.)

224 When the last adjective in the series is closely connected in thought with the noun, so that the first adjective modifies the combined idea of the final adjective plus the noun, do *not* separate the adjectives by a comma.

(*Continued on page 52.*)

The house was surrounded by an *old stone* wall. (A stone wall that is old.)
Mr. Howard is working on the *annual financial* statement. (A financial statement that is annual.)

Note: Two simple tests are useful in deciding whether the rule in ¶ 223 or ¶ 224 applies. If *and* can be inserted between the adjectives or if the adjectives can be reversed, insert commas. (See also ¶¶ 510–512.)

We came to the end of the *long, hot, dusty* walk. (Long and hot and dusty.)
An *old winter* hat. (One could not say *a winter old hat.*)

IDENTIFYING, APPOSITIVE, OR EXPLANATORY EXPRESSIONS

225   Words, phrases, and clauses that identify or explain other terms should be set off by commas. (See also ¶ 234.)

Mr. Clark, *the president,* is retiring on Monday, *June 30.*
We will meet on March 18, *Tuesday, at ten o'clock,* in my office.
San Francisco, *the second largest city on the Pacific Coast,* has an excellent harbor.
Our first thought, *to run to the nearest exit,* would have resulted in panic.
Mr. Green, *the salesman who led the group,* is to be the new manager.
He will begin work on January 2, 1965, under the terms of the contract.
The letter should have been addressed to Portland, *Maine,* rather than Portland, *Oregon.*
She enjoys outdoor sports, *such as tennis and golf.*
Business transacted on credit is based on two factors, *sales and collections.*
His latest book, *"Color and Design,"* sells for $3.

226   When the identifying or explanatory term is very closely connected with the principal noun, so that the sense would not be complete without the added explanation, no commas are required.

My sister *Nancy* was graduated from high school in June.
Mary *herself* wrote the essay.
The year *1950* marked the end of the first half of the twentieth century.
The word *accommodate* is often misspelled.
She enjoys such outdoor sports *as tennis and golf.*
His book entitled *"Color and Design"* sells for $3.

INTERRUPTIONS OF THOUGHT; ADDITIONAL CONSIDERATIONS

227   Words, phrases, or clauses that are parenthetic (asides) or that mention an additional consideration should be separated from the rest of the sentence by commas.

She has received, *so I was told,* a letter of commendation from the mayor.
The exhibit, *if I remember correctly,* contained only modern art.
Our lighting equipment, *you must admit,* is most inadequate.
His record is outstanding, *particularly in the field of electronics.*
Our executives, *as well as our staff,* acclaimed the decision.

CONTRASTING AND OPPOSING THOUGHTS

228   Contrasting and opposing expressions (these often begin with the words *but* or *not*) should be set off by commas. (See illustrations, page 53.)

He had changed his methods, *not his objectives,* we noticed.

The more even your typing touch, *the more pleasing the results.*

PHRASES MODIFYING THE SAME WORD

229   Co-ordinate phrases modifying the same word should be separated by commas.

> This book is *as well written as,* though *less exciting than,* his other books.
>
> I have no *time* for, nor *interest in,* that subject.
>
> This course of action is the *wisest, if not the most expedient,* one under the circumstances.

Caution: The full intervening expression, not just a portion of it, must be enclosed in commas.

OMITTED WORDS (usually verbs)

230   Use a comma to indicate the omission of a word or words that are clearly understood from the context. (In the following sentences, omitted words are enclosed in parentheses.) (See also ¶ 245.)

> Some modern novels are factual; others, (are) mere fiction.
>
> The English test was given to all students; the history test, (was given) to a selected group.
>
> Something is wrong. What, (is wrong) we don't know.
>
> A payment of half the purchase price is due on delivery of the goods; the balance, (is due) in three months.

FOR CLARITY

231   Note how the use of the comma prevents misreading.

> As you know, nothing came of the meeting. (*Not:* As you know nothing came of the meeting.)
>
> "Prescriptions filled reasonably, accurately." (Meaning reasonably and accurately. *Not:* "Prescriptions filled reasonably accurately.")

232   *Sometimes* it is even necessary to separate a subject and predicate.

> All any insurance policy is, is a contract for services.

DIRECT ADDRESS

233   Names and words used in direct address must be set off by commas.

> You cannot deny, *Mr. Monroe,* that you made that statement.
>
> No, *sir,* I did not see him.
>
> *Mr. Chairman,* I rise to a point of order.

RESIDENCE AND POSITION

234   Use commas to set off a phrase denoting the residence or position of a person; also, academic degrees, religious orders, and such personal-name suffixes as *Jr., Sr., 3d* (or *III*), and *Esq.* (See also ¶ 225 and ¶ 509.)

> Mr. Lee, *of San Francisco,* will represent our company at the convention. (*Note:* A recent trend is to omit the commas in sentences of this type.)
>
> I suggest that you write to Mr. Paulson, *manager of our Portland office.*
>
> Mr. L. B. Kelly, *Sr.,* sailed for Europe today.
>
> We were represented in court by Henry E. Stevens, *Esq.,* of New York.

WITH INC. AND LTD.

235   Insert a comma before *Inc.* and *Ltd.* in company names unless the official name of the company is written without a comma. In a sentence, a comma also follows the abbreviation. (See also ¶ 509.)

> Field Hats, Ltd.
> The Book-of-the-Month Club, Inc., should be notified.

WITH QUOTATION MARKS

236   A *brief* direct quotation should be preceded by a comma. (See also ¶¶256, 294.)

> The telegram reads, "Arrive six tonight."

237   An indirect quotation, either short or long, requires no comma. (See also ¶ 278.)

> The telegram said that he would arrive at six.
> The boy said that he had been given the directions by his teacher.

238   Expressions that break into a quotation to indicate its source are enclosed in commas. (See ¶¶ 293–295.)

239   When a comma and a closing quotation mark fall at the same point in a sentence, the comma is *always* placed inside the closing quotation mark. (The reason for this rule is typographical, to give a more pleasing appearance to the page.)

> The author of that article, "Office Etiquette," will lecture tonight.
> It's a case of "if you want a job done, do it yourself," I suppose.

SOME CAUTIONS

In the sentences in ¶¶ 240–243 the bars indicate points at which commas are often incorrectly inserted. Many of these errors result from punctuating by ear rather than according to sentence structure. (See also ¶¶ 207–209, 220, 223, 224, 226.)

240   Do not insert a *single* comma between a subject and its verb.

> The *woman* with the red hair/ *is* an author.
> *That he is one of the outstanding scientists in America/ has been conceded* for years.

241   Do not insert a comma *after* a co-ordinating conjunction.

> I passed all my exams, and/ I have found a job.

Exception: See third sentence in ¶ 245.

242   Do not insert a single comma between a verb and its object or complement.

> On his first day in office the mayor *dismissed/ the police chief.* (Object.)
> Within one week, the Congressman *had introduced* a *sales-tax bill/* and a restrictive *labor bill* in the House. (Compound object.)
> We hope that *you will visit our store soon/* and that *you will like our merchandise.* (Compound object.)
> She *seems/ honest, sincere,* and *capable.* (Complement.)
> In the war he *had been/ enlisted man* and *officer.* (Complement.)

➤ **See** also ¶¶ 218, 220–222 for incorrect use of comma *in a series.*

243 Do not insert a comma after the day of the month unless the sentence structure demands a comma at that point. (See also ¶¶ 220, 225.)

> We received your letter of May 8/ about the damaged shipment. (Essential.)
> *But:* We received your letter of May 8, in which you ask for a price quotation. (Nonessential.)

➤ **See** also ¶¶ 196, 197 for commas with *questions within sentences;* ¶¶ 401c, 420, 423–425 for commas in *figures;* ¶¶ 326, 327 for commas *with parentheses.*

➤ *The Semicolon*

INDEPENDENT CLAUSES—CONJUNCTION OMITTED

244 When a conjunction (*and, but, or, nor*) is omitted between two independent clauses, separate the clauses by a semicolon.

> The author practiced tolerance; his critic merely advocated it.
> The union was willing to compromise; the management was not.

COMPOUND SENTENCES

245 A semicolon is used to separate the independent clauses in a compound sentence when either or both of the clauses contain internal punctuation, such as a comma.

> The committee, as I pointed out yesterday, has taken no action; and our constitutional rights are being ignored.
> After he returned, he entered college; but he was not a good student.
> We are taking over an entire group of adjacent buildings; and, in order to give us time to move our stock, our store will be closed until Monday. (Some writers omit the comma after *and* in sentences of this type.)
> (Without the internal punctuation, commas could have separated the clauses in these sentences; for example: We are taking over an entire group of adjacent buildings, and our store will be closed until Monday.)

(See *Exception* in ¶ 206.)

SUBORDINATE CLAUSES

246 When several subordinate clauses (often introduced by *that*) are used in the same relationship to the main clause, the clauses are *usually* separated by semicolons and *must be* separated by semicolons if there is internal punctuation.

> Many modern writers believe that our cultural patterns are breaking down; that our social institutions are degenerating; and that intolerance will wreck our world. (Three noun clauses used as the object of the verb *believe.*)

IN A SERIES

247 If the items of a series contain commas, separate the members of the series by semicolons.

> Invitations have been sent to our sales managers in Portland, Oregon; Seattle, Washington; Salt Lake City, Utah; and Los Angeles, California.

ADVERBIAL CONNECTIVES (conjunctive adverbs)

248   When independent clauses are joined by one of the following adverbial connectives (also known as conjunctive adverbs), place a semicolon before the connective and a comma after it. (See ¶ 249.)

accordingly	consequently	in fact	on the contrary
at least	furthermore	moreover	otherwise
besides	however	nevertheless	therefore

The motion was voted down; *moreover,* it was voted down by a large majority.

We are moving to the suburbs; *consequently,* our budget must provide for increased commutation fare.

The Atlanta district showed a better business last year; *therefore,* we are increasing their staff.

Test: Adverbial connectives are transitional terms and not pure conjunctions. In deciding whether to use a comma or a semicolon in sentences of this type, notice that these connectives may appear *within* the clause, whereas co-ordinating conjunctions, such as *and* or *but,* will fit only at the *beginning* of the clause.

Costs have increased; *however,* we have made a modest profit.

Costs have increased; we have, *however,* made a modest profit.

Costs have increased, *but* we have made a modest profit.

249   The one-syllable adverbial connectives *hence, still, then, yet, thus,* and *so* usually do not require a comma after them unless the connective demands special emphasis.

The flood had receded; *yet* many remained homeless.

Several of the items you ordered are out of stock; *so* we are holding the entire order until the missing items have been received.

You shouldn't be without this soap powder another day; *so,* the first thing tomorrow morning ask your grocer to send you a package.

Note: Some writers also omit the comma after some of the adverbial connectives listed in ¶ 248, depending on the emphasis intended.

BEFORE WORDS INTRODUCING ENUMERATIONS

250   When enumerations, lists, and explanations are introduced by the following words and expressions, place a semicolon before the expression and a comma after it. (See also ¶¶ 252–254, 320, 321.)

for example (abbrev., e.g.)	that is (abbrev., i.e.)	namely
for instance	that is to say	to wit

The secretary has three important duties; *namely,* attending meetings, writing the minutes, and sending out notices.

Examinations will be given for a number of different positions; *for example,* typist and general clerk, secretary, office manager, and bookkeeper.

Note: Some writers use a colon instead of a semicolon in constructions like these.

251   However, if the above terms are part of a parenthetical expression, the sentence may be punctuated in either of two ways: (*a*) by placing a comma before the introductory expression as well as after the enumeration; or (*b*) by placing a dash in both places.

> *a.* A careless office worker, *for example,* a poor stenographer, should not be tolerated.
> *b.* A careless office worker—for example, a poor stenographer—should not be tolerated.

➤ **See** ¶ 311 for semicolons *with quotation marks;* ¶ 328 for semicolons *with parentheses.*

➤ *The Colon*

BEFORE LISTED ITEMS

252 Place a colon after *the following, as follows, thus,* and *these* when these expressions introduce listed items.

> The *following* students were absent today: Davis, Hall, and Lloyd.
> The essential courses are *as follows:* shorthand, typewriting, and English.
> The requirements were *these:* a college degree, three years' experience in the field, and freedom to travel abroad.
> The *following* rules should be observed in writing checks:
> 1. Write them in ink.
> 2. Leave no empty spaces on lines that are to be filled in.
> 3. Make no changes or erasures in an amount of money.

253 Even if the introducing expression is implied, not stated, use the colon.

> The house has several attractive features: cross ventilation in every room, a one-and-a-half-story living room, and two terraces.
> Wanted: Camera in exchange for portable radio.

254 However, the colon is *not* used in the following cases:

a) If the sentence in which the introductory expression occurs is a fairly long sentence, and especially if the expression occurs near the beginning of that sentence.

> We are sorry to be obliged to set *the following* restrictions on the return of merchandise, because many customers have abused the privilege. Goods cannot be returned after five days, and price tags must not be removed.

b) If the sentence containing the introductory expression is followed by another sentence.

> Campers will find that *the following* small items will add much to their enjoyment of the summer. These articles may be purchased from a store near the camp.

> | | |
> |---|---|
> | Flashlight | Hot-cold food bag |
> | Small camera | Fishing line |

c) When a list is informally introduced. (A verb usually precedes such informally introduced items.)

> This set of china includes 8 dinner plates, 8 tea plates, 8 cups and saucers, a platter, and a vegetable dish.
> The terminal marks of punctuation are the period, the question mark, and the exclamation point.

BEFORE AN EXPLANATORY SENTENCE

255   When a sentence explains, illustrates, or supplements the thought of the sentence immediately preceding it, the sentences are separated by a colon.

> And don't forget one thing: nothing can take the place of experience.
>
> Everything about this wallpaper suits me: the design is well balanced, and the colors are pleasing.

In sentences of this type, the second sentence is usually not capitalized, because the two sentences are so closely related in meaning. In some cases, however, if the material following the colon demands emphasis, or if it is introduced as a formal rule, the word following the colon may be capitalized.

> In law, there is a fundamental difference between a boardinghouse and a lodginghouse: A boardinghouse may furnish both food and shelter, whereas a lodginghouse furnishes shelter but not food.

BEFORE QUOTATIONS

256   A long direct quotation is preceded by a colon.

> Doctor Post, on his return from Europe yesterday, said: "If the free peoples of the world are to remain free, they must rally to a cause that will unite them."

257   *No colon* is used before a long indirect quotation.

> Doctor Post, on his return from Europe yesterday, said that the free peoples of the world must rally to a cause that will unite them.

IN EXPRESSIONS OF TIME AND IN PROPORTIONS

258   When hours and minutes are expressed in figures, separate the figures by a colon, as *8:25.* (No space precedes nor follows this colon.)

Note: In railroad timetables the separation is usually indicated by a period.

259   A colon is used to represent the word *to* in proportions, as *2:1.* (No space precedes nor follows this colon.)

IN LITERARY REFERENCES

260   The colon is used to separate certain items in bibliographies, the style varying with authors and publishers. One common arrangement is shown here; another, in the Reference list at the end of this Manual.

> Rosenberg, R. Robert. *College Business Mathematics,* Third Edition. New York: McGraw-Hill Book Company, Inc., 1961.

Frequently, a colon separates the volume number from the page number, especially when the volume number is indicated in arabic numerals.

> *Today's Secretary,* 1:25   *The New International Encyclopedia,* 15:157

Note: No space precedes nor follows colons in bibliographies.

> **❯ See** ¶ 312 for colons *with quotation marks;* ¶ 328 for colons *with parentheses.*

➤ *The Dash*

The dash is a more prominent and emphatic mark of punctuation than the comma, the semicolon, or the colon. Under certain conditions it may be used instead of any one of those marks. It also has distinct uses of its own. It should not be used indiscriminately, however.

INSTEAD OF COMMAS

261 When a parenthetic element requires more emphatic separation from the balance of the sentence than commas would indicate, dashes are preferred to commas.

> We have every intention that our agents—as well as the transportation companies and the public—shall receive a fair decision in this matter.
>
> There is a typographical error in one of the paragraphs—the second one.

262 When a parenthetic element contains commas within itself, dashes are preferred to commas for setting it off.

> The storm extended the entire length of the Atlantic Coast—from Eastport, Maine, to Key West, Florida—in hurricane force.

INSTEAD OF A COLON

263 The dash is often used instead of a colon to introduce a list of items, especially when the introductory word that precedes the list is implied only.

> Men own, on the average, three coats—an overcoat, a topcoat, and a raincoat—and five pairs of trousers.

INSTEAD OF A SEMICOLON

264 The dash may be substituted for a semicolon before a word or a phrase that introduces an example or an explanation. (See also ¶ 251.)

> That scientific book is out of date—for example, it contains nothing on uranium.

BEFORE SUMMARIZING WORDS

265 Use a dash before such words as *these* and *all* when these words summarize a preceding list of details.

> A lawn mower, a rake, and a spade—*these* are the tools I need most.
>
> Juniors, seniors, postgraduate students—*all* met in one big class.

TO INDICATE A BREAK OR AN AFTERTHOUGHT

266 In advertising matter and sales letters especially, a dash is often used to show a break in thought or an afterthought.

> Here's luxury food in a jiffy—economical, too!

TO SHOW HESITATION

267 In reports of speeches or of conversations, hesitation, faltering speech, or stammering is indicated by a dash.

> Mr. Case: The work on the Lawson dam was begun—oh, I should say—well, about May 1—perhaps May 8—anyway, it was under way by July.

WITH REPETITIONS

268 A word or a phrase repeated for emphasis may be set off by a dash.

> We like to consider ourselves the vital link—the link that translates your wishes into actualities.

TO INDICATE OMISSIONS

269 In confidential correspondence it is sometimes desirable not to include a complete name. In such cases a long dash (consisting of three or four hyphens) is often used to indicate the omitted portion of the name.

> I should like your candid opinion of the rumor, heard by both Mr. S_____ and me, that the T_____ Company is bringing out a new machine this fall.

BEFORE THE SOURCE OF A QUOTATION

270 When a quoted extract is followed by the name of the author or the title of the work, or both, a dash precedes the credit.

> "When more than one spelling or form is given, the one printed first is in general to be preferred."
> —*Webster's New Collegiate Dictionary*
> "All things come round to him who will but wait."
> —*H. W. Longfellow*

TYPING

271 The dash is made by striking the hyphen key twice, with no space before, between, or after the hyphens.

272 The dash should be placed at the end of a line rather than at the beginning of a new line.

WITH OTHER MARKS OF PUNCTUATION

273 The only mark of punctuation that may be used before an *opening dash* is a period following an abbreviation.

> The shipment was sent c.o.d.—as you requested.

274 When material that is set off by dashes falls at the end of a sentence, the closing sentence punctuation (a period, question mark, or exclamation point) replaces the *closing dash*.

275 When material that is set off by dashes falls within a sentence and the material demands a question mark or an exclamation point, that punctuation mark is retained *before the second dash*. Other marks of punctuation are omitted.

> The representative of the Hitchcock Company—do you know whom I mean?—called this morning.
> The representative of the Hitchcock Company—of course you know whom I mean!—called this morning.

➤ *Quotation Marks*

FOR DIRECT QUOTATIONS

276 Enclose the exact words of a speaker or a writer in double quotation marks. (See page 61 for illustrative sentences.)

> When I asked her if she could come, she simply replied, "No."
> We will feature the ad, "Good books add so much to a good vacation."
> "I don't like the last paragraph in that letter," fumed Mr. Williams.

277   A brief direct quotation is preceded by a comma (see ¶ 236); a long quotation, by a colon (see ¶ 256).

278   Do *not* enclose indirectly quoted words in quotation marks. Indirect quotations are usually introduced by *that*. Often, however, the *that* is understood.

> She simply said that she could not go. (She simply said she could not go.)
> The publisher advertised that good books were welcome gifts.

279   If a quoted extract consists of more than one sentence, do *not* put quotation marks around each sentence of the extract.

> "I hereby tender my resignation. I have reached what is considered a good age to retire. It is time for a younger man to take over."

280   When *etc.* follows a quotation, do not include *etc.* within the quotation marks.

> At least one ad in the paper this morning started with, "What is so rare as a day in June?" etc.

281   Quoted extracts that will make three or more typewritten lines may be handled in one of the following ways.
   a) Type the extract single spaced in a shorter line length than used for the remainder of the material. Do *not* enclose the extract in quotation marks. This style is preferred by many. (See Letter Style 3a.)
   b) Type the extract in the same line length and spacing as the remainder of the material.
      (1) If the extract consists of one paragraph only, place quotation marks before and after the paragraph.
      (2) If the extract consists of two or more paragraphs, place a quotation mark at the start of each paragraph but after the *last* one only.
      (3) Change any quotation marks within the extract to single quotation marks.

> "When writing a letter that grants a request, the writer usually follows this order:
> "First, he expresses appreciation for the writer's interest in the company's product or service.
> "Next, he gives the exact information requested and, if possible, additional information of interest.
> "Finally, he expresses willingness 'to be of further help.' "

282   In copying a long letter, the best plan is to copy the letter on a separate sheet headed "Copy." No quotation marks are required.

283   In copying short letters and telegrams, type the opening quotation mark before the date line, but not before the complimentary closing nor signature line. The closing quotation mark follows the signature—not the last word of the letter or telegram.

284   In typing poems, place quotation marks at the beginning of each stanza and at the end of the last stanza. (See also ¶ 313*b*.)

285   Do not enclose well-known proverbs and sayings in quotation marks.

> We shall be traveling again next year, thus proving our belief in the theory that a rolling stone gathers no moss.

286   If only a portion of a quotation is woven into a sentence:
   a) No comma precedes the quotation.
   b) The first word of the extract is not capitalized—unless it is a proper noun or a proper adjective or begins a sentence in the extract.

> We feel that "American know-how" is responsible for the improvement.

   c) The quotation marks are placed around only the exact words being quoted—not around any rearrangement of the original words.

> That reply could not have come from a "voice with a smile."
> He said he would decide when he had "all the facts." (The original statement probably was, "I will decide when I have all the facts.")

287   Words omitted from any part of a quoted extract are indicated by three periods (four at the *end* of a sentence).

> "Although interjections . . . occur freely in conversation, they are of negligible importance in commercial correspondence. . . ."

   a) When the omission occurs at the beginning of a quoted portion, the first word of the quotation is not capitalized unless it so appears in the original material.

> The author of our English textbook believes that ". . . the structural principles of our language must be mastered."
> A recent survey revealed that ". . . This English course is required for graduation."

   b) If one or more paragraphs are omitted, the omission may be indicated by three asterisks typed on a line by themselves.

*   *   *

288   In copying quoted matter, follow the style of the extract exactly in punctuation, spelling, capitalization, hyphenization, style of figures. This is especially important in legal papers.

DIALOGUES, CONVERSATIONS, AND PLAYS

289   In quoting dialogues and conversations, start the remarks of each speaker as a new paragraph, no matter how brief.

> "Are those the only styles you can show me?" the customer inquired.
> "I'm afraid so," replied the salesman, "but I can order anything shown in this catalogue for you."
> "How long would it take to get the items?"
> "Two weeks."

290   In plays and court testimony, where the name of the speaker is indicated, quotation marks are not needed.

> George: What you say is impossible!
> Henry: I tell you it's true!
> George: I must have more proof than your word before I'll believe it.

QUOTATIONS WITHIN QUOTATIONS

291 A quotation within another quotation is enclosed in single quotation marks—made by the apostrophe key.

> "Tanned skin became a fashionable 'must' about twenty or twenty-five years ago."

292 If a quotation appears within the single-quoted matter, revert to double quotation marks for the inner portion.

> "Bulletin to Staff: 'Secretaries must indicate "Foreign Mail" on airmail letters destined for foreign countries.'"

Note: Single quotation marks are used as the symbol for *feet* in technical matter. (See ¶ 404.)

INTERRUPTIONS IN QUOTATIONS

When such interruptions as *he said* (indicating the source of the quotation) are included, the following rules apply.

293 If the expression *precedes* the quotation, the expression is followed by a comma if the quotation is short; by a colon if it is long. (See ¶¶ 236, 256.)

294 If the expression *follows* the quotation, a comma and the closing quotation mark follow the quotation.

> "Your child loves music just as he loves his toys," the circular began.

However, if the quotation ends with a question mark on an exclamation point, either of those marks would be used before the closing quotation mark instead of a comma.

> "Do you know why Ethel seems so sad?" he asked.

295 If the expression *interrupts* the quotation, a comma and the closing mark precede the interrupting expression and another comma follows it. The quotation continues with an opening quotation mark and the first word in small letters.

> "For the fifth successive week," the report began, "we can chalk up increased sales in our New England territory."

When the continuation is a new sentence, however, the interrupting expression is followed by a period and the sentence is started with a capital letter.

> "We will go," he said. "However, we shall be late."

WORDS DEFINED

296 When a word or an expression is accompanied by its definition, the expression is enclosed in quotation marks.

> "Erythema" is simply the medical term for "sunburn."

297 Words and phrases accompanied by such expressions as *so-called, known as, marked, entitled, signed, the word,* and similar phrases are also enclosed in quotation marks. (See page 64 for illustrative sentences.)

The carton was marked "Fragile."
The words "carton" and "cartoon" have quite different meanings.
The book entitled "How to Study" sells for $2.50.

Note: In material that is set in type, italic type is often used instead of quotation marks for such words and phrases.

WORDS WITH SPECIAL INTERPRETATIONS

298 Technical or trade terms, when used in nontechnical material, should be enclosed in quotation marks.

In glancing through the book, I noticed that many of the small illustrations had "run-arounds."

299 Humorous or ironical words or expressions are enclosed in quotation marks.

They serve "fresh" vegetables all right—fresh out of the can!

300 Slang or poor grammar, purposely used, is enclosed in quotation marks.

That music is too "long hair" for me.
Things "ain't what they used to be" here.

301 Translations of foreign words are enclosed in quotation marks.

A *faux pas* is, literally, "a false step"; hence a mistake.

TITLES OF PUBLICATIONS

➤ **See** ¶ 375 for the *capitalization of words* in the titles of publications.

302 *Titles of books, booklets, long (book-length) poems, and pamphlets* may be arranged according to the following plan.
a) In *letters,* they may be enclosed in quotation marks.

Every secretary will find "Etiquette in Business" helpful.

Or they may be underscored without quotation marks.

Every secretary will find Etiquette in Business helpful.

Or they may be typed in all capitals without quotation marks.

Every secretary will find ETIQUETTE IN BUSINESS helpful.

b) In material that is *to be set in type*—such as an article, the manuscript for a book, an advertisement—book titles should be underscored and not enclosed in quotation marks. The underscoring indicates to the printer that the title is to be set in italics.

Practical Business Psychology, by Laird and Laird, is fascinating.

303 *Titles of periodicals* (magazines, newspapers, annuals) are simply capitalized in letters.

Have you seen the magazine for secretarial students, Today's Secretary?

(*Rule continues on page 65.*)

But if the material is *to be set in type,* they are underscored.

Why don't you consult the classified advertisements in <u>Publishers' Weekly</u>?

Most publishers prefer all capitals for titles of their own periodicals.

The best magazine for secretarial students is TODAY'S SECRETARY.

304 Titles of types of literary productions are enclosed in quotation marks.

a) *Essays and articles:* I am reading "How to Relax before an Examination."

b) *Plays and scenarios:* "South Pacific" enjoyed amazing popularity.

c) *Lectures and sermons:* Please reserve a ticket for the lecture on the "Life and Work of Beethoven."

d) *Poems:* Could you recite "The Boy Stood on the Burning Deck" if you were asked to?

e) *Mottoes and toasts:* "Eureka" (I have found it) is the motto of California.

f) *Musical compositions:* The concert opened with Ravel's "Bolero."

g) *Paintings and sculptures:* What an enormous canvas "Washington Crossing the Delaware" is!

h) *Divisions of books (titles of parts, sections, chapters, lessons, tables, charts):* Part I, "Vocabularly Building," starts with a lesson on "Getting Acquainted with Your Dictionary."

   Refer to Chapter V, "The Effective Business Letter," the section headed "The Basis of All Letter Writing."

   Exception: The words *Part, Section, Chapter, Lesson, Preface, Contents, Appendix, Index* are simply capitalized—not quoted—when they refer to the respective parts of a specific book.

   The author, in his Preface, acknowledged the editor's contribution.

   Several important topics were omitted from the Index.

Note: Names of *ships, airplanes,* and *trains* are enclosed in quotation marks: the "Queen Mary," the "Columbine," the "Twentieth Century Limited."

WITH PERIODS

305 The period is *always* placed *inside* the closing quotation mark, whether the quotation is a single word, a phrase, a clause, or a sentence.

Canceled checks are checks that have been paid by the bank and stamped "Paid." (A single word.)

Mr. Chalmers drew a draft on Mr. Stuart, payable "six months after date." (A phrase.)

Mr. Williams urged John to apply for the position and assured him that "this is a golden opportunity." (A clause.)

Just as I was leaving his office, Mr. Brown called, "Miss Ward, I need five copies of that agreement." (A sentence.)

Note: If the preceding sentence had ended with a quoted question or exclamation, no concluding period would have been required.

Just as I was leaving his office, Mr. Brown asked, "Miss Ward, do you think you can make five good copies of that agreement?"

Just as I was leaving his office, Mr. Brown snapped, "Miss Ward, remember I want five *good* copies of that agreement!"

WITH QUESTION MARKS

306   The question mark is placed *inside* the closing quotation mark *if only the quoted material is a question.*

> He asked, "Did you really enjoy reading that book?"
>
> "Did you really enjoy reading that book?" the man asked. (Notice that in this sentence no other mark of punctuation, such as a comma, is required after the closing quotation mark.)

307   The question mark is placed *outside* the closing quotation mark *if the entire sentence is a question.*

> Did Ray say, "I'll never drive at such a fast speed again"?

When the question ends with a *quoted* question, however, only *one* question mark is needed—outside the closing quotation mark.

> Was that the advertisement that started, "Why pay more"?
>
> The stenographer asked, "Was the check marked 'Insufficient Funds'?"

WITH EXCLAMATION POINTS

308   The exclamation point is placed *inside* the closing quotation mark if the exclamation point is part of the quotation.

> My boss's favorite direction is, "This is a rush job!"

309   The exclamation point is placed *outside* the closing quotation mark if the exclamation point is not part of the quotation.

> That unfair decision carries out the policy, "The customer is always right"!

WITH COMMAS

310   The comma is *always* placed *inside* the closing quotation mark. (See ¶ 239.)

WITH SEMICOLONS

311   The semicolon is *always* placed *outside* the closing quotation mark.

> He said, "I will mail them today"; however, that was a week ago, and they have not arrived.

WITH COLONS

312   The colon is *always* placed *outside* the closing quotation mark.

> Please get these supplies from the shelf marked "Editorial": 1 box of letterheads, 6 soft pencils, 1 typewriter eraser.

TYPING

313   *a)* In a list, any opening quotation mark should clear the left margin, so that the first letter of the item will align with other items.

> I need the following stationery items:
> > Paper clips
> > Rubber bands
> > "Fragile" labels
> > White cord

b) In poems, opening quotation marks at the beginning of stanzas should clear the left margin, so that the first letters of rhyming lines will be in alignment. (See also ¶ 284.)

314 Quotation marks are used for ditto marks and as symbols for *feet* and *inches* in technical works. (See ¶ 404.)

➤ *Parentheses*

EXPLANATORY MATTER

315 Use parentheses to enclose explanatory matter or comments that are independent of the main thought of the sentence. Such matter may be a single word, a group of words, or an entire sentence.

> We are disappointed at the very small number (five) of acceptances of our invitation. (A single word.)
>
> Bids are requested for repaving Sutton Avenue (formerly Lombard Street) in the town of Chester. (A group of words.)
>
> We regret that from now until the end of the year (our fiscal year starts January 1) we can make no further loans. (A sentence.)

Caution: Be sure that any sentence containing parenthetic matter can be read without the parenthetic matter; that is, such matter must not tie in with the construction of the sentence.

316 Prefer commas or dashes when the explanatory matter is not so completely independent of the sentence. (See ¶¶ 225, 261.)

REFERENCES

317 Use parentheses to enclose references and directions.

> Because of unusually heavy expenditures (see attached financial report), we are not in a position to make further changes this year.

318 The name of an authority for a statement may be enclosed in parentheses.

> Last week, average market prices advanced 0.3 per cent. (Bureau of Labor Statistics)

➤ **See** ¶ 270 for arrangement of source of a *quoted* extract.

CONFIRMING FIGURES

319 In legal work and in bids and similar business papers, figures that confirm spelled-out numbers are often enclosed in parentheses.

➤ **See** ¶¶ 199, 201 for parentheses *around question marks* and *exclamation points within sentences.*

WITH ENUMERATED ITEMS

320 Enclose in parentheses numbers or letters that accompany enumerated items appearing within a sentence. (See also ¶¶ 250, 252–254.)

> We require the following information to complete our record of Mr. Rice's experience: (1) number of years with the Western Meat Company, (2) a description of his duties there, and (3) the number of promotions he received.
>
> Please include in your expense account: (a) cost of hotel room; (b) cost of meals, including tips; (c) amount spent on transportation.

321 Subdivisions in outlines are often enclosed in parentheses. When there are many gradations, it is sometimes necessary to use a single closing parenthesis mark to provide another grade.

<pre>
    1. Basic weaves   I. . . . .
        a. Plain   A. . . . .
            (1) Basket   1. . . . .
            (2) Ribbed   a. . . . .
        b. Twill   (1) . . . .
            etc.   (a) . . . .
                                              1) . . . .
</pre>

WITH PERIODS

322 When a parenthetical remark that falls at the end of a sentence is a part of the sentence, place the sentence period *outside* the closing parenthesis mark.

> The meeting was held in Portland (Oregon).

If, in a sentence of this type, the parenthetical matter requires a question mark or an exclamation point, that mark or point is placed *inside* the closing parenthesis mark. The period punctuating the entire sentence is placed *outside* the parenthesis mark.

> The meeting was held in Portland, Oregon (or was it Portland, Maine?).
> The meeting was held in Portland, Oregon (notice, not Portland, Maine!).

323 If the closing parenthetical matter is a complete sentence:
  a) The sentence preceding the parenthetical matter closes with its own punctuation mark.
  b) The parenthetical matter opens with a capital and closes with its own closing punctuation mark *inside* the closing parenthesis mark.
  c) No punctuation follows the closing parenthesis mark.

> Local businessmen charge that the proposed bond issue will raise the tax rate. (They present no proof of this.) No one wishes this outcome.

WITH QUESTION MARKS AND EXCLAMATION POINTS

324 If a sentence that is a question or an exclamation closes with a parenthetic remark, the question mark or exclamation point *follows* the closing parenthesis mark.

> On these bills, what was the voting record of Green (Republican) and Murray (Democrat)?
> What a reprehensible act (and we mean just that)!

325 If the closing parenthetical matter is a complete question or a complete exclamatory sentence:
  a) The sentence preceding the parenthetical matter closes with its own punctuation mark.
  b) The parenthetical matter opens with a capital and closes with a question mark or an exclamation point *inside* the closing parenthesis mark.
  c) No punctuation follows the closing parenthesis mark.

> He spoke at length on his favorite topic. (How could I stop him?)
> This will be our last issue. (Yes, the magazine was not a success!)

WITH COMMAS

326   If a comma is required at the point where a parenthesis occurs, place the comma *outside* the closing parenthesis mark.

> Call me tomorrow (Thursday), and I will give you more definite information.

327   *Never* insert a comma *before* the opening parenthesis mark.

WITH SEMICOLONS AND COLONS

328   If a semicolon or a colon is required at the point where a parenthesis occurs, place the semicolon or colon *outside* the closing parenthesis mark.

> I wrote to him (as I said I would); however, he has not answered.
> I inserted this ad in the Times (New York): Lost May 5 vicinity Radio City platinum bracelet.

➤ *The Apostrophe*

329   The use of the apostrophe is covered in the following paragraphs:
  a) Forming possessives, ¶¶ 492–509.
  b) Forming contractions, ¶ 430.
  c) Forming plurals of figures, letters, symbols, and so on, ¶¶ 486, 487.
  d) Indicating the omission of figures in dates, ¶ 410.
  e) The single quotation mark, ¶¶ 291, 292.

➤ *Miscellaneous Marks of Punctuation*

ASTERISK (*)

330   The asterisk is used to refer the reader to a footnote, which usually is placed at the foot of a page. Such references are frequently used in advertising matter.

> "Because they won't let you wear it unless it fits." *
> _____
> * Reg. U. S. Pat. Off.

  a) When the asterisk and some other mark of punctuation fall at the same point in a sentence, the asterisk *follows* the punctuation mark, with no intervening space.
  b) In the footnote itself, leave one space after the asterisk.

331   Asterisks are used to replace words that are considered unprintable.

> We were shocked to hear Mr. Scott refer to Mr. Frost as a ****.

➤ **See** ¶ 287*b* for the use of asterisks to *indicate omissions*.

332   If your typewriter does not have an asterisk key, a fair substitute can be made by striking a small *v* over a capital *A*.

DIAGONAL LINE (/)

333   The diagonal line occurs in certain abbreviations and symbols.

> B/L bill of lading   D/W dock warrant   C/o care of

334 The diagonal is used in writing fractions, as *4/5,* and in some code and serial numbers, as *2S/394756.*

335 In the expression *and/or,* the diagonal indicates that the words joined by the symbol may be used interchangeably.

> My mother *and/or* I have access to the safe deposit box. (Means that *either* my mother *or* I may open the box; or my mother *and* I together may open it.)

336 No space precedes or follows the diagonal.

BRACKETS ([ ])

337 A correction or an insertion in a quoted extract should be enclosed in brackets.

> "During the height of the storm, winds exceeded 55 miles an hour [the local weather station recorded 60 miles an hour], with gusts up to 65 miles an hour."
>
> "And with this thought, ladies and gentlemen, I close my talk." [Great applause.]

338 If brackets do not appear on the typewriter keyboard, leave a space at the point where each mark should appear and insert the marks in pen after the paper has been removed from the machine.

UNDERSCORE

339 The underscore is used to emphasize words and to display words in titles and headings; also, in matter that is to be set in type, to indicate any words that are to be italicized, such as foreign words and phrases.

340 Underscore as a unit whatever should be stressed as a unit—individual words, whole titles, or whole expressions. Solid underscores are frequently used in business, particularly when typing on an electric typewriter. (*Exception:* The solid underscore is not used when typing a stencil.) Punctuation marks following underscores should not be underscored, but punctuation marks within a continuously underscored selection should be underscored.

341 Techniques in underscoring.

a) Use the backspacer to underscore five or fewer characters.

b) If more than five characters are to be underscored consecutively, draw the carriage back by hand.

c) If underscoring will appear in several places in one typewritten line, type the entire line and then draw the carriage back by hand and underscore the appropriate portions in the line.

d) With an electric typewriter, use the mechanism for repeating underscores automatically, instead of typing individual underscore strokes.

SYMBOLS NOT ON THE TYPEWRITER

Typewriters used to prepare technical matter usually contain special keys for the symbols that occur most frequently. Without special keys, the following substitutions may be constructed.

342 "Degrees" after figures, as *75° F.,* may be made by using the ratchet release to raise the symbol above the line, striking the small letter *o,* and returning to the normal line spacing.

343 To make the English pound sign (£), strike a capital *L,* backspace, and strike a small letter *f* over the *L.*

344 For the multiplication sign, type small letter *x.* (In measurements, small *x* is used for *by.*) (See also ¶ 404.)

345 For a minus sign, use the hyphen with a space before and after it.

346 If other mathematical signs (plus, division, and equal signs) are not on the machine, they may be inserted by hand. Space once before and after these signs.

TYPEWRITER SPACING WITH PUNCTUATION MARKS AND AFTER ABBREVIATIONS

347 Punctuation marks

Period
Two spaces after the end of a sentence.
One space after an abbreviation within a sentence. (See also ¶ 348.)
No space after a decimal point.

Question Mark and Exclamation Point
No space *before* either.
One space *after* either if *within* a sentence. Two spaces *after* either at the end of a sentence. (See ¶¶ 198, 201.)

Comma
No space *before*—ever.
One space *after,* unless a closing quotation mark immediately follows the comma.
No space *after* commas within numbers.

Semicolon
No space *before;* one space *after.*

Colon
No space *before.*
Two spaces after within a sentence. (See also ¶¶ 258–260.)
No space before or after in bibliographies, expressions of time (*8:20 p.m.*), or proportions (*2:1*).

Parentheses
Opening parenthesis mark
a) One space *before* when parenthetic matter is within a sentence.
b) Two spaces *before* when parenthetic matter follows a sentence. In this case parenthetic matter starts with a capital and closes with its own sentence punctuation. (See ¶ 323*c.*)
c) No space *after.*
Closing parenthesis mark
a) No space *before.*
b) One space *after* when parenthetic matter is within a sentence.
c) Two spaces *after* when parenthetic matter is itself a complete sentence and another sentence follows. (See ¶ 323*c.*)

Apostrophe

No space *before* either within or at the end of a word.

Space *after* only if it is at the end of a word within a sentence.

Dash

No space *before, between,* or *after* two hyphens used to type a dash.

Quotation Marks

No space between quotation mark and material enclosed, nor between single and double quotation marks. (See also ¶¶ 313, 314.)

Asterisk and Diagonal Line (/)

One space *after* asterisk in a footnote. (See ¶ 330.)

No space *before* or *after* diagonal line.

348 Abbreviations

Abbreviation within a sentence—one space *after* the period.

Abbreviation *at the end* of a *sentence.*

a) If the sentence requires a period, use *only one* period.

> The books were audited by Robert T. Graves, C. P. A.

b) If the sentence requires a question mark or an exclamation point, no space between the period and the other mark.

c) If the sentence ends with a parenthetical expression that closes with an abbreviation, use this style:

> Please call tomorrow afternoon (we close at 5:30 p.m.).

One space between capital letters representing abbreviations of personal names; as *Mr. L. B. Anders.*

No space within abbreviations consisting of small letters; as *f.o.b.; a.m.*

When an abbreviation consists entirely of capital letters, as *C. O. D.,* or of capitals and small letters, as *Ph. D.,* space once after each period.

SECTION 6

When to capitalize

Do not capitalize unless there is a reason for doing so. The following rules represent standard, accepted usage. Authorities differ on certain details, however, and many offices have their own preferences. Employees in such offices, of course, should follow those preferences.

BASIC RULES

349 Capitalize the first word of:

a) Every sentence and of any words or group of words used as a sentence.

> The trial resumes tomorrow. To answer your question. No.

b) Direct quotations.

> Mr. Tead then announced, "The debate will be resumed tomorrow," and hurriedly left the room.

(1) Indirect quotations are *not* capitalized. (See ¶ 278.)
(2) For the capitalization of fragments of quotations that are grammatically joined to the words that precede them in a sentence, see ¶ 286.

c) An independent question within a sentence. (See ¶ 197.)
d) Lines of poetry.

> Life is a leaf of paper white
> Whereon each one of us may write
> His word or two, and then comes night.
> —*James Russell Lowell*

e) Each item in an outline. (See example in ¶ 321.)

350 Capitalize every *proper noun and adjective;* that is, the name of a particular person, place, or thing, or an adjective referring to that name.

George (n.)	South America (n.)
Georgian (adj.)	South American (adj.)
Supreme Court of the United States	

a) Capitalize popular *descriptive names* that are sometimes used in place of the real proper names.

> the Father of his Country (for George Washington)
> the Granite State (for New Hampshire)
> the Windy City (for Chicago)

b) Do *not* capitalize words that were originally proper names but are no longer identified with those names; that is, names that have become common nouns.

plaster of paris	french dressing	turkish towel	ampere
derby hat	japan (varnish)	india ink	watt

351 Capitalize a common noun when:
a) Used alone as a well-known short form of a *specific* proper name.

> the Canal (the Panama Canal)   the Lakes (the Great Lakes)

b) The use of the common-noun element of a long proper name will avoid awkward repetition. In such cases, the full name has ordinarily been mentioned first.

> According to the recommendations of the Interstate Commerce Commission, the .... We find that the Commission also recommends ....

c) The dictator refers to "the Company" in place of the full name of the concern.

> The Company has always held that ...

Note, however, the absence of capitalization in *our company, this company,* where *company* does *not* replace the full name.

Important Note: Most of the rules that follow are applications of rules in ¶¶ 350 and 351.

> ➤ **See** ¶¶ 108, 122 for capitalization in *salutations* and *complimentary closings.*

PERSONAL NAMES AND TITLES

> ➤ **See** ¶ 76c for the capitalization of names with such prefixes as *Mc*, etc.

352 Capitalize official titles of honor and respect when they *precede* personal names.

a) Executive titles

President Arthur Orwell, of Cromwell University   Chairman Stevens
Secretary-Treasurer Owens   Supervisor Reid

b) Professional titles

Professor George Hamilton Booth   Dean Atkinson

c) Civic titles

Governor Otto Kerner   Ambassador Francis E. Willis
Chief Justice Earl Warren   Prime Minister Diefenbaker

d) Military and naval titles

General J. Lawton Collins   Commander Alan C. Lloyd

e) Religious titles

Pope John   Cardinal Spellman
Rabbi Silverman   The Reverend John S. Wyman

f) Family titles

Uncle John   Dad   Mom

Do *not* capitalize family titles when they are preceded by a possessive pronoun.

My father will sign it. (*But:* Ask Father to sign it.)

353 When these titles *follow* the name in sentences, do not capitalize the titles unless they refer to high government officials.

Dr. Arthur Orwell, president of Cromwell University
Mr. Thomas Wentworth, chairman of the Executive Committee
Mr. Wallace Pierce, comptroller of the Aero Company
Alexander Hamilton, Secretary of the Treasury under Washington

354 In the *inside address* of a letter and on an *envelope,* capitalize all titles whether they precede or follow the name. (See ¶¶ 78–84.)

355 Capitalize a title when it refers to a specific person and is used in place of that person's name.

Did you hear the President's address last night? (Meaning the President of the United States.)

(*See page 75 for exception.*)

But: Our president (meaning of an organization or company) resigned.
I hope, Senator, you will support our organization.

Do *not* capitalize such words as the following when they occur without
a personal name or are not used in place of a name.

professor	manager	minister	superintendent
secretary	priest	director	

356 In minutes of meetings and in rules and bylaws, capitalize titles of
officeholders.

The Secretary's minutes were read and approved.

357 Do not capitalize *former* and *late* used with titles, nor *ex-* and *-elect*
joined to titles.

the late President Roosevelt   ex-President Hoover   Governor-elect Ott

NAMES OF ORGANIZATIONS

358 Capitalize the names of firms, companies, associations, societies, com-
missions, committees, bureaus, boards, departments, schools, political
parties, conventions, fraternities, clubs, and religious bodies.

the McGraw-Hill Book Company, Inc.	the University of Montana
the Young Women's Christian Association	the Republican Party
the Democratic National Committee	the American Legion Convention
the New York State Board of Education	the Masons
the Board of Directors	the Town and Country Club
our Credit and Collection Department	the American Red Cross

359 Capitalize *the* preceding the name of an organization only when it is
part of the legal name of the organization.

The Investment Company of America   The Associated Press

Do *not* capitalize *the* when the name is used as a modifier or is abbreviated; as *the Associated Press report, the AP.*

360 Capitalize the common-noun element in the name of an organization
when the common noun is used as a substitute for the full name. (See
also ¶ 351*b* and *c*.)

We are not now accepting applications for membership in the Club. (Meaning, for example, *the Stuart Athletic Club.*)

361 In other cases do *not* capitalize a common noun used alone as a general
classification.

Send the report to our New York *office,* not to this *office.*
I was graduated from *high school* in 1955.
The work in a *credit department* is highly confidential. (But: The
Credit Department reports a satisfactory rating.)
I would not join any *club,* as I do not enjoy group activity.

COMMERCIAL PRODUCTS

362 Capitalize trade-marked names, brand names, proprietary names, commercial products, and market grades. The common noun following the name of a product is usually capitalized by the *manufacturer* or *advertiser.*

Fab	Hotpoint Dishwasher	Choice lamb (market grade)
Ivory Soap	Kislav Gloves	Winter wheat (market grade)

363 Some trade names are so commonly used that they are erroneously considered common nouns. They should, however, be capitalized.

Mimeoscope Vaseline Photostat Pyrex Adrenalin

Exception: The words *mimeograph* and *mimeographed.*

NAMES OF GOVERNMENT BODIES

364 Capitalize the names of countries; international organizations; national, state, county, and city bodies and their branches.

the Republic of Panama	the Court of Appeals of the State of
the United Nations Organization	Wisconsin
Congress	the Department of the Interior
the House of Representatives	the Interstate Commerce Commission
the Appropriations Committee	the Police Department
the Illinois Legislature	the Bureau of Sanitation

365 Capitalize the shortened name of a governmental body when:

a) The short form is generally recognized.

The House (of Representatives) the Army the Administration (Federal)

b) The full name has been mentioned earlier.

the Division (as the Division of Postal Savings)
the Corporation (as the Federal Deposit Insurance Corporation)
the Commission (as the Commission of Fine Arts)

366 The words *federal, government, union, nation,* and *commonwealth* are usually capitalized when they refer to a *specific* country.

A senator is introducing a bill to provide control by the Government of all railroads. (Meaning the United States Government.)
Many economists do not believe in government control of railroads.
He is on the Federal payroll.
He was accredited to the Greek Government.
Alaska became the forty-ninth state of the Union.
Our Nation's first census was taken in 1790. (Meaning the United States.)

NAMES OF PLACES

367 Capitalize the names of definite geographic localities (states, cities, mountains, rivers, valleys, parks, oceans, harbors) and of streets and buildings.

Montana	the Atlantic Ocean	U. S. 101
the Rocky Mountains	Death Valley	the Empire State Building
the Mississippi River	New York Harbor	the East Side

368 Capitalize the word *city* only when it is a part of the corporate name of the city; as in *Kansas City* but, *the city of San Francisco.*

369 Capitalize *state* when it follows the name of a state, or when it is used in place of the name of the state. (See also ¶ 350*a*.)

> He has moved to New York State.
> He is an employee of the State. (Meaning of some one state.)
> The state of Alaska is the largest state in the Union.
> I do not know in what state they are incorporated.
> Several Canadian families have recently moved to the States. (Meaning the United States.)

370 Capitalize *the* only when it is a part of the official name of a place; as *The Hague.*

POINTS OF COMPASS

371 Capitalize the points of the compass only when they designate definite localities.

> The industry I refer to is in the West.
> The North is proud of its industrial achievements.
> Do you have a map of the Northern Hemisphere?
> He lives on the West Coast.

372 Do not capitalize words that merely indicate points of the compass or directions.

> The birds fly south in winter. (Direction.)
> The west coast of the United States borders on the Pacific. (Descriptive.)
> We had a true northern winter. (Adjective—general description.)

DAYS OF WEEK, HOLIDAYS, SEASONS

373 Capitalize names of the days of the week, months, holidays, and religious days.

> This year Columbus Day, October 12, falls on a Friday.
> In 1956 Easter fell on April 1.

374 Capitalize the names of the seasons only when they are personified.

> Come, gentle Spring.
> Our order for fall merchandise was mailed today.

TITLES OF PUBLICATIONS

375 Capitalize all words except articles (*a, an,* and *the*), conjunctions, and short prepositions (*of, in, by, with*) in the titles of publications and their divisions.[1] (See ¶¶ 302–304 for illustrations.)

a) Capitalize *the* preceding the name of a book only if *the* is a part of the book title.

> I obtained much practical help from "The Secretary at Work."
> I use the "Gregg Shorthand Dictionary Simplified" every day.

---

[1] It will be noted that this Manual capitalizes only the first word of section heads. This style reflects a growing tendency in modern typographic design. The rule given in ¶ 375, however, is the accepted standard practice.

b) Ordinarily, do not capitalize *the* preceding the name of a magazine or newspaper.

> This clipping is from the New York Times.

c) Prepositions of seven or more letters are often capitalized in titles; as "A Trip Through the Panama Canal."

HISTORICAL EVENTS, PERIODS, AND DOCUMENTS

376   Capitalize the names of important historical events, movements, periods, specific treaties, bills, acts, and laws. Do not capitalize the names of centuries or decades.

the American Revolution	the Act (referring to a specific act)
the Battle of the Bulge	the Treaty of Versailles
the Middle Ages	the twentieth century
the Reciprocal Trade Agreements Act	the fabulous forties

RACES, PEOPLES, LANGUAGES, RELIGIONS

377   Capitalize the names of races, peoples, tribes, religions, and languages.

> Negroes   Chinese   the Sioux Indians   Sanskrit   Judaism

HEAVENLY BODIES

378   Do not capitalize the names of heavenly bodies unless they are used in connection with the names of other planets or stars that are always capitalized.

> The moon was hidden behind a cloud.
> They are studying Mercury, Arcturus, the Sun, Mars, and the Earth.
> The earth revolves on its axis.

COURSES OF STUDY AND SUBJECTS; ACADEMIC DEGREES

379   Capitalize the names of *courses;* but do *not* capitalize mere names of subjects, except for any proper nouns or adjectives in the subject name.

English Literature II	typewriting
Fundamentals of Design	American history

Do not capitalize academic degrees used as general designations; as a *bachelor of arts degree.*

NOUNS WITH NUMBERS OR LETTERS

380   Usually capitalize a noun followed by a number—either roman or arabic—or a letter that indicates position in a sequence. Nouns that refer to minor divisions, such as *page, note, verse,* or *line,* are not capitalized. It is not necessary to use *No.* before such numbers. (See also ¶ 426.)

Act I	Column 1	line 4	Policy 394857
Appendix A	Diagram 4	Lot 2	Room 501
Article 2	Exercise 8	note 1	Section 1
Book III	Exhibit A	page 158	Table 7
Car 8171	Figure 9	paragraph 1a	Track 2
Chapter V	Illustration 19	Part III	Unit 2
Chart 3	Invoice 00487	Plate XV	verse 3
Class 4	Lesson 20	Platform 3	Volume II

COMPOUND WORDS

381 Capitalize the individual words that make up a compound word that appears in a *heading* or a *title* as they would be capitalized were they not hyphenated. In *running matter,* the second element is capitalized only if it is a proper noun or a proper adjective.

> How to Keep That Up-to-Date Look   Profit-Sharing Plans
> There are many dialects among English-speaking people.

ADVERTISING MATERIAL

382 Words that are not ordinarily capitalized are often capitalized in advertising correspondence and material in order to obtain emphasis. (But, unless you work in an advertising office, be cautious!)

> Come in to see our Tropical Worsteds, Wool Crash, and Gabardine Suits.

LEGAL CORRESPONDENCE

383 In legal documents many words are capitalized that ordinarily would be written in small letters: references to parties, the name of the document, special provisions, and sometimes spelled-out amounts of money.

> Whereupon, I, the said Notary, at the request of the aforesaid, did PROTEST, and by these presents do publicly and solemnly PROTEST, as well against Maker and Indorser of said note . . .

CAPITALIZING AFTER A COLON

384 Ordinarily, the first word in a list of items that follows a colon in a sentence is not capitalized. When the items are tabulated, however, the first word in each item is capitalized.

> He enumerated the four levels of the city's educational system: grade school, junior high school, high school, junior college.
> I need the following office supplies:

> | | |
> |---|---|
> | Paper clips | Address labels |
> | Rubber bands | File folders |

➤ **See** ¶ 255 for capitalization after a colon that *introduces an explanatory sentence.*

ABBREVIATIONS

For the capitalization of abbreviations, see ¶ 454.

SECTION 7

How to write numbers

Numbers are written in figures more often in business letters than in any other type of composition. Almost every number that is used is inserted for quick reference, for clearness, or for emphasis. As with capitalization, authorities differ regarding certain rules and many offices have their own preferences. For the style of hyphenization of spelled-out numbers, follow the rules in ¶¶ 521, 522.

GENERAL RULES

Important Note: Rules 385–392 are basic; the remaining rules are modifications to suit individual cases.

385   In *business letters* write all *exact numbers above ten* in figures.

> The boat carried 35 passengers.
> We will mail four cases today.
> We are sending 100 copies of our new bulletin to you.

> **➤ See** ¶ 149 for the use of figures in social correspondence.

386   Spell out *approximate* numbers if they are round numbers in even units. (See "advertising and sales letters" below.)

> Yes, *fifty* to *sixty* will be ample.
> We expect an enrollment of about *five hundred* this fall. (*But:* We expect an enrollment of over *550* this fall.)
> *But:* The company has assets of more than $6,000,000. (See ¶ 393.)

If a round number is over a thousand, use this shorter form:

> About *twelve hundred* books were sent. (*Not:* one thousand two hundred.)

In *advertising and sales letters,* even round numbers are usually written as figures for emphasis.

> Over 5,000 copies have been sold since the first of the month.

387   If several numbers occur in a connected group within a sentence, write *all* numbers, including those under ten as well as round numbers, in figures.

> We ordered 28 chairs, 16 tables, 9 desks, and about 20 typewriters. (*But:* Only five dresses and eleven suits were damaged.)

388   Use figures for *all* numbers in statistical and tabular work.

389   Very large numbers *are sometimes written* in the following styles: *15 billion, 10 million dollars, $10 million.* (But see ¶ 393 for amounts of money in *all other instances.*) This style can be used only when the hundreds and thousands are even amounts. Such numbers as *7,845,700* and *$1,510,110,000* must be written in full.

390 Always spell out numbers that begin a sentence.

> Four glasses were broken.
> Five hundred persons attended the lecture.

If the numbers are large (would require more than two words when spelled out), rearrange the wording of the sentence if possible.

> The company sent out 298 circulars. (*Instead of:* Two hundred ninety-eight circulars were sent out.)
> Our salesmen had a bad year in 1954. (*Instead of:* 1954 was a bad year for our salesmen.)

> ❯ **See** also Note in ¶ 522 on style of spelled-out large numbers.

391 Spell out ordinals (*first, second, third,* etc.) except in certain styles of dates. (See ¶ 66.)

> Mr. and Mrs. Bliss celebrated their twenty-fifth wedding anniversary.

392 Never divide a figure at the end of a line.

DATES

> ❯ **See** ¶¶ 63–67 for the use of *figures in dates.*

MONEY, MARKET QUOTATIONS

393 In *business correspondence,* write all amounts of money in figures.

> $5 $9.50 $1,750 $10,500,000   10 cents   £3 4s 6d   2 lire

394 Do not include the decimal point nor ciphers in even amounts of dollars that occur in the *body of a letter.*

> Enclosed is our check for $125 in payment of legal services rendered.

In tabulations, however, if any amount in the column contains cents, add the decimal point and two ciphers to the even amounts to maintain a uniform appearance.

$150.50
25.00
8.05

395 Repeat the dollar sign before each amount in a series of dollar amounts.

> Small country homes for sale; price range, $5,000–$20,000.

396 When amounts under $1 appear in the body of the letter, write the word *cents* after the figures.

> For today only, we offer two toothbrushes for 39 cents.

The form ¢ may be used in technical matter containing many price quotations.

> Wholesale prices for food commodities yesterday: coffee, 55¢; cocoa, 36¢; sugar, 5¢; butter, 61¢.

397 Do not use the style of *$.75* in sentences, except when the amount of cents occurs in a series of other money amounts that include dollar signs.

> I am sure that customers will not pay more than 50 cents for this item.
> Prices for the principal grains were as follows: wheat, $2.31; corn, $1.50; oats, $.78; rye, $1.58.

398   Write indefinite sums of money in words.

> Several million dollars will be needed to start the project.
> He contributed nearly a thousand dollars. (*But:* He contributed $1,000.)

399   In legal documents amounts of money are spelled out, the amount being repeated in numerals in parentheses.

> Three Hundred and Fifty Dollars ($350)

400   Write stock-market quotations and brokerage descriptions in figures.

> ABC 3s at 98¼   DEF pf 7 170 down 1½ points

DECIMALS, PERCENTAGES, PROPORTIONS

401   Always write decimals in figures; as *99.87; .01.*
   a) For technical exactness, a cipher may precede a decimal fraction, as *0.66,* to indicate that the writer has not overlooked the fact that this fraction is less than one whole number.
   b) Likewise, in such decimals as *7.280,* the final cipher indicates that the computation has been carried to three decimal places.
   c) Never insert a comma in a decimal; *1.486543.*

402   Express percentages in figures, preferably with *per cent* written as two words. (*Percent* is also allowable.)

> The store allowed a discount of 10 per cent.
> Our terms are 2 per cent 10 days, net 30 days.

In a succession of percentages, *per cent* follows the last number only.

> Price reductions range between 20 and 50 per cent.

   a) The % symbol may be used after the figure:
      (1) When percentages occur frequently, as in statistical and account-ing matter. Note that the symbol follows *each* figure.

> In our Women's Ready-to-Wear Department, sales last year were propor-tioned as follows: dresses, 50%; coats and suits, 30%; blouses, 15%; skirts, 5%.

      (2) In tabulations, invoices, and interoffice memorandums.
   b) Fractional percentages may be written as common fractions (*5½ per cent, 66⅔%*) or, especially in technical work, as decimals (*5.5 per cent, 66.66%*).

403   Always write ratios and proportions in figures.

> a ratio of 5 to 1 (or 5:1)   a 50–50 chance to recover

MEASUREMENTS

404   In *business correspondence,* use figures for dimensions, measures, weights, degrees, distances, capacities, and market quotations.

> The room was 15 by 30 feet. (In technical matter or tabular work, the form is usually *17 x 22* or *5′ 3″ x 6′ 10″,* a space being left before and after the *x.*)
> The can will hold 10 gallons of paint.
> Your order for one pair of tennis shoes, size 6, has been delayed.
> The temperature reached 90 degrees.

405   When a weight, capacity, measure, etc., consists of several words, do not separate the words by commas. The quantity is considered a single unit.

> The baby weighed 6 pounds 14 ounces.
> The punch bowl holds 4 quarts 1 pint.
> My oculist told me I have 20/20 vision.

> **➤ See** ¶¶ 442, 443 for the abbreviation of units of measurement.

HOUSE, STREET, AND ZONE NUMBERS

> **➤ See** ¶¶ 90, 92, 100 for the use of figures in *house, street,* and *zone numbers.*

TIME AND AGES

406   Spell out the time of day when the word *o'clock* or any other informal style is used.

> The store opens at ten o'clock.
> They are coming at ten.
> The picture starts at a quarter to eight.
> My appointment is for three-thirty tomorrow afternoon.

407   When the precise time is given or when *a.m.* or *p.m.* is used, write the time in figures. (See also ¶ 441.)

> She did not appear until 9:22!   The boat sails at 11:30 a.m.

a) Do not include two ciphers when the even hour is mentioned, unless the time appears with another figure containing minutes.

> The train leaves at 7 p.m., EST. (Meaning Eastern Standard Time.)
> The ticket window will be open from 6:00 to 8:30 p.m. tomorrow.

b) Do not use *a.m.* or *p.m.* unless figures are used; do not use either abbreviation with *o'clock.*

> tomorrow afternoon (*not:* tomorrow p.m.)
> at ten o'clock (*not:* 10 a.m. o'clock)

c) Omit spaces in *a.m.* and *p.m.*

d) Noon and midnight are designated as follows: *12 noon* or *12 N.; 12 midnight.*

408   Write numbers representing periods of time in words, except when such numbers are used in discount and credit terms and in interest rates.

> Mr. Albert Hill was a member of our sales staff for fourteen years.
> I will meet you in twenty minutes.
> Mr. Clark was entitled to 7 per cent interest on the $250 for 60 days.
> A payment on your loan will be due in 60 days.

409   Spell out names of centuries and decades. (See ¶ 376.)

410   Express class graduation years and well-known years in history by two figures preceded by an apostrophe.

> the class of '50   the spirit of '76

411 Express ages in words unless they are given accurately in years, months, and days.

> Mary is nineteen years old.
> My brother is 19 years 4 months 17 days old.

Note that, as with weights and measures (see ¶ 405), no commas separate the parts of such expressions.

NUMBERED SESSIONS OF CONGRESS, MILITARY BODIES, POLITICAL DIVISIONS

412 Spell out numbers of sessions of Congress.

> The bill was passed by the Seventy-eighth Congress.

413 Spell out numbers in names of military divisions.

> The Twenty-second Regiment was sent to Hawaii.

414 Spell out numbers in names of political divisions.

> He was a candidate in the Twenty-third Assembly District.

FRACTIONS

415 Spell out fractions standing alone. (See also ¶ 524.)

> At least two-thirds of the books in my library are reference books.

416 When spelling out mixed numbers, include the word *and* between the words representing the whole number and the fraction; as *three and three-fourths.*

417 When forming fractions that do not appear on the typewriter, use the diagonal bar. Separate the whole number from the fraction by a space (*not* by a hyphen.)

> The rate of interest was 3 7/8 per cent.

418 In the same sentence, do not mix built-up fractions like the above with those that appear on the typewriter.

> The rate of interest is now 3 7/8 instead of 3 1/2 per cent. (*Not:* 3½.)

NUMBERS IN COMPOUND ADJECTIVES

419 When a compound adjective before a noun contains a number, the expression is hyphenated like any compound modifier. (See ¶ 510.)

> The lake is a 2-mile drive from here.
> They have agreed to accept the 60-day draft.
> We have a four-month (*or* a four months') option on the property.

A prepositional phrase that contains a number does not require a hyphen.

> There is a distance of 2 miles between the towns.

TWO NUMBERS COMING TOGETHER

420 When one number follows another, separate the numbers by a comma.

> In 1951, 400 cases were reported.
> On page 7, 90 cents was the price listed for that item.

421   If two numbers form one item, however, spell out one of them—usually the one that, when spelled out, would be the shorter word—and express the other number in figures.

> two 8-inch boards   500 four-page leaflets.

NUMBERS PRECEDED BY NOUNS

Note: For the capitalization of nouns, as *Chapter, Figure, page,* etc., used with numbers, see ¶ 380.

NUMBERS REPRESENTING A SEQUENCE

422   Use a hyphen to indicate the omission of the word *to* between two numbers that represent a sequence.

> pages 18–28   1945–1950 (*but:* from 1955 to 1965)
> May 15–20   Chapters I–III

423   Use a comma to separate two or more separate numbers that do not indicate a continuous sequence or period.

> pages 18, 20, 28   1945, 1950, 1952   May 15, 20, 25

COMMAS IN LARGE NUMBERS

424   In figures of four or more digits, use commas to separate thousands, millions, billions.

> $2,375.88   147,300 $1,275,478   4,300,000,000

425   Do *not* use commas in large serial numbers, house numbers, telephone numbers, page numbers, dates, and decimals.

> Serial No. 3954746   page 1246   46.9999
> 8760 Sunset Drive   ORchard 7–3765   1957

NO. OR # BEFORE FIGURES

426   When the word *number* is followed by a figure, write *No.* (plural *Nos.*) or # before the figure (preferably *No.* in the body of a letter). At the beginning of a sentence, spell out *Number.* (See also ¶ 90.)

> Our check covers the following invoices: Nos. 592, 653, and 654.
> Number 81275 has been assigned to your new policy.
> Please buy me two spools of #70 white thread.

ROMAN NUMERALS

427   Roman numerals are used chiefly for the important divisions of literary and legislative material, and in dates on public buildings.

> Volume I, Chapter X   Expressed in roman numerals, 1957 is
> Part II   written MCMLVII.

For methods of forming roman numerals, consult the dictionary.

Note: Pages in the front section of a book, as the Preface, Contents, etc., are customarily numbered in small roman numerals: *iii, vi, ix,* etc. Other pages are numbered in arabic numerals: *3, 6, 9,* etc.

PLURALS OF NUMBERS

428 Form the plurals of figures by adding an apostrophe and *s.* (See also ¶ 487.)

> We plan to print this book in 64's.

SECTION 8

When to abbreviate

DIFFERENCE BETWEEN ABBREVIATIONS AND CONTRACTIONS

429 An *abbreviation* is a shortened form of a word or a group of words, used to save space. It is followed by a period. (For example, *acct.,* for *account; f.o.b.,* for *free on board.*)

Note: Some abbreviations have become accepted as words and are written without periods; as *ad* for *advertisement.*

430 A *contraction* also is a shortened form of a word or a group of words; but an apostrophe is inserted at the exact point where letters are omitted, and *no* period follows the contraction (unless the form falls at the end of a sentence). (Examples: *nat'l,* for *national; doesn't,* for *does not.*)

a) Sometimes the same shortened form is used either as an abbreviation or as a contraction; as *mfg.* and *m'f'g; handkf.* and *h'dk'f.*

  Hint: In such cases prefer the abbreviation and avoid shifting to strike the apostrophe.

b) Contractions are used more often in informal writing than in business letters.

c) Some words formerly written with the apostrophe are now recognized as complete words; as *phone.*

FUNDAMENTAL RULES

431 Use abbreviations and contractions sparingly.

432 Be consistent. Do not abbreviate sometimes and spell out other times in the same letter, report, or manuscript.

433 When you do abbreviate, use the generally accepted forms found in the dictionary, such as *C. I. F.* (cost, insurance, freight), *cwt.* (hundredweight), and *f.o.b.* (free on board).

NAMES AND TITLES OF PERSONS

➤ **See** ¶¶ 76–84 for names and titles used with a person's *full name.*

434 In sentences, when the surname only is used, all titles except *Mr., Mrs.,* and *Messrs.* should be spelled out.

(*See page 87 for illustrative sentences.*)

Mrs. Ames, may I present *Professor* King.

The program was planned by *Chairman* Kennedy and *Doctor* Ross.

But: The original suggestion came from *Dr.* Herbert Mann.

➤ **See** ¶¶ 85–88 for the writing of *firm names.*

NAMES OF ORGANIZATIONS AND GOVERNMENT AGENCIES

435 Names of well-known societies and associations (trade, fraternal, charitable, professional) and names of railroads are often abbreviated. The trend is to omit the spaces between the letters of such abbreviations.

N.A.M.	National Association of Manufacturers
I.O.O.F.	Independent Order of Odd Fellows
C.O.S.	Charity Organization Society
Y.M.H.A.	Young Men's Hebrew Association
D.L.&W.	Delaware, Lackawanna & Western

436 Initials of the names of various Government agencies and international organizations are usually written without spaces and without periods.

FCC	Federal Communications Commission	ITO	International Trade Organization
SEC	Securities and Exchange Commission	UN	United Nations

437 Initials of names of labor organizations are also usually written close without periods.

AFL-CIO American Federation of Labor and Congress of Industrial Organizations.

Note: Some publishers, however, use periods in abbreviations of the type discussed in ¶¶ 436 and 437.

➤ **See** ¶¶ 91–104 for the abbreviation or the spelling out of *names of streets, cities, counties, states,* and *countries.*

DAYS, MONTHS, YEAR DATES, TIME ZONES

438 Always spell out names of days of the week and months of the year.

439 If space is very limited in a table or list, the following abbreviations *may* be used.

Sun.	Thurs.	Jan.	Apr.	Oct.
Mon.	Fri.	Feb.	Aug.	Nov.
Tues.	Sat.	Mar.	Sept.	Dec.
Wed.				

May, June, and *July* should not be abbreviated.

440 *A. D.* (an abbreviation of *anno Domini,* Latin for "in the year of our Lord") and *B. C.* ("before Christ") are written in all capitals, with a period following each letter. In each case, no comma separates the abbreviation from the year.

a) *A. D.* precedes the year; as *A. D. 1776.*

b) *B. C.* follows the year; as *100 B.C.*

441 The standard time zones are abbreviated as follows: *EST, CST, MST,* and *PST.* When daylight saving prevails, the forms *EDST, CDST, MDST,* and *PDST* are used. (See also ¶¶ 406, 407.)

MEASUREMENTS: WEIGHT, LENGTH, CAPACITY, AREA, VOLUME, TEMPERATURE, TIME

442 In general correspondence and in isolated usages, spell out units of measure.

> 5 pounds of sugar   1 yard of ½-inch-wide ribbon
> a 1-quart saucepan   a 20-degree drop in temperature

443 In technical and scientific work, on invoices, and wherever measurements occur very frequently, these terms are usually abbreviated.

> a room 10 ft. 6 in. x 19 ft. 10 in.   or   10′6″ x 19′10″
> Heat 1½ oz. of _____ and 4 oz. of _____ for 2 hrs. at _____°F.

444 Abbreviate *a.m.* and *p.m.* in expressions of time. Small letters are preferred for these abbreviations. (See also ¶ 407.)

445 In single occurrences, compass directions are spelled out.

> We purchased a lot at the southwest corner of Green and Union Streets.

446 Compass points included in street names are spelled out; as *East 123d Street.* (See also ¶¶ 93, 94.)

447 In technical work (real estate, legal, nautical), compass points are abbreviated thus:

> S.   south   SW.   southwest   SSW.   south-southwest

If the directions occur very frequently, the periods are often omitted.

NAMES OF RADIO AND TELEVISION BROADCASTING STATIONS AND SYSTEMS

448 The names of radio and television broadcasting stations and systems are written in capitals without spaces and without periods.

> Station KFRC   Station WPIX—Channel 11
> Station WQXR—FM   NBC

CHEMICAL, MATHEMATICAL, AND BUSINESS SYMBOLS

449 Do not use a period after the symbols used to represent chemical elements and formulas.

> K (potassium) H_2O (water)   NaCl (sodium chloride—salt)

450 Do not use a period after such mathematical symbols as *log, tan,* and in technical work after such phrases as *rpm* (revolutions per minute).

451 Neither *IOU* nor *SOS* is written with periods or spaces. Neither is an abbreviation.

452 *O.K.,* also *O.K.'d* and *O.K.'ing* are preferably written with periods. (See also ¶ 486.)

ORDINALS

453 Do not place a period after an ordinal, as *1st, 2d, 3d,* and so on. (See also ¶ 66.)

> ➤ **See** ¶¶ 483–487 for forming the *plurals* of abbreviations and symbols; ¶ 509 for the *possessives* of abbreviations.

CAPITALIZATION AND HYPHENIZATION

454   Abbreviations follow the capitalization and hyphenization of the full words for which they stand.

e.o.m.	end of month	a.m.	ante meridiem
ft.-lb.	foot-pound	R.I.	Rhode Island

➤ **See** ¶ 348 for spacing with abbreviations and for abbreviations with other marks of punctuation.

SECTION 9

Helps for the puzzled speller

BASIC RULE

The basic rule in spelling is: *When in doubt, consult the dictionary.* (See ¶¶ 21–29.) Be sure that you do not find some other word that is pronounced or spelled very much like the one you are looking up, such as those in the list in ¶ 611. Reading the definition and the illustrative sentences will help you determine whether you have found the right word.

The Merriam *Webster's New Collegiate Dictionary* is the authority for the spellings in this and other sections of this Manual. Wherever two spellings are allowable, only the preferred form (the first form) is given here.

WHEN A FINAL CONSONANT IS DOUBLED

455   One-syllable words double the final consonant if:
a) The word ends with a single consonant (pla*n*).
b) The consonant is preceded by a single vowel (pl*a*n).
c) The suffix to be added begins with a vowel (plann*ed*).

   stop   stopping   bag   baggage   ship   shipper

   Exception: gas   gaseous

456   Words of more than one syllable double the final consonant if:
a) The word ends with a single consonant (defe*r*).
b) The consonant is preceded by a single vowel (def*e*r).
c) The accent is on the last syllable of the root word (de*fer*).
d) The suffix to be added begins with a vowel (deferr*ed*).

   begin   beginning   transfer   transferred (*but:* transferable)

Exception: If the accent *shifts* to the first syllable of a word when a suffix beginning with a vowel is added, the final consonant is not doubled.

   defer   deferred (*but:* deference)

WHEN A FINAL CONSONANT IS NOT DOUBLED

457 Do not double the final consonant when a suffix beginning with a vowel is added to a word that ends in a *single consonant* and that is not accented on the last syllable (as *benefit*).

profit	profited	differ	differing
cancel	canceled	canceling (*but:* cancellation)	

458 Do not double the final consonant when a suffix beginning with a vowel is added if: (*a*) the final consonant is preceded by *more than one vowel,* or (*b*) the word ends in *more than one consonant.*

defeat	defeated	confirm	confirming

459 Words ending in *double consonants* usually retain both consonants when suffixes are added.

skill	skillful	install	installment

FINAL SILENT E

460 Words ending with silent *e* usually *drop* the *e* before a suffix beginning with a *vowel.*

use	usage	judge	judging
force	forcible	desire	desirous

Exceptions:

notice	noticeable	manage	manageable
advantage	advantageous	mile	mileage

461 Words ending with silent *e* usually *retain* the *e* before a suffix beginning with a *consonant.*

manage	management (*but:* managing)
like	likeness (*but:* likable)

Exceptions:

judgment	acknowledgment	truly	ninth	wholly

WHEN FINAL Y IS CHANGED TO I

462 Words ending in *y* preceded by a *consonant* usually change the *y* to *i* before *any suffix* except one beginning with *i.*

ordinary	ordinarily	heavy	heaviest

463 Words ending in *y* preceded by a *vowel* usually retain the *y* before *all terminations.*

obey	obeyed	annoy	annoyance

Exceptions:

pay	paid	day	daily
lay	laid	slay	slain

464 EI AND IE WORDS

Put *i* before *e*
Except after *c*

Or when sounded like *a*
As in *neighbor* and *weigh.*

I before e				*After c*	
chief	field	niece	pier	deceive	ceiling
brief	yield	variety	fierce	receipt	receive

Sounded like a		*Exceptions:*		
freight	their	seize	weird	forfeit
weight	heir	height	ancient	financier

WORDS ENDING IN -ABLE AND -IBLE

465 The more usual ending is *-able*. However, some of the most commonly used words end with *-ible*.

advis*able*	prob*able*	receiv*able*	sal*able*	valu*able*
collect*ible*	divis*ible*	flex*ible*	permiss*ible*	suscept*ible*

WORDS ENDING IN -CEDE, -CEED, -SEDE

466 Only *one* word ends in *-sede: supersede.*

Only *three* words end in *-ceed: exceed, proceed, succeed.* (Note, however, that derivatives of these three words are spelled with only one *e: excess, procedure, success.*)

All other words ending with the syllable pronounced "seed" are spelled *-cede: precede, secede, recede.*

WORDS ENDING IN -ISE, -IZE, AND -YZE

467 The most usual ending is *-ize*. However, some of the most commonly used words end with *-ise.*

apolog*ize*	author*ize*	critic*ize*	real*ize*	summar*ize*
advert*ise*	compromi*se*	exerc*ise*	merchand*ise*	superv*ise*
anal*yze*	paral*yze*			

➤ *Formation of Plurals*

When you are uncertain as to the plural form of a word, consult the dictionary. Irregular plurals and alternative forms of plurals are shown. If no plural is shown, the plural is formed in the regular way. If the word is not included in the dictionary, form the plural the simplest way—by adding *s* or *es*, according to the rules in ¶¶ 468 and 469.

468 Plurals are regularly formed by adding *s* to the singular form.

park	parks	employee	employees

NOUNS ENDING IN S OR AN S SOUND

469 When the singular form ends with *s* or an *s* sound (*ss, x, ch, sh, z*), the plural is formed by adding *es* to the singular.

gas	gases	church	churches
business	businesses	dispatch	dispatches
Jones	the Joneses	sash	sashes
annex	annexes	quartz	quartzes

470 Words ending in silent *s* do not change their forms in the plural.

one corps	two corps

NOUNS ENDING IN Y

471 When a noun ends in *y* preceded by a *consonant,* the plural is formed by changing the *y* to *i* and adding *es* to the singular.

| company | companies | necessity | necessities |
| vacancy | vacancies | authority | authorities |

Note: The plural of a proper noun ending in *y* is formed simply by adding *s; as Lucy, all the Lucys.*

472 When a noun ends in *y* preceded by a *vowel,* the plural is formed by adding *s* to the singular.

| attorney | attorneys | *Exception:* soliloquy | soliloquies |

NOUNS ENDING IN O

473 Nouns ending in *o* preceded by a *vowel* form their plurals by adding *s* to the singular.

| studio | studios | radio | radios |

474 Some singular nouns ending in *o* preceded by a *consonant* form their plurals by adding *es* to the singular.

| potato | potatoes | embargo | embargoes |

475 Some nouns ending in *o* have two plural forms. (The preferred form is given first.)

| cargo | cargoes, cargos | proviso | provisos, provisoes |

NOUNS ENDING IN F, FE, OR FF

476 The plurals of most nouns that end in *f, fe,* or *ff* are formed by adding *s* to the singular.

| brief | briefs | safe | safes |
| handkerchief | handkerchiefs | tariff | tariffs |

477 Some commonly used nouns ending in *f* or *fe* form their plurals by changing the *f* or *fe* to *ve* and adding *s.*

| half | halves | shelf | shelves |
| wife | wives | knife | knives |

IRREGULAR PLURALS

478 In some nouns the plurals are formed by a change of vowels.

| woman | women | foot | feet |
| mouse | mice | goose | geese |

479 A few plurals end in *en.*

| ox | oxen | child | children |

COMPOUNDS

480 The plurals of hyphenated or two-word compounds are formed by adding the plural sign to the chief element of the compound.

(*See examples on page 93.*)

man-of-war	men-of-war	notary public	notaries public
court-martial	courts-martial	bill of lading	bills of lading

a) When a hyphenated compound consists of a noun and a preposition, the noun portion is pluralized.

looker-on	lookers-on	passer-by	passers-by

b) When neither element of a hyphenated compound is a noun, the final element of the word is pluralized.

go-between	go-betweens	tie-in	tie-ins
write-up	write-ups	hand-me-down	hand-me-downs

481   When a compound noun is a solid word, the sign of the plural is added at the end.

cupful	cupfuls	businessman	businessmen
stepchild	stepchildren	courthouse	courthouses

TITLES AND PERSONAL NAMES

482   Titles and personal names may be pluralized as follows:

the Misses Mercer *or* the Miss Mercers
the Doctors Crane *or* the Doctor Cranes

(See also Note in ¶ 471.)

ABBREVIATIONS, LETTERS, FIGURES, SYMBOLS

483   The plurals of most abbreviations are formed by adding *s* to the singular.

dept.	depts.	yr.	yrs.	lb.	lbs.	Co.	Cos.

484   The abbreviations of many units of weight and measure, however, are the same in both the singular and plural

oz.	(for *ounce* and *ounces*)	ft.	(for *foot* and *feet*)
deg.	(for *degree* and *degrees*)	min.	(for *minute* and *minutes*)

485   The plurals of a few single-letter abbreviations consist of the same letter doubled.

p.	(for *page*)	f.	(for *and the following page*)
pp.	(for *pages*)	ff.	(for *and the following pages*)

486   The plural of an abbreviation made up of separate letters is formed by adding an apostrophe and *s* to the abbreviation.

C. P. A.'s	C. O. D.'s	f.o.b's	N.P.'s O.K.'s

Note: The apostrophe is also used to form *O.K.'d, O.K.'ing, X'd, X'ing,* and similar terms. (See also ¶ 452.)

487   The plurals of letters, numerals, symbols, signs, and words referred to as words are formed by adding an apostrophe and *s.*

C	four C's	–	the –'s	IOU	IOU's
7	all the 7's	if	the if's	1900	the 1900's

Note: Some authorities do not use the apostrophe if no confusion would result from its omission.

(*Rule continues on page 94.*)

In forming the plural of a word that already contains an apostrophe, the *s* alone is added; as *the do's and don'ts.*

NOUNS HAVING THE SAME SINGULAR AND PLURAL FORM

488 Some nouns have the same form for both the singular and the plural.

cattle	pains (care)	politics	Japanese
deer	odds	corps	Portuguese
sheep	species	Chinese	wheat

NOUNS ALWAYS SINGULAR

489 Some nouns are always singular.

civics	economics	news	music
mathematics	aeronautics	measles	whereabouts

NOUNS ALWAYS PLURAL

490 The following nouns have no corresponding singular forms in the same sense.

ashes	doings	means (income)	scissors
assets	goods	paraphernalia	spectacles
auspices	grounds	premises	statistics
belongings	headquarters	proceeds	wages
brains	hysterics	remains	winnings
credentials	leavings	scales	works

PLURALS OF FOREIGN NOUNS

491 Many nouns of foreign origin have been given English plurals, some retain their foreign plurals, and still others have two plurals—an English and a foreign. In general, the foreign forms are used in formal, scientific, and technical matter. If you are not sure of the plural of a foreign noun, consult your dictionary. These words are used frequently in business.

Singular	*English plural*	*Foreign plural*
addendum		addenda
alumna (fem.)		alumnae
alumnus (mas.)		alumni
analysis		analyses
basis		bases
crisis		crises
criterion	criterions	criteria
datum		data
formula	formulas	formulae
index	indexes	indices
memorandum	memorandums	memoranda
parenthesis		parentheses
terminus	terminuses	termini

➤ *Formation of Possessives*

492 Usually an *s*-ending noun that is followed immediately by another noun is in the possessive form.

the employee's record (meaning "the record of the employee")
the Harms's merchandise (meaning "the merchandise of the Harms store")

(Rule continues on page 95.)

But do not mistake a modifier ending in *s* for a possessive. (See also ¶ 497.)

> sales effort (*sales* modifies *effort;* the meaning is not "effort of sales")
> the Harms survey (meaning a survey made for the Harms store)
> the Forbes account; the George Reynolds estate

To test such cases, substitute some other word that does not end in *s* for the doubtful word (as the *publicity* effort). If the substituted word does not require the possessive, the doubtful word does not.

SINGULAR NOUNS

493   To form the possessive of a singular noun *not* ending in *s,* add an apostrophe and *s* to the noun.

> a boy's coat   Joe's record

494   To form the possessive of a singular noun that ends in *s* or an *s* sound, add an apostrophe and *s* if a new syllable is formed in the pronunciation of the possessive.

> my boss's desk   Charles's pen
> the witness's testimony   Mr. Jones's book

If the addition of *s* would make an *s*-ending word hard to pronounce, it is permissible to add the apostrophe only.

> Mr. Hawkins' order   Simmons' factory   Mr. Phillips' pen

(Not all authorities agree on this exception.)
Caution: In forming the possessive of any noun ending in *s*, do not place the apostrophe before the final *s* of the noun.

> Mr. Burns's message (*not:* Mr. Burn's message)

PLURAL NOUNS

495   To form the possessive of a *regular plural,* add only an apostrophe.

> students' marks   attorneys' offices
> the witnesses' testimonies   the Joneses' contributions

496   To form the possessive of *irregular plurals,* add an apostrophe and *s.*

> men's suits   children's shoes

Hint: To avoid mistakes in forming the possessive of plural nouns, form the plural first; then apply the rule in ¶ 495 or 496, whichever fits.

Singular	Plural	Plural possessive
boy	boys	boys'
boss	bosses	bosses'
child	children	children's

497   When a plural noun is more of an adjective than a true possessive, the apostrophe may be omitted. Such nouns describe rather than show possession. (See also ¶ 492.)

> teachers college   ladies night   Texas legislature

PRONOUNS

498   The possessive forms of *personal pronouns* and of *who* do not require the apostrophe. Each pronoun has its own special possessive form.

I: my, mine	she: her, hers	they: their, theirs
you: your, yours	it: its	who: whose
he: his	we: our, ours	

Caution: Guard against confusing personal possessive pronouns with similarly spelled contractions; for example:

its with *it's,* which means "it is" (See ¶ 592.)
theirs with *there's,* which means "there is"
whose with *who's,* which may mean either "who is" or "who has"

499   Form the possessive of *indefinite pronouns* according to the regular rules.

one's choice   the other's claim   anybody's guess   the others' claims

COMPOUND NOUNS

500   Form the possessive of compound nouns, whether hyphenated or two words, by adding the apostrophe and *s* to the last member of the compound.

my mother-in-law's will	anybody else's job
the secretary-treasurer's hours	the attorney general's power

Note: Instead of using the plural possessive of a compound noun, it is usually preferable to rephrase the sentence.

This agrees with the statements of both attorneys general.

JOINT OR INDIVIDUAL OWNERSHIP

501   To form the possessive of two or more nouns that represent joint ownership, add the sign of the possessive to the *final* noun.

Bruce & Hall's Department Store   Tom and Ed's boat

502   To indicate separate ownership by two persons, add the sign of the possessive to both nouns. (The repetition of *the* clearly indicates separate ownership.)

the buyer's and the seller's signatures

NOUNS IN APPOSITION

503   Sometimes a noun that ordinarily would be in the possessive is followed by an explanatory word. In such cases, add the sign of the possessive to the explanatory word only.

That is Miss Case, the file clerk's, responsibility.

Note: If this form results in awkwardness, the possessive may be changed to an *of* phrase.

That is the responsibility of Miss Case, the file clerk.

POSSESSIVE STANDING ALONE

504   Sometimes the noun that the possessive modifies is merely understood.

> Please call for my order at the grocer's (store).
> Mary's (transcript) was the best transcript handed in.

POSSESSIVE INCORRECT FOR INANIMATE THINGS

505   Properly, the possessive form should be applied only to nouns and pronouns that refer to persons or animals.

> the salesman's quota   the bird's song

506   When reference is to inanimate things, an *of* phrase should be used.

> the hood of the car (*not:* the car's hood)
> the terms of the contract (*not:* the contract's terms)

507   In many common expressions that refer to time and measurements, however, and in phrases implying personification, the possessive form has come to be accepted usage. (See also ¶ 419.)

> one day's notice   a dollar's worth   a stone's throw
> an hour's work   several dollars' worth   for heaven's sake
> two years' progress   at arm's length   for conscience' sake

PRECEDING A VERBAL NOUN

508   When a noun or a pronoun denoting a person or an animate thing precedes a gerund (the *ing* form of a verb used as a noun), the noun or pronoun should be in the possessive form.

> I am opposed to *your* entering that school.
> Was there a report of the *salesman's* being recalled?
> The *dog's* barking awakened us.

ABBREVIATIONS

509   Form the possessive of an abbreviation by placing the apostrophe and *s* after the period if the abbreviation is singular; only an apostrophe if it is plural. (See ¶¶ 234 and 235.)

> the C. P. A.'s audit   Allen Bros.' sale
> George Thompson, Inc.'s stationery   Mr. John Smith, Jr.'s new house
> the A. & V. Co.'s ad   the M. D. s' diagnoses

Note: The comma is omitted after *Inc.'s* and *Jr.'s* in order to bring the possessive element as near to the object possessed as possible.

➤ **See** ¶ 88 for the names of organizations that contain nouns in the possive case.

SECTION 10

One word, two words, or hyphenated?

Some compound words are written as one solid word; others, as two separate words; and others are hyphenated. Authorities do not agree on the rules; moreover, practice gradually changes. An up-to-date dictionary is the only sure guide. (*Caution:* See ¶ 512.) However, the following rules should help you be consistent in compounding.

COMPOUND ADJECTIVES

510 When two or more words are used as a one-thought modifier *before* a noun, the modifier is hyphenated. (For exceptions, see ¶ 517.)

a well-known book	a hard-and-fast rule
in first-class condition	a never-to-be-forgotten event
a one-way street	a change-of-address card
a 10-foot board	the Chicago-Seattle route
high-grade securities	a would-be authority

511 Do not confuse true compound adjectives with constructions in which two or more *independent* adjectives precede a noun. (See also ¶¶ 223, 224.)

a distinguished public orator   recognized accounting procedures

In such constructions as these, the *first* adjective modifies the idea expressed by the second adjective plus the noun.

Special Hint on ¶¶ 510 and 511: If you have difficulty deciding whether to apply ¶ 510 or ¶ 511, try asking yourself such questions as these:

"Is it a four building?" No. "Is it a story building?" No. Therefore it must be a *four-story* building.

"Is it a far model?" No. "Is it a superior model?" Yes. Therefore it must be a *far superior* model.

512 When a one-thought modifier *follows* the noun, the construction of the sentence usually changes and *no hyphen* is needed. The compound adjective becomes either a predicate adjective or a prepositional phrase that is clear without a hyphen.

A book that is up to date in that field will be well received. (An up-to-date book in that field will be well received.)

An author who is well known will speak at the luncheon. (A well-known author will speak at the luncheon.)

(*Continued on page 99.*)

The check mentioned above has not been received. (The above-mentioned check has not been received.)

I need a board 10 feet long. (Please get me a 10-foot board.)

She types at a speed that is more than average. (She types at a more-than-average speed.)

Important Exception: In some cases, however, the hyphenated form is necessary even in the predicate to make the one-thought meaning clear. Usually these forms consist of an adjective or a noun plus a noun to which -ed has been added, or an adjective or a noun plus a participle.

an old-fashioned virtue	Honesty is not old-fashioned.
a quiet-spoken man	He is quiet-spoken.
an awe-inspiring view	The view was awe-inspiring.

An up-to-date dictionary includes compound adjectives of this type that are always hyphenated.

513 Modifiers that contain adverbs ending in *ly* as their first element are not hyphenated. The *ly* indicates that the first word modifies the second, and therefore the hyphen is not needed.

a poorly constructed house	a privately owned corporation
a highly valued employee	a poorly arranged office

514 Note, however, that some *adjectives* end in *ly*. Compounds containing such adjectives require a hyphen.

a friendly child	a snarly dog
a friendly-looking child	a snarly-sounding dog

515 When one of the words in a compound modifier ends in the comparative or the superlative ending *er* or *est,* no hyphen is needed, as the ending shows the relationship of the two words. The second element of such compounds most often ends in *ed*.

a high-priced car	a small-sized umbrella
a higher priced car	the smallest sized umbrella

However, when adjectives are compared irregularly, the hyphen is used in the comparative and superlative forms.

a well-paying job	a better-paying job	the best-paying job

516 When a two-word proper noun is used as an adjective before a noun, the hyphen is not used.

New York traffic	a South American country
Supreme Court decision	a Western Union telegram

But, when one or both of the proper nouns before a noun consist of two words, the combined form is hyphenated.

the Chicago–St. Louis express	the New York–San Diego flight

517 There is a tendency to omit the hyphen from certain frequently used one-thought modifiers that are instantly clear without the hyphen.

(*Continued on page 100.*)

a high school student	a life insurance premium
an income tax blank	the dining car menu
civil service requirements	long distance calls
a safe deposit box	real estate advertising

Also, in special industries and businesses, hyphens are omitted from modifiers that would be hyphenated in more general correspondence. Many offices supply their stenographers with the forms to be used.

low voltage supplies	new car sales
radar data processing	cold storage warehouse

518 When a series of hyphenated adjectives has a common basic element and this element is omitted in all but the last term, a "suspending" hyphen follows each adjective. (Be sure to space after the first hyphen.)

long- and short-term securities	(long-term and short-term securities)
left- and right-hand margins	hard- and soft-coal dealers

10- and 20-year bonds

COMPOUND NOUNS AND COMPOUND VERBS

519 Compound nouns are usually either one solid word or two words. There are some exceptions, however.

   a) Some unusual combinations that represent a single unit of thought are hyphenated.

   go-between   know-how   give-and-take   old-timer   man-hour

   b) Some compounds that, if solid, would result in a confusing combination of letters are hyphenated.

   trade-in   tie-up   follow-up   make-up   (*but:* setup)

Note: When used as verbs: *follow up   make up   set up*

520 A compound verb built up from an adjective and a noun or from an adjective and a verb is hyphenated.

   dry-clean   quick-freeze   blue-pencil   cross-examine

NUMBERS

521 Hyphenate spelled-out compound numerals below 100; as *ninety-nine.*

522 When numbers over 100 are spelled out, do not insert a hyphen between *hundred* and *thousand* and the rest of the number.

   one hundred twenty-five
   five thousand seven hundred twenty-five

Note: Some persons insert the word *and* in large written-out numbers like the above. As the word is not used in writing large amounts of money on checks, however, or in other business usages, it seems preferable to treat all cases the same way.

523 When *dates* are written in words, as in formal invitations and in some legal documents, the form is *nineteen hundred and fifty-seven.*

524 When a fraction is spelled in words, the numerator and the denominator should be separated by a hyphen, unless either the numerator or the denominator already contains a hyphen.

one-half the vote	five thirty-seconds
a two-thirds majority	twenty-five sixty-fourths

Note: Figures are clearer for long, awkward forms.

5/32ds	25/64ths

525 One-thought modifiers containing numbers are written in accordance with ¶¶ 510 and 512.

➤ **See** ¶ 422 for the use of the hyphen in numbers representing a sequence.

PREFIXES AND SUFFIXES

526 In general, when the first element of a compound is a prefix or the last element is a suffix, no hyphen is used.

Prefixes		*Suffixes*
*after*thought	*post*script (but: *post* office)	king*dom*
*ante*date	*pre*dawn	thought*ful*
*anti*climax	*re*organize	neighbor*hood*
*bi*annual	*semi*annual	account*ing*
*by*laws (*but: by*-product)	*step*mother	heart*less**
*extra*territorial	*sub*division	child*like**
*fore*most	*super*abundant	excite*ment*
*hyper*critical	*there*by	costli*ness*
*inter*office	*ultra*critical	lone*some*
*mono*plane	*under*current	back*ward*
*non*essential	*up*take	leader*ship*
*over*confident	*where*as	

* If, in the addition of these suffixes, the result is three *l*'s in succession, the hyphen is used; as *bell-like, shell-less.*

527 Compounds with *self* are hyphenated.

self-confidence	self-addressed	(*but:* selfsame)

528 A hyphen is inserted when the last vowel of a prefix is the same as the first vowel of the word to which it is joined or when such a joining would result in a confusing sequence of letters.

co-operate	pre-election	anti-intellectual
re-education	semi-invalid	co-worker

529 In several words beginning with *re,* in which *re* means "again," the hyphen is needed to distinguish the words from other identically spelled words of different meanings.

to re-mark the ticket	as he remarked to me
to re-form the class	to reform a sinner
to re-cover a chair	to recover from an illness
to re-collect the slips	to recollect the mistake

530 When a prefix is added to a word that begins with a capital, a hyphen follows the prefix. (See list on page 102.)

un-American	mid-January	pre-Revolutionary
non-Asiatic	trans-Canadian	pro-Continental

TITLES

531 Civil, military, and naval titles of two or more words are not hyphenated.

Chief of Police Murphy	Lieutenant Colonel Clark
Consul General Boyd	Rear Admiral Byrd
General Manager Henderson	Attorney General Bradford

Exceptions: Compound titles containing *ex, Vice,* and *elect* are hyphenated. (See also ¶ 357.)

ex-President Hoover   Vice-President Johnson   Governor-elect Smith

When *ex* is used with words other than names, no hyphen is used, as *ex officio.*

532 If a title represents two offices, however, it is hyphenated.

Secretary-Treasurer McDermott

➤ **See** ¶ 381 for rules governing the *capitalization* of compounds.

➤ **See** ¶¶ 480, 481, 500 for rules governing the formation of *plurals* and *possessives* of compounds.

SOMETIMES ONE WORD, SOMETIMES TWO WORDS

533 Several common compounds may be written either as one solid word or as two separate words, depending on the meaning.

a) *Almost* and *all most*

The plane was *almost* (an adverb meaning "nearly") three hours late.
We are *all most* (all very much) pleased with the new working schedule.

b) *Already* and *all ready*

The order had *already* (an adverb meaning "previously") been shipped.
The order is *all ready* (all prepared) to be shipped.

c) *Altogether* and *all together*

He is *altogether* (an adverb meaning "entirely") too lazy to be a satisfactory employee.
The papers are *all together* (in a group) on Mr. Green's desk.

d) *Always* and *all ways*

She has *always* (at all times) done her work well.
We have tried in *all ways* (by all means) to keep our employees satisfied.

e) *Anyone* and *any one*

Anyone (that is, anybody) could follow those directions.
Any one (that is, any person of a group) of us could have made the same mistake.

Hint: Any one (also *every one, no body,* and *some one*) is usually followed by *of.*

f) *Anyway* and *any way*

> *Anyway* (an adverb meaning "in any case"), we can't spare him now.
> If we can help in *any way* (*way* is a noun), please phone.

g) *Everyday* and *every day*

> The new stenographer soon mastered the *everyday* (an adjective meaning "ordinary" or "daily") routine of the office.
> He has called *every day* (each day) this week.

h) *Everyone* and *every one*

> *Everyone* (that is, everybody) likes to be popular.
> *Every one* (that is, each person without exception) of the men was paid.

(See Hint in *e*.)

i) *Indifferent* and *in different*

> She was an *indifferent* (an adjective meaning "without interest") worker.
> He liked our idea, but he wished it expressed *in different* (other) words.

j) *Indirect* and *in direct*

> *Indirect* (an adjective meaning "not direct") lighting is very satisfactory in an office.
> This order is *in direct* conflict with the policy of this company.

k) *Into* and *in to* (See ¶ 608.)

l) *Maybe* and *may be*

> If we don't receive a letter today, *maybe* (an adverb meaning "perhaps") we should wire the company.
> Mr. Brown *may be* (a verb) in his office tomorrow.

m) *Nobody* and *no body*

> There was *nobody* (no person) at the information desk when I arrived.
> *No body* (group) of employees is more co-operative than yours.

(See Hint in *e*.)

n) *None* and *no one* (See also ¶ 567.)

> *None* of the offers proved acceptable.
> *No one* in the room could answer the question.

o) *Someone* and *some one*

> *Someone* (somebody) called you early this morning.
> *Some one* (some particular person) of the stenographers mislaid the carbon copy of that letter.

(See Hint in *e*.)

p) *Sometime, sometimes,* and *some time*
Sometime is an adverb meaning at an unspecified or indefinite time, usually in the future.

> The order will be shipped *sometime* next week.

Sometimes, also an adverb, means "now and then."

Sometimes reports are misleading.

Some time is a two-word phrase (*some,* an adjective, modifying *time,* a noun). The phrase usually refers to the passage of time.

It took me *some time* to complete the job. (Hint: If the word *little* can be mentally inserted between the *some* and *time,* the two-word phrase is correct.)

q) *Whoever* and *who ever*

Whoever (no matter who) is elected secretary should write that letter at once.

Who ever made such a statement? (*Ever* is an adverb.)

SECTION 11

How to divide words

Wherever possible, avoid dividing a word at the end of a line. (Some offices even follow the rule of never dividing a word.) Sometimes, nevertheless, it is necessary to carry over part of a word. Too many divisions, however, are unattractive.

Note: The hyphenated forms of the words used to illustrate the following rules should not be confused with hyphenated compound words. (See Sec. 10.)

BASIC RULES

534 Words may be divided *only* between syllables.

535 Careful pronunciation will aid you in determining the structure of a word. In many cases it is necessary to consult the dictionary to verify syllable structure. (See ¶ 26.) Note these distinctions.

rec-ord (an official copy)	pres-ent (a gift)
re-cord (to make an official copy)	pre-sent (to make a gift)

536 Divide a word as it is naturally divided in pronunciation rather than according to derivation.

knowl-edge (*not:* know-ledge)   prod-uct (*not:* pro-duct)

537 The following rules explain why certain divisions are preferred.

ONE-SYLLABLE WORDS

538 Never divide one-syllable words. Even when *-ed* is added to some words, they still remain one-syllable words and so cannot be divided.

weight	thought	strength	scheme
passed	trimmed	weighed	shipped

WORDS CONTAINING THREE, FOUR, OR FIVE LETTERS

539   Do not divide words of only three, four, or five letters, even when they contain more than one syllable.

     ago   upon   idea   rely   begin   index

ONE-LETTER SYLLABLES

540   Do not divide a one-vowel *beginning* or *ending* syllable from the rest of the word.

     *a*mount   *i*dentify   bacteri*a*   pian*o*

541   A one-vowel syllable that occurs *within* a word should *not* be carried over to the new line.

     criti-cal   sepa-rate   simi-lar   regu-lar

TWO-LETTER SYLLABLES

542   Avoid dividing after a two-letter syllable, and never carry over only two letters.

     *le*galize   *se*curity   count*er*   satis*fy*

Exception: If absolutely necessary, division may be made after two-letter prefixes.

     ad-joining   *de*-tract   *by*-stander   *ir*-rational
     in-convenient   *re*-affirm   *un*-important   *im*-possible

TWO CONSONANTS BETWEEN TWO VOWELS

543   As a general rule, when two consonants come together between two vowels, divide between the consonants.

     advan-tage   impor-tance   struc-ture   finan-cier

A SINGLE CONSONANT BETWEEN TWO SINGLE VOWELS

544   When a single consonant comes between two single vowels, if the first vowel is short and accented, keep the consonant with the first syllable, as *băl-ance, prŏd-uct.* If the vowel is long, keep the consonant with the second syllable, as *sē-dan, prō-duction.*

DOUBLE CONSONANTS

545   As a rule, when double consonants occur at the point where two syllables join, divide between the consonants. (See also ¶¶ 547, 548.)

     mil-lion   drug-gist   pas-senger   inflam-mable
     neces-sary   recur-rence   pos-sible   recom-mend

PREFIXES AND SUFFIXES

546   Words beginning with a prefix of three or more letters are preferably divided *after* the prefix. Words ending with a suffix of three or more letters may be divided *before* the suffix. (See *Exception,* ¶ 542.)

     intro-duce   *sub*-sistence   *pro*-motion   *trans*-lation
     advis-*able*   collec-*tion*   ambi-*tious*   benefi-*cial*

547   If a *suffix* is added to a word that ends in a double letter, divide before the suffix.

sell-ers   full-est   fulfill-ing   careless-ness

548   When a final consonant is doubled before a suffix, divide between the consonants, provided the last part of the word forms a separate syllable.

ship-ping   omit-ted   begin-ning   refer-ring

But: occurred, referred, shipped

COMPOUND WORDS

549   Both hyphenated compounds and solid-word compounds should be divided only between the elements of the compound.

Hyphenated Words		*Solid Compounds*	
self-control	self-control	businessman	business-man

DATES AND OTHER FIGURES; NAMES

550   Avoid dividing the following elements. If *necessary,* however, divide according to the following rules and the correspondingly lettered illustrations that follow.

a) Dates: Between the day and year.
b) Street addresses: Between the name of the street and *Street, Avenue, etc.*
c) Names of persons: Between the given name and surname.
d) Names of places: Between the city and the state.
e) Very long titles: Between the title and the name.
f) Before a mark of enumeration and the matter to which it refers.

Illustrations

a) _____September 21, 1961 _____

b) _____South Mountain Avenue_____

c) _____William E. Roberts_____

d) _____Cincinnati, Ohio_____

e) _____The Reverend Henry S. Brewester_____

f) _____ ... these points: (1) all cards to ....

551   *Never* divide the following:

a) Abbreviations or contractions. Also, do not separate an abbreviation from a preceding figure to which it applies; as *3 p.m.*
b) Figures or amounts of money.
c) Units of measure from the figures with which they belong; as *7 miles.*
d) A person's initials or his title (as *Mr.*) from his surname.
e) The abbreviation of a degree (as *Ph. D.*). Also do not separate degrees or such abbreviations as *Jr.* from a name.

GENERAL PRECAUTIONS

552   Do not allow more than two consecutive lines to end in hyphens.

553   Do not divide the last word in a paragraph.

554   Do not divide the last word on the first page of a two-page letter or on any page.

SECTION 12

Your grammar is showing

→ *Subject and Verb*

555 A verb must agree with its subject.

556 A singular subject requires a singular verb; a plural subject, a plural verb.

> *She is* ready to leave the office.
> The *men are* ready to move the safe.

> The *gloves* she lost *were* white.
> The *pair* of gloves she lost *was* white.

A plural verb is always required after *you,* even when *you* is singular, referring to only one person.

> *You were* very kind to me during my illness.

Note: Although *s* added to a *noun* indicates the plural form, *s* added to a verb indicates the third person singular.

> He *favors* the move.   They *favor* the expansion.

557 Guard against making the verb agree with an intervening plural object of a preposition *or any intervening plural* instead of with the true subject.

> The lost *box* of new letterheads *has* not been found. (In the phrase *of new letterheads, letterheads* is the object of *of.*)
> The *prices* of the new model *vary* with the dealer.
> *One* of the items ordered *has* been delivered. (See also ¶ 558.)
> Her *experience* as adviser to boys and girls *gives* her understanding.

558 The verbs following the various expressions containing the words *one of* are chosen in accordance with these rules.

a) The simple form *one of* or *one of the* is followed by a singular verb, to agree with the subject *one.* (See ¶ 557.)

> *One* of the books *has* been lost.
> *One* of the reasons for his resignation *is* poor health.

b) The phrases *one of those who* and *one of the things that,* however, are followed by plural verbs because these phrases contain words introducing relative clauses. In the subordinate clause the subject is the relative pronoun *who* or *that,* and a relative pronoun agrees with its antecedent in number.

> He is one of those who *favor* increasing the staff. (*Favor* agrees with *those.*
> In the phrase *one of those who, those* is the plural object of the preposition
> *of.* In the subordinate clause *who favor increasing the staff,* the relative pronoun *who* is the subject and must agree with its antecedent *those.*)

(*Continued on page 108.*)

She is one of our employees who *are* never late. (*Are* agrees with *employees.*)
I ordered one of the skirts that *were* advertised. (*Were* agrees with *skirts.*)
John is one of our men who *are* going with me. (*Are* agrees with *men.*)

Exception: When *only* precedes such phrases, however, the meaning is singular and a singular verb is required.

John is the *only* one of our men who *is* going with me.

559 The insertion of phrases introduced by *with, together with, as well as, in addition to, along with, besides, including,* and so on after the subject does not affect the number of the verb. If the subject is singular, a singular verb is required; if plural, a plural verb.

Mrs. Smith, with her son and daughter, *is* going to the theater this evening.
Our chief *competitor,* as well as ourselves, *is* obliged to raise prices this fall.
The *decoration* of the room, including the drapes and rugs, *is* most pleasing.
The *ornaments,* along with the clock, *are* to be sold.

560 If the subject consists of *two singular words* connected by *and* or by *both . . . and,* the subject is plural and so requires a plural verb.

Mr. Johnson *and* Mr. Bruce *have* received promotions.
Both the collection *and* the delivery of mail *are* to be curtailed.

The repetition of *the* makes it doubly clear that two different items are meant.

Exceptions:

a) If a subject consisting of two singular nouns connected by *and* refers to the same person or thing, a singular verb is used.

The *secretary and treasurer* (one officer) *is* reading the minutes.
Corned beef and cabbage is our Monday special.

b) When two subjects connected by *and* are preceded by *each, every, many a,* a singular verb is used.

Each man and boy *is* expected to meet his obligation.
Every hat, suit, and topcoat *is* marked for reduction.
Many an office boy and clerk *has* become an executive in his company.

561 If the subject consists of *two singular* words connected by *or, either . . . or,* or *neither . . . nor,* the subject is singular and requires a singular verb.

Tom *or* John *has* the stapler.
Either July or August *is* a good vacation month.
Neither our Credit Department *nor* our Accounting Department *has* a record of the transaction.

562 If the subject is made up of both singular and plural words connected by *or, nor, either . . . or, neither . . . nor, not only . . . but also,* the verb agrees with the nearer part of the subject.

Neither the *salesmen nor* the *buyer is* in favor of the system.
Neither the *buyer nor* the *salesmen are* in favor of the system.
Not only the *teachers but also* the *superintendent is* in favor of the plan.

563   Plural verbs are required for many nouns that have no singular form. (See ¶ 490.)

> The *proceeds* of the concert *are* to be given to the fund for blind veterans.
> The *goods are* being shipped today.

564   The following rules govern the form of verb to be used with a collective noun. (A *collective noun* is a word that represents a group of persons, animals, or things; for example, *army, audience, board, cabinet, class, committee, company, corporation, council, department, firm, group, majority, public, society, school.*)

a) If the group is thought of as acting as a unit, the verb should be singular.

> The *Board* of Directors *meets* Friday.
> The *committee has* agreed to submit its report on Monday.
> The *firm is* one of the oldest in the field.

b) If the members of the group are thought of as acting separately, the verb should be plural.

> The *committee were* not in agreement on the action to be taken.
> The *audience were* cheering and laughing—even crying.

c) *Company names* may be either singular or plural according to the meaning. The plural form emphasizes the individual personnel making up the company. If a company is referred to as *they,* a plural verb is required. If a company is referred to as *it,* a singular verb is used.

> Morris & Company *have* the reputation of going to any length to retain the good will of a customer. As a result, *they* seldom *lose* a customer.
> The Elite Corporation *is* located at 12th and Market Streets.
> The Rice Company *has* lost *its* lease.

d) When nouns expressing *periods of time, amounts of money,* or *quantities* are considered as a single unit, singular verbs are used.

> *Three months is* too long a time to wait.
> That *$10,000 was* an inheritance from my uncle.
> Yes, *3 yards is* ample for a dress.

e) After such expressions as *one-half of, two-thirds of, a part of, a majority of* (see also ¶ 569):

(1) Use a *singular verb* if a *singular noun* follows the *of.*

> *Three-fourths of* the mailing list *has* been checked.
> A *part of* the building *is* closed.
> A *majority of* 2,000 *indicates* his popularity.

(2) Use a *plural verb* when a *plural noun* follows the *of.*

> *Two-thirds of* our customers *live* in the suburbs.
> *Part of* the walls *are* to be papered.
> The *majority of* our students *live* at home.

f) The expression *the number* has a singular meaning and demands a singular verb; *a number* has a plural meaning and demands a plural verb.

> *The number* of orders still to be filled *is* estimated at nearly a hundred.
> *A number* of our staff *are* going on vacation today.

565 When a noun has a foreign plural form, a plural verb must be used with the plural form. (See ¶ 491.)

> *These memoranda are* inaccurate. (*But: This memorandum is* reliable.)
> *Parentheses are* required around such references. (*But:* The closing *parenthesis was* omitted.)
> The *media* by which we reach our clientele *are* advertisements in quality magazines and radio broadcasts.

Note: There is a growing tendency to use a singular verb after *data.*

> The data (*were* or *was*) prepared by the Research Committee.

566 The words *each, every, either,* and *neither* used as pronouns or as adjectives are always singular and require singular verbs. (See also ¶ 560*b*.)

> *Each is* eating his lunch. (Pronoun.)
> *Each employee is* responsible for closing his window in the evening. (Adjective.)
> *Every child sits* quietly. (Adjective.)
> *Neither* of the women *is* eligible. (Pronoun.)
> *Neither* woman *is* eligible. (Adjective.)

However, if a parenthetical *each* follows a plural noun or pronoun, the verb should be plural.

> The members *each feel* their responsibility.
> They *each have* high expectations.
> Twelve *each* of these items *are* required.

To test the correctness of such sentences, omit the *each.*

567 The following words and their compounds are always singular and require a singular verb.

body (*anybody, everybody, nobody, somebody*)
thing (*anything, everything, nothing, something*)
one (*anyone* or *any one, everyone* or *every one, no one, nobody*)

> *Everyone is* required to register in order to vote.
> *No one is* entitled to have his debts canceled.
> *Something tells* me I'm wrong!
> "*Nobody knows* the trouble I've seen."

Note: Even when two of the above words are joined by *and,* the singular verb is still required.

> *Anyone and everyone is* entitled to a fair hearing.

None was formerly considered a singular word and required a singular verb. In modern usage, however, *none* usually takes a plural verb unless a singular idea is clearly meant. (See page 111 for illustrations.)

None of the bond paper *was* used.
None of the packages *were* well wrapped.
None were injured. (Meaning none of the passengers.)

Note: No one is often used to stress the singular idea.

No one is better prepared than he.

568 The following words are plural in meaning and require plural verbs: *both, few, many, others, several.*

Several members *were* invited, while *others were* overlooked.
Both those books *are* out of print.
Many were asked, but *few were* able to come.

569 *All, any, some, more, most* may be singular or plural depending on the meaning. (See also ¶ 564e.)

All the typing *has* been finished.
All the reports *have* been handed in.
Some were acceptable. (Meaning some of the reports.)
Is there *any* (ice cream) left? *Are* there *any* (cookies) left?
Most of the stock *has* been sold, but *more* of these suits *are* due.
Some of the food *seems* too high priced.
Some of the items *seem* too high priced.

570 In sentences in which the verb precedes the subject, the verb should be made to agree with the subject nevertheless.

On the results of this survey *depend* the *extent and the type* of campaign we shall wage.
To Mr. Richards *have* fallen the *responsibilities* of personnel manager.
Attached *are* two carbon *copies.*
Here *is* the *invoice.*

571 In sentences beginning with *there is* or *there are,* the real subject also follows the verb. *There is* should be used when the real subject is singular; *there are,* when it is plural.

There is a vast *difference* between the two plans. (Subject is *difference.*)
There are a great many *angles* to this problem. (Subject is *angles.*)

572 Book and magazine titles are considered singular.

"Trade with Our Neighbors" *is* a best seller.

573 Do not use *don't* in the third person singular. Use *doesn't. Don't* is a contraction for *do not.*

He *doesn't* talk easily.
She *doesn't* take her work seriously.
It *doesn't* seem right to penalize him.

➤ *Verb Problems*

In addition to the problem of making verbs agree with their subjects, which was discussed in ¶¶ 555–573, transcribers encounter several other problems connected with verbs.

PRINCIPAL PARTS

574 The principal parts of a verb are the three simple forms upon which all tenses and other modifications of the verb are based.

    a) In most verbs, the past and the past participle are formed simply by adding *d* or *ed* to the present form.

Present	Past	Past participle
fill	filled	filled
manage	managed	managed

    b) In many frequently used verbs, however, a different form is used for the past and the past participle.

Present	Past	Past participle
choose	chose	chosen
do	did	done
forget	forgot	forgotten
see	saw	seen
sing	sang	sung
write	wrote	written

    The dictionary includes the past and the past-participle forms for all irregular verbs. If you are in doubt about any form, consult the dictionary.

    c) The past-participle form, if used as a part of a verb phrase, must *always* be used with one or more helping (or auxiliary) verbs.[1] The most common helping verbs are:

be	could	have	has	might	shall	will
can	do	may	had	must	should	would

    They *have* sung. (*Not:* They sung.)   They *might have* sung.
    He *has filled* the container.   He *should have filled* the container.

575 The first principal part of the verb (the *present*) is used:

    a) To express the *present time.*

        We *fill* all orders promptly.   They *do* what is expected of them.

    b) To make a statement that is *true at all times.*

        Water *seeks* its own level.

    c) Combined with *will* or *shall,* to express *future time.*

        We *shall order* our spring goods next week.
        They *will do* what is expected of them.

576 The second principal part of the verb (the *past*) is used to express *past time.*

        We *filled* the order yesterday.
        They *did* what was expected of them.

    No helping verb is used with this form.

---

[1]A past participle used alone becomes an adjective; as, "The song *sung* by the soprano was too sentimental." A past participle used as part of a verb phrase is a part of the principal verb; as, "The song *was sung* by the soprano."

577 The third principal part of the verb (the *past participle*) is used:

  a) To form the *present perfect tense*. This tense indicates action that has been completed at some *indefinite time before the present time*. It is made up of the helping verb *have* or *has* combined with the past participle.

> We *have filled* the orders. (*Not:* We have filled the orders yesterday.)
> She *has done* what was expected of her.

  b) To form the *past perfect tense*. This tense indicates action that was completed *before another past action*. It is made up of the helping verb *had* combined with the past participle.

> We *had filled* the orders before we saw your letter.
> They *had done* the job before we arrived.

  c) To form the *future perfect tense*. This tense indicates action that will be completed *before a certain time in the future*. It is made up of the helping verbs *will have* or *shall have* combined with the past participle.

> We *shall have filled* the orders by that time.
> They *will have done* the job by that time.

A CONDITION CONTRARY TO FACT, AN UNCERTAINTY, OR A WISH

578 Use *were* to express a condition that is contrary to fact, an uncertainty, or a wish. Clauses beginning with *as if* and *as though* commonly introduce uncertainties.

> If Miss Bruce *were* here, she would know. (Contrary to fact.)
> We saw a streak in the material, as if the goods *were* faded. (Uncertainty.)
> I wish I *were* going on a long vacation. (Wish.)

FORMS OF INFINITIVE

579 Infinitives have only two tense forms—the present and the perfect.

  a) The perfect infinitive is used to express action that has been completed before the time of the main verb.

> I *am* sorry *to have caused* you so much trouble last week. (*But:* I *am* sorry *to be unable* to recommend a suitable man.)

  b) The present infinitive is used in all other cases.

> I *planned to leave* early. (*Not:* to have left. In the past of which you write, you were planning to leave early.)

580 Do not insert a word or a phrase between the parts of an infinitive—that is, between *to,* the sign of the infinitive, and the verb—unless an awkward construction would result otherwise.

> It was impossible *to see* even a foot ahead. (*Not:* to even see.)
> We are able *to fill* our orders completely. (*Not:* to completely fill.)

➤ **See** also *Infinitive* in Glossary.

AGREEMENT OF TENSES

581 The verb in the subordinate clause of a sentence should agree with the verb in the main clause, unless the subordinate clause expresses a general truth.

> Mr. Eaton *said* that the offer *was withdrawn* today.
>
> Mr. Eaton *said* that the offer *had been withdrawn* before the meeting last Monday.
>
> The teacher *pointed out* that all persons under twenty-one *are* legally considered minors. (General truth.)

TROUBLESOME VERBS

582 The following verbs require watching.

Bring—take. Bring indicates motion toward the speaker. (*Hint:* Connect the *i* in *bring* with you yourself, *I*.)

> Please *bring* me the morning paper.

Take indicates motion away from the speaker. (*Hint:* Connect the *a*'s in *take* and in *away*.)

> I will *take* this file to Mr. Walter.

Come—go. Choice depends on location of speaker. *Come* indicates motion *toward; go,* motion *away from.* (See also *Bring—take.*)

> Tomorrow Dad will *come* home, and I shall *go* to the meeting with him.
>
> A salesman speaking to a customer: Perhaps it is not convenient for you to *come* to the store tomorrow.
>
> Anyone outside the store speaking: Perhaps it is not convenient for you to *go* to the store tomorrow.

Lay—Lie. Lay means "to put; to place." It refers to some person as placing something in a reclining position. Its principal parts are *lay, laid, laid.* This verb requires an object to complete its meaning.

> Please *lay* the *box* on the shelf.
>
> I *laid* the *letter* on his desk.
>
> I *had laid* two other *letters* there yesterday.
>
> The dress *was laid* in the box. (A passive construction implying that someone *laid the dress* in the box.)
>
> He always *lays* the *blame* on his assistants. (Puts the blame.)

Lie means "to rest or stay; to take a position of rest." It refers to a person or thing as either assuming or being in a reclining position. Its principal parts are *lie, lay, lain.* This verb does *not* require an object—the meaning of the verb is complete.

> The invalid *lies* on a couch.
>
> Our dog *lay* before the fire all evening.
>
> The beautiful dress *has lain* on the dirty floor.

Test: In deciding whether to use *lie* or *lay* in a sentence, substitute the word *place* for the word in question. If it does not fit, then use some form of *lie.*

> I will (*lie* or *lay?*) down now. (You could not say: "I will place down now." Therefore, the word must be *lie.*) "I will *lie* down now."

(*Continued on page 115.*)

I (*laid* or *lay?*) the pad on his desk. I *placed* (*laid*) the pad on his desk.

Note: The verb *lie,* meaning "to tell a falsehood," and having regularly formed principal parts (*lie, lied, lied*), is seldom confused with the pairs just studied.

Learn—teach. Learn means "to acquire knowledge." *Teach* means "to impart knowledge to others."

> I *learned* my lesson well.
> I plan to *teach* shorthand at the summer session.

Leave—let. Leave (principal parts, *leave, left, left*) means "to move away." *Let* means "to permit" or "to allow."

> I now *leave* you to your own devices.
> Mr. Maxwell *left* on the morning train.
> *Let* me see the last page.

Test: In deciding whether to use *let* or *leave,* try substituting *permit* and *depart.* If *permit* fits, use *let;* if *depart,* use *leave.*

May—can (*might—could*). *May* and *might* imply permission or possibility; *can* and *could,* ability or power.

> You *may* send us a dozen cans of paint on trial. (Permission.)
> The report *may* be true. (Possibility.)
> *Can* he present a workable plan? (Has he the ability?)
> Mr. Pratt said I *might* (permission) have the time off if I *could* (power) finish my work in time.

Raise—rise. Raise (principal parts, *raise, raised, raised*), meaning "to cause to lift, to lift something," requires an object.

> The soldier *raises* the *flag.*
> The teacher *raised* the *shade* in the late afternoon.
> Most growers *have raised* the *price* of coffee.
> Our rent *has been raised.* (A passive construction implying that someone *has raised* the rent.)

Rise (principal parts, *rise, rose, risen*), meaning "to ascend, to move upward by itself, to get up," cannot be used with an object.

> Mr. Chairman, I *rise* to a point of order.
> The sun *rose* at 6:25 this morning.
> The river *has risen* to flood level.

Test: Remember, you cannot "rise" anything.

Set—sit. Set (principal parts, *set, set, set*), when it means "to place something somewhere," the meaning most often confused with *sit,* requires an object.

> May I *set* another *place* at the table?
> I *set* my *suitcase* down and hailed a taxicab.
> I *have set* my *alarm* for six o'clock.

(*Continued on page 116.*)

The vase *was set* on the mantel. (A passive construction implying that someone *set* the vase on the mantel.)

Sit (principal parts, *sit, sat, sat*), meaning "to be in a position of rest, to be seated," does not require an object.

Here we *sit,* enjoying our meal.
I *sat* next to Maude at the movies.
They *had sat* at the station a full hour.

Test: Remember, you cannot "sit" anything.

Note: Set has a few other meanings in which the verb does *not* require an object, but these meanings are seldom confused with *sit.*

They *set* out on the trip in high spirits.
The sun *set* at 5:34 p.m. Wednesday.
The dress *sets* well.
Do not disturb the gelatin dessert until it *has set.*

Shall—will

1. To indicate mere *future action,* use:
   I or we shall . . . . . .
   You will . . . . . .
   He, she, it, or they will . . . . . .

I (or *we*) *shall* be glad to answer all inquiries promptly.
You will meet her at the tea this afternoon.
They (or *he* or *she*) *will* not find the trip too tiring.

> *Note:* The most common error made in the use of these verbs is the use of *will* for *shall* with *I* or *we* to express simple future action. Always say "I *shall*" unless you really mean "I am willing" or "I am determined."

We *shall* appreciate an early reply. (*Will* would mean "We are determined to appreciate.")

2. To indicate *determination, promise, desire, choice, threat,* use:
   I or we will . . . . . .
   You shall . . . . . .
   He, she, it, or they shall . . . . . .

In spite of the risk, *I will* go where I please. (Determination.)
We (or *I*) *will* not be coerced. (Determination.)
He (or *they*) *shall* not work in my department. (Determination.)
I will send my check by the end of the week. (Promise.)
We (or *I*) *will* deliver the goods today. (Promise.)
We (or *I*) *will* report you to the authorities if this is true. (Threat.)
You shall obey me! (Threat.)
He shall study, or *he shall* leave college. (Threat.)

3. To indicate *willingness* (to be willing, to be agreeable to), use *will* in all persons.

Yes, *I will* meet you at six o'clock.
Yes, *he will* meet you at six o'clock.

4. In *questions:*
    a) Always use *shall* with *I* and *we.*

  Shall I meet you at the station? *Shall we* take a taxi?

    b) With *you, he, she, it,* and *they,* use the word that is expected in the answer.

  Shall you go shopping tomorrow? (Answer expected, "I shall.")
  Will you get that report out today? (Answer expected, "I will.")
  Will he tell us when it is time? (Answer expected, "He will.")
  Shall he be penalized for this? (Answer expected, "He shall.")

Should—would.
  1. *Should* and *would* follow the same rules as *shall* and *will,* which see.

  I (or *we*) *should* like to hear from you. (Simple future.)
  You would not enjoy that experience either. (Simple future.)
  He (*she* or *they*) *would* be exhausted from the ride. (Simple future.)
  I (or *we*) *would* not permit such a demonstration. (Determination.)
  You should be required to pay for the loss if I had my way. (Threat.)

Note: In the first person, always use *should* with *like, glad,* or *pleased.*

  2. To indicate "ought to," use *should* in all persons.

  I should study tonight. (Duty.)
  You should report his dishonesty to the manager. (Duty.)
  He should pay his debts. (Obligation.)

  3. To express a condition in an *if* clause, use *should* in all persons.

  If *he should* win the prize, he will share it with his sister. (Condition.)
  If *you should* miss the train, please wire me at once. (Condition.)

  4. To indicate customary action, use *would* in all persons.

  Every day *I would* swim in the lake.
  They would only say, "No comment."
  She would practice day after day.

➤ *Pronouns*

BASIC RULE

The rules in this section are detailed applications of the following basic rule: The form of a pronoun depends on the relation of the pronoun to the other words in the sentence. Unlike nouns, pronouns have different forms to indicate these relationships.

583 Use the *nominative forms* of personal pronouns (*I, we, you, he, she, it, they*):
  a) When the pronoun is the subject of a verb.

    They are far ahead of schedule.
    We have followed your instructions.

b) When the pronoun is a predicate pronoun; that is, appears after some form of the verb *to be* (*am, is, are, was, were*).

It *is I.*	*Was* it *he* who dictated the letter?
It *was they* who called.	That "culprit" *was she.*

The following verb phrases contain forms of *to be* with various helping, or auxiliary, verbs.

can (*or* may) be	have (*or* has) been
shall (*or* will) be	shall (*or* will) have been
should (*or* would) be	should (*or* would) have been
might (*or* must) be	could have been
	might (*or* must) have been

➤ **See** ¶ 589 for special rules for pronouns with the infinitive *to be.*

584 Use the *objective forms* of personal pronouns (*me, us, you, him, her, them*):

a) When the pronoun is the object of a verb.

> They *invited* my wife and *me* for the weekend.

Hint: When you omit *my wife and,* it is obvious that the objective form *me* is the correct pronoun.

b) When the pronoun is the object of a preposition.

> This is *for you* and *me.*
> Would you like to sing a song *with* Mr. Earle and *me?*
> *Between you* and *me,* that decision is unfair.

c) When the pronoun is the subject of an infinitive. (See also ¶ 589.)

> The department head asked *him to resign.* We invited *her to call.*

585 *Who* and *whom* (or *whoever* and *whomever*).

a) These pronouns are used both as interrogative pronouns (used in asking questions) and relative pronouns (used to refer to a noun in the main clause of a sentence).

> *Who* is going? (Interrogative.)
> Mr. Sears is the man *who* is going. (Relative, referring to Mr. Sears.)
> To *whom* shall I deliver the message? (Interrogative.)
> Miss Brown, *whom* I have never met, is in charge today. (Relative, referring to Miss Brown.)

b) These pronouns may be either singular or plural in meaning.

> *Who is* talking?
> *Who are* to be selected?
> *Whom* do you prefer for this job?
> *Whom* do you prefer for these jobs?

c) *Who* (or *whoever*) is the nominative form. Use it whenever *he* (or *she, they, I, it, we*) could be used with the verb of the *who* clause.

> *Who is* at the door? (*He is* at the door.)
> *Who sang* the duet with you? (*He sang.*)

(Continued on page 119.)

The problem of *who should be* appointed secretary is still not settled. (*She should be* appointed.)
Who could it *have been?* (It *could have been he.*)
The matter of *who should pay* was not decided. (*He should pay.*)
James is the boy *who* we expect *will win.* (*He will win.*)

d) *Whom* (or *whomever*) is the objective form. Use it whenever *him* (or *her, them, me, us*) could be used with the verb of a *who* (*whom*) clause.

I need a cashier *whom* I can trust. (I can trust *him.*)
Guess *whom* we saw today? (We saw *him* today.)
Our president, *whom* all respect, is resigning. (All respect *him.*)
It depends on *whom* they mean. (They mean *him.*)
Whom were you talking about? (You were talking about *him.*)
To *whom* are you talking? (You are talking *to him.*)

e) When some such parenthetical clause as *I think, he says, we feel sure* occurs within a clause introduced by *who* or *whoever,* disregard the parenthetical clause when deciding on the form of the pronoun to be used.

Please vote for the member *who* you believe has done the most for the class. (*Who* is the subject of *has done.*)
The member *who* we thought deserved the honor will receive a scholarship. (*Who* is the subject of *deserved.*)
Who did they say was chosen? (*Who* is the subject of *was chosen.*)
We have referred your claim to our attorney, *who,* we are sure, will reply soon. (*Who* is the subject of *will reply.*)
Please write at once to *whoever* you think can supply the information desired. (*Whoever* is the subject of *can supply.*)
We have sent this order blank to all *who* we have reason to believe are interested in our book. (*Who* is the subject of *are interested.*)

586 *Who, which,* and *that.*
a) *Who* and *that* are used when referring to persons, *who* being used when the individual person or the individuality of a group is meant and *that* when a class, species, or type is meant. For example:

She is the girl *who* understands French.
He is the kind of student *that* we want.

b) *Which* is used when referring to places, objects, and animals. Careful writers use *which* to introduce nonrestrictive clauses and *that* to introduce restrictive clauses.

Machines *that* require frequent repairs are a poor investment.
The tax report, *which* is long, is now ready.

587 A pronoun must agree with its antecedent (the word for which the pronoun stands) in person, number, and gender. Study the following sentences carefully; also ¶¶ 555–573.

It is *I* who *am* at fault. (*Who* agrees in person and number with its antecedent *I;* the verb agrees with *I.*)

(*Continued on page 120.*)

It is *they* who *are* at fault.

It is people like *you* who *make* laws necessary.

If a *worker* is justified in his contention, *he* should be heard.

If *Americans* wish to travel in foreign countries, *they* must obtain passports.

Why not have *each student* write *his* version of the accident?

Why not have *all students* write *their* versions of the accident?

a) When the antecedent is a singular word applying to either sex, a masculine pronoun is used.

> *Each* person should hold *his* own ticket.
> *Each boy and girl* should hold *his* own ticket.

b) Sometimes, for exactness, *his or her* is substituted for *his.*

> *Each boy and each girl* must hold *his or her* own ticket.

588   When a pronoun follows *than* or *as* in a comparison that is not a complete clause, the correct form of pronoun is determined by mentally supplying the words that are missing.

> They type better than *I.* (Meaning *than I do.*)
> The South High School players are as strong as *we.* (*As strong as we are.*)
> I like you better than *him. (Than I like him.*)

589   Pronouns after *to be.* ¶ 584c states that the objective form of a pronoun is used when the pronoun is the subject of an infinitive. The following special rules govern the selection of the pronoun to be used with the infinitive *to be.*

a) If *to be* has a subject, that subject, like the subject of any infinitive, is in the objective case—and the pronoun that follows the infinitive is *also* in the objective form.

> They believe the *visitors* to be *us.* (*Visitors,* the subject of *to be,* is in the objective; therefore, the predicate pronoun following *to be* is objective, *us.*)
> They took *Mary* to be *me.*
> *Whom* do you take *him* to be? (You do take *him* to be *whom?*)
> *Whom* do you consider to be the more expert draftsman? (You do consider *whom* to be the more expert draftsman?)

b) But, if the infinitive *to be* has no subject, then the pronoun that follows *to be* is in the nominative case, to agree with the subject of the sentence.

> The *caller* was thought to be *I.* (*I* agrees with the subject of sentence, *caller.*)
> *They* were thought to be *we.*
> *Who* was he thought to be? (*He* was thought to be *who?*)

590   The *self-* or *selves*-ending pronouns (*myself, yourself, himself, herself, itself, ourselves, themsclves*) should be used:

a) To emphasize or to intensify a noun or pronoun already expressed.

> The *director himself* arranged the program.
> *I myself* am bewildered.
> *I* will write him *myself.*

b) To reflect the action expressed by the verb back on the subject.

> *He* found *himself* the only one in favor of the move.
> *We* have satisfied *ourselves* as to the wisdom of the action.

c) But not in place of simple personal pronouns.

> The tickets are for Miss Barnest and *me* (*not:* myself).
> Henry and *I* (*not:* myself) can distribute all the mail.

591 When a pronoun identifies a noun or another pronoun, the identifying pronoun is either nominative or objective, depending on whether the word explained is nominative or objective.

> Mr. Clark called *us,* Ruth and *me,* into his office. (Since *us* is objective, the explanatory pronoun *me* is also objective.)
> The explanation was for the *newcomers,* Marie and *me.* (Was for *me.*)
> The exceptions were the *newcomers,* Marie and *I.* (Exception was *I.*)
> Let's *you* and *me* go to the picnic. (*Let's* is a contraction for *let us.* Since *us* is the objective form, the explanatory pronouns *you* and *me* are also objective.)
> Mr. Hoyt sent *us* boys on an errand.
> *We* boys are going on an errand.

To test such expressions, omit the explanatory word; for example, *boys.*

592 *Its* and *it's. Its* is a possessive pronoun, meaning "of it." It never takes an apostrophe. *It's* is the contraction for *it is.* To test for the correct form, try to substitute *it is* in the sentence. If you cannot do so, then the personal pronoun *its* is the desired word.

> The nation should protect *its* resources.
> *It's* time for the bell.

➤ **See** ¶ 498 for other possessive personal pronouns.

593 A pronoun that modifies a gerund, or verbal noun (an *ing*-ending form of a verb that is used as a noun), should be in the possessive form.

> We shall appreciate *your* shipping the order at once.

THE INDEFINITE, EDITORIAL, OR PROFESSIONAL WE

594 Dictators often use *we* instead of *I* to avoid any seeming overemphasis on themselves.

> A physician: It is *our* opinion that the patient may be discharged, provided he returns home by ambulance.
> An executive: *We* shall be glad to prepare the necessary legal forms.

➤ *Adjectives and Adverbs*

595 Only an adverb can modify an adjective.

> The price is *considerably* (*not:* considerable) higher than I can pay.

596 When the word following a verb describes the *subject* of the sentence, an adjective is used. *Linking verbs* (the various forms of *appear, be, become,* *seem*) and the verbs of the *senses* (*smell, sound, taste, feel, look*) in most cases are followed by adjectives.

He looks *well*.	The *tree* grew *tall*.
He looks *bad*.	*Sugar* tastes *sweet*.
He feels *bad*.	The *typing* looks *neat*.
He is *well*.	Her *voice* sounded *strong*.
He became *famous*.	*She* appeared (or seemed) *shy*.

Test: If *is, are, was, were* can be substituted for the verb, choose the adjective.

He *looks happy*.   He *is happy*.

597 When the word following a verb refers to the *action of the verb*, an adverb is used.

He *reads slowly* but he *talks rapidly*.
She *entered* the room *timidly*.
Read the directions *carefully*.
We guarantee *to ship* the goods *promptly*.
She *was injured badly* in the accident.
I *tasted* the new dish *hesitatingly*.
She *felt* the old fabric *cautiously*.
He *sounded* the rising bell *punctually*.

Test: If "in a . . . manner" can be substituted for the *ly*-ending word, choose the adverb.

He looked *sharply* (in a sharp manner) at the intruder.

598 Several of the most frequently used adverbs have two forms.

deep, deeply	slow, slowly
direct, directly	cheap, cheaply
loud, loudly	quick, quickly

The choice is largely a matter of usage. The *ly* forms are more formal; the shorter forms, more emphatic.

He proceeded *slowly* up the steep path. Drive *slow*.

Direct and *directly* differ slightly in meaning, however.

Send the goods *direct* to me. (Meaning straight, without detour.)
He was *directly* responsible for the dissatisfaction. (Meaning without anyone or anything intervening.)

599 Although -*ly* is the usual sign of an adverb, several adjectives also end in *ly; as costly, orderly, timely, motherly, fatherly, friendly, neighborly*.

Check the stock in an *orderly* fashion.
Her offer to help the new clerk was a *friendly* gesture.

600 Also, a few frequently used *ly*-ending words are both adjectives and adverbs; as *cowardly, early, likely, only*.

I expect a reply by an *early mail*. (Adjective.)
The explosion *occurred early* in the day. (Adverb.)

(*Continued on page 123.*)

That was a *cowardly position* for him to take. (Adjective.)
He *acted cowardly* all during the trial. (Adverb.)

601　Problems of comparison.

a) When referring to *two* persons, places, or things, use the comparative form; when referring to *more than two,* the superlative form.

> That is the *finer* piece of linen. (Only two pieces are involved; hence the comparative form.)
> This is the *finest* piece of linen I could find. (Many pieces are involved; hence the superlative form.)
> Of the two positions open, you have chosen the *more* promising.
> That is the *more* efficient of the two methods.
> This is the *most* efficient method that could be devised.

b) The comparative degree of two-syllable adjectives and adverbs may be formed either by adding *er* to the positive form or by inserting either *more* or *less* before the positive form.

> happy: happier, more happy　　　often: oftener, less often

The superlative degree of adjectives and adverbs containing three or more syllables is always formed by inserting either *most* or *least* before the positive degree.

> acceptable: most acceptable　　　desirable: least desirable

c) Some adjectives and adverbs, from their very meanings, allow no comparison; as *square, round, unique, completely, universally, correct, perfect, always, never, dead.* Such words may be modified in meaning, however, by such adverbs as *hardly, nearly,* or *almost,* in order to suggest an approach to the superlative.

> That design is *very nearly unique.*
> She is *almost always* on time.
> This is the *most nearly perfect* example.

d) Avoid double comparisons.

> cheaper (*not:* more cheaper)　　　unkindest (*not:* most unkindest)

e) A few adjectives have irregular comparisons.

Positive	*Comparative*	*Superlative*
bad or ill	worse	worst
good or well	better	best
far	farther, further	farthest, furthest
late	later, latter	latest, last
little	less	least
many, much	more	most
_____	inner	innermost, inmost
_____	outer	outermost, outmost

f) When comparing one person or thing with the group of which it is a part, use the comparative degree and the word *other*.

> This coffee has a better flavor than any *other* coffee on the market.
> There were more accidents on July 4 than on any *other* day this summer.

Failure to include the word *other* is a very common error.

g) After the superlative degree use *all,* not *any.*

> He is *tallest* of *all* the contestants.
> Mary is the *most reliable* of *all* our staff.

602 The adverbs *only, nearly, almost, ever, scarcely, merely, too, also* should be placed as close to the word modified—usually before—as possible. The wrong position of the adverb may change the entire meaning of the sentence.

> Our list of depositors now numbers *almost* 50,000. (*Not:* almost numbers.)
> *Only* the Board of Directors can nominate the three new officers. (Cannot be nominated by anyone else.)
> The Board of Directors can *only* nominate the three officers. (They cannot elect.)
> *Only* Robert liked her. (No one else liked her.)
> Robert liked *only* her. (Robert liked no one else.)
> Robert *only* liked her. (Robert didn't love her.)

SOME TROUBLESOME ADJECTIVES AND ADVERBS

603 The following words deserve watching. (See also ¶ 612.)
Badly. Avoid using for *a great deal* or *very much.*

> Mr. Tead wants *very much* (*not:* badly) to meet Mr. Scott.

Different—differently. When the meaning is "in a different manner," use the adverb *differently.*

> I wish the story had ended *differently.*
> I understand it *differently.*
> My mother looked at the episode *differently.*

After linking verbs and verbs of the senses, the adjective *different* is correct. (See ¶ 596.)

> That music sounds completely *different.*
> You look *different* in that hairdo.
> He seems (appears) *different* since his promotion.

Extra. Do not use for *unusually.*

> She had an *unusually* (*not:* extra) fine opportunity.

Fewer—less. *Fewer* refers to number. *Less* refers to degree or amount.

> *Fewer* accidents (a smaller number) were reported than was expected.
> *Less* effort (a smaller degree of) was put forth by the organizers, and thus *fewer* people (a smaller number of) attended.

Good—well. *Good* is an adjective. *Well* may be an adverb or an adjective. In the sense of "in good health" or "to make a favorable impression," *well* is an adjective. (See ¶ 596.)

> Marie had *good* grades in school. (Adjective.)
> I will do this work as *well* as I know how. (Adverb.)

(Continued on page 125.)

He admits he does not feel *well* today. (Adjective.)
Miss Keith looks particularly *well* in that hat. (Adjective.)

Hardly. The adverb *hardly* is negative in meaning. Therefore, no other negative should be used with it.

> You *could hardly* (*not:* couldn't hardly) expect that to happen.

Kindly. Often meaningless in letters when no act of kindness is intended. Such expressions as "Thank you very much," "Will you please . . ." are preferable.

Only. The adverb *only* is negative in meaning. Therefore, no other negative should be used with it. (See ¶ 602 for placement of *only*.)

> I use this letterhead *only* for foreign correspondence. (*Not:* I do not use this letterhead only for foreign correspondence.)

Quite. Often erroneously used in the sense of "rather," "very," or "somewhat," instead of in its true sense of "completely," "entirely."

> The play was *rather* (*not:* quite) short.
> The lecture was *very* (*not:* quite) interesting.
> You are *quite* mistaken.

Quite a few and *quite a little* are considered colloquial.

Real—really. *Real* is an adjective; *really,* an adverb. Do not use *real* for *very* or *really.*

> The ring is set with *real* diamonds. (Adjective.)
> I was *really* ashamed of her. (Adverb.)
> It is *very* (*not:* real) cool today.

Scarcely. The adverb *scarcely* is negative in meaning. Therefore, no other negative should be used with it. (See ¶ 602 for placement of *scarcely*.)

> She *scarcely* (*not:* didn't scarcely) recognized me.

Sure—surely. *Sure* is an adjective; *surely,* an adverb.

> I am *sure* that I did not make that mistake. (Adjective.)
> I was *surely* glad to learn that the mistake was not mine. (Adverb.)

Very. Preferably *very* should not be used immediately before a past participle. Insert some such adverb as *much.* *Very* may modify an adjective, however.

> We were *very much pleased* (*not:* very pleased) with your order.
> It is a *very disappointing* showing. (Modifies an adjective.)

➤ *Prepositions*

➤ **See** ¶ 584*b* for selection of the correct pronoun to follow a preposition.

WORDS REQUIRING CERTAIN PREPOSITIONS

604 Usage requires that certain words be followed by certain prepositions. Some of the most frequently used words are listed on page 126.

agree *with* a person; *on* a course; *to* a proposal
apply *for* a position; *to* a person
correspond *with* a person; *to* or *with* a thing
different *from* (*than* is British usage)
employed *for* a purpose; *at* a salary; *on* or *in* an undertaking
independent *of*
interested *in*
liable *for* debts; *to* authority
regard: *in* or *with* regard (not: regards) *to; as* regards
proceed *to* a place; *with* a matter begun
respect: *in* or *with* respect *to* (not: *in* respect *of*)
stay *at* home (not: *to*)
wait *on* a customer; *for* a person or thing; *at* a place

SUPERFLUOUS PREPOSITIONS

605 Do not use prepositions that are not needed. (See *Up* in ¶ 608.) Note that the prepositions in the following sentences add nothing to the meaning.

Where is she (*at*)?
Where did that paper go (*to*)?
The new stenographer seems to be (*of*) about sixteen years of age.
She could not help (*from*) crying.
I don't remember (*of*) your saying that.
His house is opposite (*to*) hers.
The chair is too near (*to*) the desk.
Let us meet *at about* one o'clock. (Omit either *at* or *about*.)

OMITTING PREPOSITIONS

606 Conversely, do not omit essential prepositions.

a couple *of* books (*not:* a couple books)
Of what use is this gadget? (*Not:* What use is this gadget?)

PREPOSITIONS AT THE END OF SENTENCES

607 A sentence may or may not end with a preposition, depending on the emphasis and effectiveness desired.

Weak: I wish I knew the magazine that that article appeared *in*.
Stronger: I wish I knew the magazine *in which* that article appeared.
Stilted: It is difficult to know *about what* he is thinking.
Natural: It is difficult to know what he is thinking *about*.

Short questions frequently end with prepositions.

How many can I count *on*?   What is this good *for*?

SOME TROUBLESOME PREPOSITIONS

608 See also ¶ 612.

All (*of*). Do not use *of* after *all* unless the following word is a pronoun. (See also *Both*.)

All the men belong to the softball team.

(*Continued on page 127.*)

All of us belong to the softball team.
All of us girls belong to the Girls Club.

Among. Use *among* when referring to more than two persons or things. (See also *Between.*)

There is a lively contest going on *among* the salesmen.

At—in. Both *at* and *in* are used in reference to places. In general, *in* is used for larger places; *at,* for smaller places.

He lives *in* New York and works *at* Macy's.

At—to. Use *at* to denote position; *to,* to indicate movement toward.

You'll find her *at* home.   He is going *to* Detroit next week.

Beside—besides. (See ¶ 611.)

I sat *beside* my teacher at the concert.
Besides, we need your support of the measure.

Between. Ordinarily, *between* should be used in reference to *two* persons or things. (See also *Among.*)

The territory is divided evenly *between* the two salesmen.

However, *between* may be used of more than two persons or objects in order to bring each person or object into the relation expressed.

The three children had but $1 *between* them.
There are distinct differences *between* New York, Chicago, and Dallas.
In packing china, be sure to place paper *between* the plates. (*Not:* between *each* of the plates.)

Both (*of*). Do not use *of* after *both* unless the following word is a pronoun.

Both of them are wrong.   *Both* girls are wrong.

From—off. Use *from* with persons; *off* with things.

I heard the news *from* Margaret.
I could scarcely lift the typewriter *off* the desk.

Off of and *off from* are redundant.

The papers fell *off* (*not:* off of or off from) the desk.

In, into, in to. In implies position within; *into* implies motion from without to within; *in to* is a two-word phrase in which *in* is an adverb.

The correspondence is *in* the file.
He walked *into* the outer office.
All sales reports are to be sent *in to* the sales manager.
Mr. Green came *in to* see me.

On, onto, on to. On and *onto* are very similar in meaning, but in most cases *on* is the better word. In the two-word phrase *on to, on* is an adverb.

(*See page 128 for illustrative sentences.*)

Next, place the carbon sheet *on* the onionskin.

Sew the bow *on* (rather than *onto*) the side of the hat.

We will now pass *on to* the next problem.

On, upon, up on. *On* and *upon* are interchangeable, although *upon* is a little more formal and emphatic. In the two-word phrase *up on*, *up* is an adverb.

I will place the note *on* his desk.

His statements were based *upon* scientific data.

It will be necessary to step *up on* the stool.

On is often misused for *of* in such expressions as "a sale *on* shoes" instead of "a sale *of* shoes."

Up. Many verbs (for example, *end, rest, confess, settle, burn, drink, eat, tear*) contain the idea of "up"; therefore, the preposition *up* is unnecessary. In the following sentences, the *up* is not needed and should be omitted.

I'd like to settle (up) my bill.

The electrician will connect (up) the fan.

Let's divide (up) the sandwiches.

Can you help me lift (up) this case?

➤ *Sentence Structure*

PARALLEL STRUCTURE

609   Express parallel (that is, co-ordinate) ideas in parallel form.

a) Adjectives should be paralleled by adjectives, nouns by nouns, infinitives by infinitives, subordinate clauses by subordinate clauses, etc.

Not: Our new course is challenging and an inspiration. (Adjective and noun.)

But: Our new course is *challenging* and *inspiring*. (Two adjectives.)

Not: This machine is inexpensive, efficient, and it is easily operated. (Two adjectives and a clause.)

But: This machine is *inexpensive, efficient,* and *easily operated*. (Three adjectives.)

Not: The seniors have already started reviewing and to cram. (Participle and infinitive.)

But: The seniors have already started *reviewing* and *cramming*. (Two participles.)

Note: Parallelism is especially important in tabulations.

Not: The duties of the committee hostess are:
1. To greet guests
2. Ordering refreshments
3. Arrangement of flowers

But: The duties of the committee hostess are:
1. To greet guests
2. To order refreshments
3. To arrange the flowers

b) Correlative conjunctions (*not only . . . but also, both . . . and, either . . . or, neither . . . nor, whether . . . or,* etc.) should be followed by elements in parallel form.

> *Not:* She is not only proficient in shorthand but also in typing.
> *But:* She is proficient not only *in shorthand* but also *in typing.*
>
> *Not:* I have sent a telegram both to Chicago and San Francisco.
> *But:* I have sent a telegram to both *Chicago* and *San Francisco.*
>
> *Not:* He would neither apologize nor would he promise to reform.
> *But:* He would neither *apologize* nor *promise to reform.*

DANGLING MODIFIERS

610 Sometimes modifiers are attached to no word in a sentence; sometimes, to the wrong word. Such modifiers are called *dangling modifiers.* They may be participial phrases, infinitive phrases, gerund phrases, or elliptical clauses. They may start, or they may end, a sentence. The fault may be corrected by supplying the word that the phrase modifies or by making the phrase into a clause.

a) Participial phrases

> *Not:* Answering your question, the damage was slight.
> *But:* Answering your question, we are glad to report the damage was slight.
>
> *Not:* I caught a glimpse of the fugitive, running to the window.
> *But:* Running to the window, I caught a glimpse of the fugitive. *Or:* I ran to the window and caught a glimpse of the fugitive.

b) Infinitive phrases

> *Not:* To obtain satisfactory carbon copies, unwrinkled carbon paper must be used.
> *But:* To produce satisfactory carbon copies, the typist must use unwrinkled carbon paper.
>
> *Not:* This coupon should be mailed at once to obtain the free booklet.
> *But:* You should mail this coupon at once to obtain the free booklet.

c) Gerund phrases

> *Not:* In passing the store windows, many new spring models were on display.
> *But:* In passing the store windows, I noticed many new spring models on display.
>
> *Not:* The desk should be cleared of papers before going out to lunch.
> *But:* You should clear your desk of papers before going out to lunch (*or* before you go out to lunch).

d) Ellipitical clauses (clauses from which the subject and predicate have been omitted)

> *Not:* If ordered before May 1, a 5 per cent discount will be allowed.
> *But:* If the goods are ordered before May 1, a 5 per cent discount will be allowed.
>
> *Not:* When four years old, my father had an important promotion.
> *But:* When I was four years old, my father had an important promotion.

SECTION 13

Words often confused

611   The following selected list of similar-sounding and similar-looking words contains two types of word groups: (1) words that are pronounced *exactly alike,* though spelled differently, and for which the shorthand outlines are therefore identical; and (2) words that look and sound *somewhat alike,* and for which the shorthand outlines may be very nearly the same. Word groups are marked by dots.

➤ **See** ¶ 533 for words similar in sound that are sometimes one word and sometimes two words; as *already, all ready.*

The brief definitions are intended to suggest basic distinctions in meaning. They are not complete definitions. For those, consult your dictionary.

• *accede*	to comply with		• *allusion*	an indirect reference
exceed	to surpass		*illusion*	an error of vision
• *accent*	stress in speech or writing		*delusion*	an error of belief
			elusion	adroit escape
ascent	act of rising		• *altar*	part of a church
assent	consent		*alter*	to change
• *accept*	to take; to receive		• *annul*	to cancel
except	to exclude		*annual*	yearly
• *access*	admittance		• *ante-*	a prefix meaning "before"
excess	surplus			
• *ad*	shortened form of *advertisement*		*anti-*	a prefix meaning "against"
add	to join		• *antecedents*	preceding things; ancestors
• *adapt*	to adjust			
adept	proficient		*antecedence*	priority
adopt	to choose		• *appraise*	to set a value on
• *addition*	something added		*apprise*	to inform
edition	one of a number of printings		• *area*	surface; extent
			aria	a melody
• *adherence*	attachment		*arrears*	that which is due but unpaid
adherents	followers			
• *adverse*	opposing		• *arrange*	to put in order
averse	disinclined		*arraign*	to call into court
• *advice*	information; recommendation; counsel		• *ascent*	(see *accent*)
			• *assay*	to test an ore or a chemical
advise	(v.) to recommend (incorrect for *inform*); to give counsel		*essay*	(n.) a treatise; (v.) to attempt
• *affect*	to influence; to change; to assume (*always a verb*)		• *assistance*	help
			assistants	those who help
			• *attain*	to gain; to achieve
effect	(n.) result; outcome; (v.) to fulfill; to bring about		*attend*	to be present at
			• *attendants*	escorts; followers; companions; associates
• *allowed*	permitted		*attendance*	presence
aloud	audibly			

• *aught*	anything (incorrect for *naught,* meaning "cipher")
ought	should; obliged
• *averse*	(see *adverse*)
• *awhile*	(adv.) for a short time
a while	(phrase) a short period of time
• *bail*	security; the handle of a pail; to dip water
bale	a bundle
• *bare*	naked; exposed; empty
bear	to carry; to endure; to produce; (n.) an animal
• *base*	(n.) foundation; (adj.) mean
bass	lower notes in music; a fish
• *bases*	plural of *base* and of *basis*
basis	foundation
• *berth*	a bed
birth	being born
• *beside*	by the side of; separate from
besides	in addition to; also
• *biannual*	occurring twice a year
biennial	occurring once in two years
• *bibliography*	list of writings pertaining to a given subject or author
biography	written history of person's life
• *billed*	charged
build	to construct
• *board*	a piece of wood; an organized group; meals
bored	penetrated; wearied
• *born*	brought into life
borne	carried; endured
• *brake*	a retarding device; to retard
break	to shatter; to divide; an opening; a fracture
• *breath*	respiration
breathe	(v.) to inhale and exhale
breadth	width
• *build*	(see *billed*)
• *bullion*	uncoined gold or silver
bouillon	broth
• *calendar*	a record of time
calender	a machine used in finishing paper and cloth
colander	a strainer
• *callous*	(adj.) hardened
callus	(n.) a hardened surface

• *canvas*	a coarse cloth
canvass	(v.) to solicit
• *capital*	(n.) a seat of government; a principal sum of money; a large-sized letter; (adj.) chief; foremost
capitol	a government building
• *carton*	a pasteboard box
cartoon	a caricature
• *casual*	incidental
causal	pertaining to a cause
• *cease*	to stop
seize	to grasp
• *cede*	to grant; to give up
seed	that from which anything is grown
• *ceiling*	top of a room; any overhanging area
sealing	closing
• *census*	statistics of population
senses	mental faculties
• *cereal*	any grain food
serial	arranged in a series
• *cession*	a yielding up
session	the sitting of a court or other body
• *choose*	to select
chose	did choose (past tense of *choose*)
chews	masticates
• *cite*	(v.) to quote; to summon
sight	a view; vision
site	a place
• *clothes*	garments
cloths	fabrics
close	to shut; the end
• *coarse*	rough; common
course	direction; action; a way; part of a meal
• *collision*	a clashing
collusion	a scheme to defraud
• *coma*	an unconscious state
comma	a mark of punctuation
• *command*	to order; an order
commend	to praise; to entrust
• *commence*	to begin
comments	remarks
• *complement*	that which completes
compliment	a flattering speech: to praise
• *comprehensible*	understandable
comprehensive	extensive
• *confidant*	a friend; an adviser (feminine form: *confidante*)
confident	sure; positive
• *confidently*	certainly; positively
confidentially	privately

• *conscience*	(n.) faculty; the sense of right and wrong	*depreciate*	to lessen in estimated value
conscious	(adj.) cognizant; sensible; aware	• *descent*	going down
		decent	proper; right
• *conversation*	a talk	*dissent*	disagreement
conservation	preservation	• *desert*	barren land; (plural) a punishment; (v.) to abandon
• *continual*	occurring in rapid and steady succession or at intervals		
		dessert	the last course of a meal
continuous	uninterrupted; unbroken	• *desolate*	lonely; sad
• *co-operation*	the art of working together	*dissolute*	loose in morals
		• *detract*	to take from
corporation	a form of business organization	*distract*	to divert the attention of
• *correspondence*	letters	• *device*	(n.) a contrivance
correspondents	those who write letters	*devise*	(v.) to plan; to convey real estate by will
corespondents	parties in divorce suits	• *die*	to cease living; a tool
• *costume*	dress	*dye*	to change the color of; that which changes the color of
custom	habit		
• *council*	an assembly	• *disapprove*	to withhold approval
counsel	an attorney; advice; to give advice	*disprove*	to prove the falsity of
		• *disassemble*	to take apart
consul	a foreign representative	*dissemble*	to disguise; to feign
		• *disburse*	to pay out
• *courtesy*	a favor; politeness	*disperse*	to scatter
curtesy	a husband's life interest in the lands of his deceased wife	• *discreet*	prudent
		discrete	separate
		• *divers*	various or sundry; plural of *diver*
curtsy	a gesture of respect		
• *credible*	believable	*diverse*	different
creditable	meritorious; deserving of praise	• *dual*	double
		duel	a combat
• *currant*	a berry	• *dying*	near death
current	belonging to the present; tide; electricity	*dyeing*	changing the color of
		• *edition*	(see *addition*)
• *deceased*	dead	• *effect*	(see *affect*)
diseased	sick	• *elapse*	(see *lapse*)
• *decree*	a law	• *elicit*	to draw forth
degree	a grade; a step	*illicit*	unlawful
• *deduce*	to infer	• *eligible*	fitted; qualified
deduct	to subtract	*illegible*	unreadable
• *defer*	to put off	• *elusion*	(see *allusion*)
differ	to disagree	• *elusive*	baffling; hard to catch
• *deference*	respect; regard for another's wishes	*illusive*	misleading; unreal
		• *emanate*	to originate from
difference	dissimilarity; controversy	*eminent*	well known; prominent
• *delusion*	(see *allusion*)	*imminent*	threatening; impending
• *depositary*	preferred in referring to the person with whom something is deposited		
		• *emerge*	to rise out of
		immerge	to plunge into
depository	preferred in referring to the place where something is deposited	• *emigrate*	to go away from a country
		immigrate	to come into a country
• *deposition*	a formal written statement	• *envelop*	(v.) to cover; to wrap
		envelope	(n.) a wrapper for a letter
disposition	temper; disposal		
• *depraved*	morally debased		
deprived	taken away from	• *equable*	even; tranquil
• *deprecate*	to disapprove	*equitable*	just; right

• *erasable*	capable of being erased
irascible	quick-tempered
• *especially*	to an exceptional degree
specially	particularly, as opposed to generally
• *essay*	(see *assay*)
• *exceed*	(see *accede*)
• *excess*	(see *access*)
• *except*	(see *accept*)
• *expand*	to increase in size
expend	to spend
• *expansive*	capable of being extended
expensive	costly
• *expatiate*	to enlarge on
expiate	to atone for
• *explicit*	easily understood
implicit	unquestioning
• *extant*	still existing
extent	measure
• *facetious*	witty
fictitious	like fiction
factitious	artificial
• *facilitate*	to make easy
felicitate	to congratulate
• *facility*	ease
felicity	joy
• *fair*	favorable; just; an exhibit
fare	cost of travel; food; to go forth
• *farther*	at a greater distance (refers to space)
further	moreover; in addition (refers to time, quantity, or degree)
• *faze*	to disturb
phase	a state in development
• *feet*	plural of *foot*
feat	an act of skill or strength
• *finale*	the end
finally	at the end
finely	in a fine manner
• *fineness*	delicacy
finesse	tact
• *fiscal*	pertaining to finances
physical	relating to the body
• *flew*	did fly
flue	a chimney
flu	short for *influenza*
• *for*	a preposition
fore	first; preceding; the front
four	numeral
• *forbear*	to bear with
forebear	an ancestor
• *forgo*	to relinquish; to let pass
forego	to go before
• *formally*	in a formal manner

formerly	before
• *forth*	away; forward
fourth	next after third
• *foul*	unfavorable; unclean
fowl	a bird
• *genius*	talent
genus	a classification in botany or zoology
• *guarantee*	to secure (preferred in verb sense)
guaranty	financial security (preferred in noun sense)
• *holy*	sacred
holey	full of holes
wholly	entirely
holly	a tree
• *human*	pertaining to mankind
humane	kindly
• *hypercritical*	overcritical
hypocritical	pretending virtue
• *illegible*	(see *eligible*)
• *illicit*	(see *elicit*)
• *illusive*	(see *elusive*)
• *imitate*	to resemble; mimic
intimate	innermost; familiar; (v.) to hint; make known
• *immerge*	(see *emerge*)
• *immigrate*	(see *emigrate*)
• *imminent*	(see *emanate*)
• *implicit*	(see *explicit*)
• *inane*	senseless
insane	of unsound mind
• *incidence*	range of occurrence
incidents	accidental happenings
• *incinerate*	to burn
insinuate	to imply
• *incite*	(v.) to arouse
insight	(n.) understanding
• *indict*	to consider guilty
indite	to compose and write
• *indigenous*	native
indigent	needy
indignant	angry
• *ingenious*	clever
ingenuous	candid
• *insoluble*	incapable of being dissolved
insolvable	not explainable
insolvent	pertaining to a person unable to pay his debts
• *instants*	short periods of time
instance	an example
• *intelligent*	possessed of understanding
intelligible	understandable
• *intense*	acute; strong; of an extreme kind
intents	aims
• *interstate*	between states
intrastate	within one state
• *irascible*	(see *erasable*)

• *its*	possessive form of *it*	*loss*	something lost
it's	contraction of *it is* (see ¶ 592)	• *magnificent*	having splendor
• *lapse*	to become void	*munificent*	unusually generous
elapse	to pass	• *mail*	correspondence
relapse	to slip back into former condition	*male*	masculine
• *last*	final	• *main*	chief; a conduit
latest	most recent; nearest in order of time	*mane*	hair on the neck of some animals
• *later*	more late; after a time	• *manner*	a way of acting
latter	second in a series of two	*manor*	an estate
• *lath*	a strip of wood	• *marital*	pertaining to marriage
lathe	a wood-turning machine	*martial*	military
• *lay*	to place	*marshal*	an official; to arrange
lie	to recline; to speak falsehood; a falsehood	• *mean*	to intend; the midpoint; unpleasant appearance
lye	a strong alkaline solution	*mien*	
• *lead*	a heavy metal (pronounced lĕd); (v.) to guide or direct (pronounced lēd)	• *meat*	flesh of animals
		• *meet*	to join
		mete	to measure
		• *medal*	a badge of honor
		meddle	to interfere
led	guided (past tense of *to lead*)	*metal*	a mineral
• *lean*	(adj.) thin; (v.) to incline	*mettle*	courage; spirit
		• *miner*	a worker in a mine
lien	a legal claim	*minor*	underage; lesser, as in size, extent, or importance
• *leased*	rented		
least	smallest	• *mist*	haze
• *legislator*	a lawmaker	*missed*	failed to do
legislature	a body of lawmakers	• *mite*	a tiny particle
• *lend*	to allow the use of temporarily	*might*	force; (v.) past tense of *may*
loan	(n.) something lent; (v.) to lend	• *mood*	disposition
		mode	fashion; method
lone	one	• *moral*	virtuous
• *lessee*	a tenant	*morale*	spirit
lesser	smaller	• *morality*	virtue
lessor	one who gives a lease	*mortality*	death rate
• *lessen*	(v.) to make smaller	• *morning*	before noon
lesson	(n.) an exercise assigned for study	*mourning*	grief
		• *naught*	a cipher; zero
• *levee*	embankment of a river	*nought*	nothing
levy	an amount collected by levying; to raise a collection of money	• *oculist*	one who treats eyes
		optician	one who makes eyeglasses
• *liable*	responsible	*optometrist*	one who measures the vision
libel	defamatory statements		
• *lightening*	making lighter	• *official*	authorized
lightning	accompaniment of thunder	*officious*	overbold in offering services
lighting	illumination	• *one*	a single thing
• *loath*	(adj.) reluctant	*won*	did win
loathe	(v.) to detest	• *ordinance*	a local law
• *loose*	free; not bound; to release	*ordnance*	arms; munitions
		• *ought*	(see *aught*)
lose	(v.) to suffer the loss of; to part with unintentionally	• *overdo*	to do too much
		overdue	past due
		• *packed*	crowded
		pact	an agreement
		• *pail*	a bucket
		pale	light colored; an enclosure

• *pain*	suffering; (pl.) care		votes for a body of
pane	window glass		persons; (v.) to register
• *pair*	two of a kind		the votes of
pare	to peel	• *poor*	needy; inadequate
pear	a fruit	*pore*	to study; to gaze in-
• *partition*	division		tently
petition	prayer; a formal writ-	*pour*	to flow
	ten request	• *populace*	the common people;
• *partly*	in part		the masses
partially	to some degree	*populous*	thickly settled
• *past*	(n.) time gone by;	• *portion*	a part
	(adj., adv., or prep.)	*proportion*	a ratio of parts; rela-
	gone by		tionship
passed	moved along; trans-	*apportion*	to allot
	ferred (past tense of	• *practicable*	workable
	pass)	*practical*	useful
• *patience*	composure; endurance	• *pray*	to beseech
patients	sick persons	*prey*	a captured victim
• *peace*	calmness	• *precede*	to go before
piece	a portion	*proceed*	to advance
• *pedal*	pertaining to the foot;	• *precedence*	priority
	a treadle	*precedents*	established rules
peddle	to hawk; to sell	• *preposition*	a part of speech
• *peer*	(v.) to look steadily;	*proposition*	an offer
	(n.) one of equal rank;	• *prescribe*	to designate
	a nobleman	*proscribe*	to outlaw
pier	a wharf	• *presence*	bearing; being present
• *perfect*	without fault	*presents*	gifts
prefect	an official	• *presentiment*	foreboding
• *perpetrate*	to be guilty of	*presentment*	a proposal
perpetuate	to make perpetual	• *pretend*	to make believe
• *perquisite*	an added privilege	*portend*	to foreshadow
prerequisite	a preliminary require-	• *principal*	chief; leading; a capi-
	ment		tal sum of money that
• *persecute*	to oppress		draws interest; chief
prosecute	to sue		official of a school
• *personal*	private	*principle*	a general truth; a rule
personnel	the staff	• *profit*	gain
• *perspective*	a view in correct pro-	*prophet*	one who forecasts
	portion	• *prophecy*	a prediction
prospective	anticipated	*prophesy*	to foretell
• *peruse*	to read	• *propose*	to suggest
pursue	to chase	*purpose*	intention
• *phase*	(see *faze*)	• *quiet*	calm; not noisy
• *physic*	a medicine	*quite*	entirely; wholly
physique	bodily structure	*quit*	to stop
psychic	pertaining to the mind	• *rain*	falling water
	or spirit	*rein*	part of a bridle; a curb
• *psychical*	mental	*reign*	to rule; the term of a
physical	(see *fiscal*)		ruler's power
• *plain*	undecorated; prairie	• *raise*	to lift something
	land	*raze*	to destroy
plane	a level surface; to	*rays*	beams
	make level	• *rap*	to knock
• *plaintiff*	party in a lawsuit	*wrap*	to enclose; a garment
plaintive	mournful	• *read*	to perform the act of
• *pleas*	plural of *plea* (a		reading
	pleading, an entreaty)	*reed*	a plant; a musical in-
please	to be agreeable		strument
• *pole*	a long, slender piece	*red*	a color
	of wood or metal	• *receipt*	an acknowledgment of
poll	(n.) the casting of		thing received

recipe	a formula for mixing ingredients	stayed	past tense and past participle of *to stay*
• recent	late	• stake	a pointed stick; a hazard; to wager
resent	(v.) to be indignant		
• relapse	(see *lapse*)	steak	a slice of meat or fish
• residence	a house	• stationery	writing materials
residents	persons who reside in a place	stationary	fixed
		• statue	a carved or molded figure
• respectively	in order indicated		
respectfully	in a courteous manner	stature	height
respectably	in a respectable manner	statute	a law
		• steal	to take unlawfully
• reverence	profound respect	steel	a form of iron
reference	that which refers to something	• strait	a water passageway; (plural) a distressing situation
• right	correct; a privilege		
rite	a ceremony	straight	not crooked; directly
wright	a workman (chiefly as a combining form)	• suit	a legal action; clothing; to please
write	to inscribe	suite	things in a connected set; a retinue
• role	a part in a play		
roll	a list; to revolve; a type of bread	sweet	having an agreeable taste; pleasing
• root	(n.) underground part of a plant; (v.) to implant firmly	• superintendence	management
		superintendents	supervisors
		• tare	allowance for weight of container
route	(n.) the way to be traveled; (v.) to send by a certain route	tear	to rip; a rent
		tear	a drop of secretion from the eye
en route	on or along the way	tier	a row or layer
rout	(n.) confused flight; (v.) to defeat utterly	• than	conjunction of comparison
• rote	repetition	then	(adv.) at that time
wrote	did write	• their	belonging to them
• sail	part of a ship's rigging; to travel by water	there	in that place
		they're	contraction for *they are*
sale	the act of selling	• theirs	possessive form of *they,* used without a following noun
• scene	a setting; an exhibition of strong feeling		
seen	past part. of *to see*	there's	contraction of *there is* or *there has*
• scent	odor	• therefor	for that thing
send	to dispatch	therefore	consequently
sent	did send	• through	by means of; from beginning to end; because of
• sealing	(see *ceiling*)		
• seam	a line of junction		
seem	to appear	threw	did throw
• seize	(see *cease*)	thorough	carried through to completion
• senses	(see *census*)		
• serge	a kind of cloth	• to	(prep.) toward
surge	(n.) a billow; (v.) to rise in surges	too	(adv.) more than enough; also
• serial	(see *cereal*)	two	one plus one
• sight, site	(see *cite*)	• track	a trail
• sleight	dexterity, as in *sleight of hand*	tract	a treatise
		• trial	examination; an experiment; hardship
slight	(adj.) slender, scanty; (v.) to make light of		
		trail	a path
. sole	one and only	• undo	to open; to render ineffective
soul	the immortal spirit		
• specially	(see *especially*)		
• staid	grave; sedate		

undue	improper; excessive	*where*	at the place in which
• *uninterested*	not taking an interest in	• *waste*	needless destruction; useless consumption; to expend uselessly
disinterested	impartial		
• *vain*	proud; conceited	*waist*	part of the body; a garment
vein	a blood vessel; a bed of mineral materials	• *wave*	a billow; a gesture; to swing back and forth
vane	a weathercock		
• *vendee*	purchaser	*waive*	(v.) to give up
vendor	seller	• *waver*	to hesitate
• *veracious*	truthful	*waiver*	the giving up of a claim
voracious	greedy		
• *veracity*	truthfulness	• *weather*	state of the atmos-
voracity	ravenousness; greedi-		phere; (v.) to come
	ness		through safely
• *vice*	wickedness; a prefix	*whether*	if
	used with nouns to	• *wholly*	(see *holy*)
	designate title of office	• *whose*	possessive of *who*
vise	a clamp	*who's*	contraction of *who is*
• *want*	lack; need	• *won*	(see *one*)
won't	contraction of *will not*	• *wright, write*	(see *right*)
wont	custom	• *wrote*	(see *rote*)
• *ware*	goods	• *your*	pronoun
wear	to have on	*you're*	contraction of *you are*
were	form of *to be*		

SECTION 14

Words and phrases often misused

612 The following words and phrases are often incorrectly used. See also ¶ 533 for compounds that are *sometimes one word, sometimes two words;* and ¶ 611 for *similar-sounding* and *similar-looking* words. See also references under *Adjectives and adverbs, Prepositions, Pronouns,* and *Verbs* in the following pages.

A—an. A is used before all consonant sounds including sounded *h* and long *u;* as *a dog, a day, a week, a home, a house, a unit, a union, a uniform, a C. P. A.* (pronounced "se p a.").

An is used before all vowel sounds except long *u* and before words beginning with silent *h;* as *an evening, an army, an omnibus, an umbrella, an umpire, an heir, an hour, an honor, an r* (pronounced "ar"), *an f.o.b. order* (pronounced "ef o b").

Herb, humble, humor, and *homage* may be pronounced with either the silent or the sounded *h;* hence either *a* or *an* may precede these words, depending on the pronunciation.

A. D. Used only with a year that is not modern. Do not use with a century only. (See also ¶ 440.) (See sentences on page 138.)

The Roman occupation of Britain began in 43 A. D.

The first century after Christ (*not:* the first century A. D.).

A—per. (See *Per—a.*)

Accidently. No such word. Use *accidentally.*

Adjectives and adverbs. See ¶ 603 for *Badly, Different—differently, Extra, Fewer—less, Good—well, Hardly, Kindly, Only, Quite, Real—really, Scarcely, Sure—surely,* and *Very.*

Alike. Do not use *both* and *alike* together; as in "Jane and Mary are *alike* (*not:* both alike) in one respect."

All-around. Prefer *all-round;* as an *all-round education.*

All right. Not *alright, all-right,* nor *allright.* When in doubt, remember that, like *all wrong, all right* is always two words.

All the. Incorrect with *farther* and *faster.* Use *as far as, as fast as.*

Allow. Do not use for *think* or *admit. Allow* means "permit."

Amount. Incorrect for *number* in such expressions as "a large amount of students." Correct for things in bulk, as "a large amount of lumber."

And etc. Never use *and* with *etc.* (See *Etc.*)

And/or. (See ¶ 335.)

And which. Use only to introduce a clause that parallels a preceding clause introduced by *which.*

> To meet our quota, we need several large orders, which we do expect next week *and which* will be credited to our department.

Anyplace. There is no such word.

Any place, every place, no place, some place. Incorrect for *anywhere, everywhere, nowhere, somewhere.*

> I cannot find it *anywhere* (*not:* any place).

Anytime. There is no such word.

Anywheres. Incorrect for *anywhere.*

Around. Substitute *about* for *around* to indicate approximate time.

> Mr. Saunders can meet you *about* ten o'clock.

As. Do not use for *that* or *whether;* as in "I do not know *that* (*not:* as) I can go."

As . . . as. Used with positive statements. (See also *So . . . as.*)

> She telephones *as* often *as* I do.

As if. Prefer to *as though* in such sentences as "It seems *as if* I checked that."

At about. Omit *at;* as in "Come *about* (*not:* at about) noon."

Awful. Correctly used, means "awe-inspiring," "majestic." Avoid in the slang sense of "serious" or as a mere intensive. Also, avoid the adverb *awfully* used to mean "very."

> Over a hundred persons were injured in that *awful* wreck.
>
> What an *unbecoming* (*not:* awful) hat Mary selected!
>
> It has been *extremely* (*not:* awfully) hot all week.

Balance. Incorrect for *remainder,* except when a bank balance is meant.

> My bank statement for May shows a *balance* of $159.50.
>
> Spend the *remainder* of your time in retyping the report.

Bank on. If possible, substitute *rely on, trust in, expect.*

Because. Do not use for *the fact that;* as in "*The fact that* (*not:* because) he is untrained may bar him from the post."

Because of. (See *Due to.*)

Behind—in back of. (See *In back of.*)

Being that. Do not use for *since* or *because;* as in "*Because* (*not:* being that) I was late, I could not get a seat."

Between you and me (I). (See ¶ 584*b*.)

Blame on. *Blame* or *put the blame on* is preferable.

Both alike. *Both* is unnecessary; as in "The dresses are *alike* (*not:* both alike)."

Both—each. *Both* means "the two taken together." *Each* refers to the individual members of a group considered separately.

> *Both* designs are acceptable.   *Each* design was considered on its merits.

But what. Prefer *that;* as in "I do not doubt *that* (*not:* but what) he will be elected."

Calculate. Do not use for *think, suppose, expect, intend.*

Cannot help (*but*). This expression is a confusion of two others; namely, *can but* and *cannot help.*

> I *can but* try.   I *cannot help* (*not:* but) feeling sorry for her.

Can't seem. *Seem unable* or *do not seem able* is preferable.

Claim. Use only in the sense of demanding on the basis of a right. Do not use for *maintain* or *assert.*

> He *claimed* his share in his aunt's property.
> He *maintains* (or *asserts*) that the charge is too high.

Class. (See *Kind.*)

Come and. Illiterate for *come to;* as in "*Come to* (*not:* and) see me."

Could of. Illiterate for *could have;* as in "I *could have* (*not:* could of) gone if I'd had the money."

Couldn't seem. *Seemed unable* or *did not seem able* is preferable.

Data—datum. (See ¶ 565.)

Different than. Not in good use. Substitute *different from;* as in "The work of senior year is entirely *different from* that of junior year."

Doesn't. (See *Don't.*)

Done. Incorrect as past tense of *do;* as in "I *did* (*not:* done) the assignment."

Don't (*do not*). Should not be used for *doesn't* (*does not*). (See ¶ 573.)

> We *don't* favor the plan.   He *doesn't* like his work.

Doubt that—doubt whether. Use *doubt that* in negative statements and in questions. Use *doubt whether* in affirmative statements. (Also see *Whether.*)

> We do not *doubt that* he is capable.
> Is there any *doubt that* the letter was mailed?
> I *doubt whether* I can go.

Doubtful. Same distinction as for *doubt.*

Due to—caused by—because of—on account of. *Due to* and *caused by* introduce adjective phrases and should modify nouns.   (Continued on page 140.)

> Her success is *due to* conscientiousness. (Modifies *success.*)
> His failure was *caused by* indolence. (Modifies *failure.*)

Because of and *on account of* introduce adverbial phrases and should modify verbs.

> He resigned *because of* ill health. (Modifies *resigned.*)
> He resigned *on account of* ill health. (Modifies *resigned.*)

Each—both. (See *Both—each.*)

Each other. Use *each other* to refer to two persons or things; *one another* for more than two.

> The two partners had great respect for *each other.*
> The four winners congratulated *one another.*

Equally as good. Use either *equally good* or *just as good.*

> His pen is newer, but mine is *equally good* (*not:* equally as good).
> My pen is *just as good* (*not:* equally as good) as his.

Etc. This abbreviation means "and other things." Therefore, do not use *and* before it. A comma both precedes and follows *etc.* (See ¶ 219.)

Every place. (See *Any place.*)

Except. When *except* is a preposition, be sure to use the objective form of a pronoun that follows; as in "Everyone has left *except* the committee and *me.*"

Fix. Greatly overused for *repair* or *arrange;* as in "The mechanic *repaired* (*not:* fixed) the typewriter."

Former. Refers to the first mentioned of two persons or things. When more than two are mentioned, *first, first mentioned,* or *first named* is preferred to *former.* (See also *Latter.*)

> This style is made in silk and in rayon, but I prefer the *former.*
> This style is made in silk, in rayon, and in wool; but I prefer the *first.*

Gotten. An old form of *got. Got* is preferable.

Guess. Avoid in the sense of *think, suppose,* or *expect.*

Have got. Often misused for *have;* as in "They *have* (*not:* have got) a television set."

Healthy. People are *healthy;* a climate is *healthful;* food is *wholesome.*

Help. Do not use *from* after *help;* as in "I couldn't *help* (*not:* help from) telling her she was wrong."

Identical with, not *identical to.*

If. (See also *Whether.*) Not in good use for *whether* in such sentences as "He doesn't know *whether* he will be able to leave tomorrow."

In back of. Substitute *behind* for *in back of.* However, *in front of* is correct.

> File that folder *behind* the "Miscellaneous" folder.
> Please mow the lawn *in front of* the house.

In regards to. Substitute *in regard to, with regard to, as regards.*

Individual. Do not use indiscriminately as a substitute for *person. Individual* refers to a single or particular person or thing as distinguished from the members of a group.

> The *individual,* not the group, must be considered.
> All *persons* whose names begin with *S* come this way!

Inside—outside. Do not use *of* after either of these words; as in "This chair may
  be used either *inside* or *outside* the house."
  Also, do not use *inside of* in reference to time. Substitute *within;* as in
  "Mr. Charles is expected *within* an hour."
Its, it's. (See ¶ 592.)
Just. Colloquial for *very;* as in "That play is *very* (*not:* just) charming."
Kind. *Kind* is singular; therefore, *this kind, that kind;* but, *these kinds, those
  kinds.* Same distinctions for *Class, Type, Sort.*
Kind of—sort of. *Somewhat* or *rather* is preferable.

> I was *somewhat* (*not:* kind of, sort of) bored.
> She seemed *rather* (*not:* kind of, sort of) tired.

Kind of (a). The *a* is unnecessary; as in "That *kind of* (*not:* kind of a) material
  is very expensive.
Last—latest. Accurately, *last* means "after all others"; *latest,* "most recent."

> Mr. Long's *last* act before leaving was to recommend Mr. Holt's promotion.
> This is the *latest* bulletin from the Weather Bureau.

Note: In practice, however, this distinction is not always observed and
both words are used as superlatives of *late.*

Latter. Refers to the second of two persons or things mentioned. When more
  than two are mentioned, *last named* or *last mentioned* is preferable to
  latter. (See also *Former.*)

> July and August are both vacation months, but the *latter* is more popular.
> July, August, and September are all vacation months; but the *last named*
> is the most popular.

Let's (*let us*). Use only when *let us* would be correct; as in "*Let's* take a picnic
  lunch."
Like—as, as if. *Like* is correct when used as a preposition, in which construction
  it takes an object.

> Mary looks *like* her mother.   My sister looks *like* me.

But *like* should *not* be used as a conjunction to mean "as" or "as if." It
should *not* introduce a subject and verb or a dependent clause.

> Mary looks *as* (*not:* like) her mother did at her age.
> It looks *as if* (*not:* like) it will rain.

These words are very often confused.

Lots of. *Many* or *much* is preferable.
May of. Illiterate for *may have.*
Memoranda, memorandum. (See ¶ 565.)
Might of. Illiterate for *might have.*
Most. Do not use for *almost. Most* is superlative.

> The ink is *almost* gone, and *almost* all the paper is gone too.

Must of. Illiterate for *must have.*
Myself, yourself, himself, and so forth. (See ¶ 590.)
Neither. Use with *nor,* not *or;* as in "She could *neither* take dictation *nor*
  answer the telephone correctly."

No good. Substitute *worthless, of no value, useless.*

No place. (See *Any place.*)

No use. Substitute *of no use, useless, of no value, unsuccessful.*

Nor. (See *Neither.*)

Nothing like. Incorrect for *not nearly.*

Nowhere near. Incorrect for *not nearly.*

Nowheres. Incorrect for *nowhere.*

Number, a or *the.* (See ¶ 564*f.*)

Of—have. The use of *of* instead of *have* in the forms *could of, would of, ought to of, should of, might of, may of, must of* is grossly illiterate.

> I *would have* (*not:* would of) gone shopping today if I had had the money.

One another. (See *Each other.*)

Opposite. Followed by *of* when used as a noun; as in "Her opinion is the *opposite of* mine."

When used as a preposition, followed by *to* or *from,* or by *neither.*

> Her opinion is *opposite to* (or *from*) mine.   She lives *opposite* the school.

Ought to of. Illiterate for *ought to have.*

Outside. (See *Inside.*)

Party. Do not use for *person,* except in legal work.

Per—a. Per, a Latin word, is frequently used in business to mean "by the," as in "$5 per hundredweight," "60 miles per hour." Whenever possible, the English *a* or *an* should be substituted, as "at the rate of 75 cents an hour," "30 cents a gallon." Do *not* use *per* in the sense of "according to" or "in accordance with."

> We are sending you samples *in accordance with* (*not:* as per) your request.

Person. (See *Individual.*)

Prepositions. See ¶ 608 for *All of; Among; At—in; At—to; Beside—besides; Between; Both of; From—off; In, into, in to; On, onto, on to; On, upon, up on;* and *Up.*

Pretend like. Omit *like.*

Pronouns. See ¶¶ 585, 586 for *Who—whom* and *Who—which—that.*

Proven. Proved is preferable.

Reason is because. Substitute *reason is that;* as in "The *reason* for the small sale *is that* (*not:* because) prices are too high."

Remember of. Of is not necessary.

Retroactive to (not *from*). "Salaries of all secretaries will be increased $5 a week *retroactive to* January 1."

Same. Do not use for *it,* except in legal work; as in "We will alter the suit and have *it* (*not:* same) ready for you by Saturday."

Seldom ever. Substitute *seldom* or *hardly ever.* If a more emphatic form is desired, *seldom if ever* or *seldom or never* is correct.

> I *seldom* eat candy.   I *seldom if ever* eat candy. (More emphatic.)

So . . . as. In negative statements and in questions implying negative answers, prefer *so . . . as* to *as . . . as.* (See also *As . . . as.*)

> The new stock is not *so* beautiful *as* the old.

Some. Some is an adjective. Do not use it as an adverb.

> I did *some* homework last night.
> I was *somewhat* (*not:* some) tired yesterday.

Some place. (See *Any place.*)
Somewheres. Incorrect for *somewhere.*
Sooner. Not good form in the sense of "rather"; as in "I'd *rather* file than type."
Sort. (See *Kind.*)
Sort of. (See *Kind of.*)
Such a. Colloquial when used to give force or emphasis to a statement.

> This is a *very* (*not:* such a) difficult job.
> It is a *great* (*not:* such a) pleasure to meet you.

Sure and. Do not use for *sure to;* as in "Be *sure to* turn left at the corner."
Suspicion. Do not use as a verb; as in "I *suspect* (*not:* suspicion) you are right."
Than—then. Than is a conjunction introducing a subordinate clause of comparison. *Then* is an adverb meaning "at that time." For choice of pronoun following *than* in a comparison that is not a complete clause, see ¶ 588.

> The compulsory retirement age is considerably lower now *than* it was *then.*

That there. Never use for *that;* as in "May I have *that* (*not:* that there) ring?"
That—which—who. (See ¶ 586.)
Them. Never use as an adjective; as in "Do not file today's letters with *those* (*not:* them) others."
These sort—these kind. Sort and *kind* are *singular.* Therefore, *this* or *that* should precede both words. (See also *Kind.*)
This here. Do not use for *this;* as in "*This* (*not:* this here) typewriter is out of order."
Through. Do not use in the sense of "finished."
Toward—towards. Both forms are correct.
Try and. Illiterate for *try to.*
Type. (See *Kind.*)
Unique. Do not use in sense of "unusual." A unique thing is one that is alone of its kind. (See ¶ 601*c.*)
Verbs. See ¶ 582 for *Bring—take, Come—go, Lay—lie, Learn—teach, Leave—let, May—can* (*might—could*), *Raise—rise, Set—sit, Shall—will, Should—would.*
Want to. Do not use in sense of *should* or *had better;* as in "You *should* (*not:* want to) develop a more optimistic outlook."
Way. Colloquial for *away.* Say, "*Away* (*not:* way) down in the southern part of the state."
Ways. Do not use for *way* in referring to distance; as in "I live a short *way* (*not:* ways) from here."
Where . . . at. Illiterate. Say, "*Where* is Mr. Brown?" (*Not:* Where is Mr. Brown at?)
Where . . . to. The *to* is redundant; as in "Where did John go (*not:* go to)?"
Whether. Prefer *see whether, learn whether, know whether* to *see if, learn if, know if.* (For *Doubt whether,* see *Doubt that.*) *Whether* is correct in indirect questions.

> He wondered *whether* you had finished the work.

Who—which—that. (See ¶ 586.)

Who—whom. (See ¶ 585.)

Without. Without may be used as a preposition, but it should not be used to mean "unless."

> Ship the desk *without* the chair.
> *Unless* (*not:* without) you make a decision soon, the job will be filled.

Worst kind—worst way. Do not use either to mean "very much."

Would better. Do not use for *had better;* as in "I think you *had better* (*not:* would better) consult a physician."

Would have. Do not use for *had* in a clause beginning with *if;* as in "If you *had* (*not:* would have) come early, you could have seen him."

Would of. Illiterate for *would have.*

You was. Illiterate for *you were.* (See ¶ 556.)

SECTION 15

Typing manuscripts, reports, and articles

Note: The information in this section applies chiefly to the typing of manuscripts for office use—such as reports and studies. For complete information regarding the special problems involved in typing manuscripts that will be set in type (such as manuscripts of books and articles), see *Gregg Typing,* Second Edition, by Rowe and Lloyd, pages 73–78, 139–141, 355–357, or the index of any modern typewriting textbook.

PAPER AND CARBONS

613   Use a good quality of paper, usually 8½ by 11 inches in size. Type on only one side of the paper.

614   Make at least one carbon copy.

MARGINS

615   Use the following margins:

a) Top margin of first page when it contains the title—2 inches.

(1) Center the title and type in all capital letters.

(2) Triple space between the title and the first line of the copy if there is no subtitle. If a subtitle appears, leave three spaces between the subtitle and the first line of the body of the manuscript.

b) Top of other pages, 1 inch above page number (1½ inches above text).

c) Left, 1¼ inches (or 1½ inches if papers are to be bound).

d) Right, 1¼ inches (or 1 inch if papers are to be bound).

e) Bottom, 1 to 1½ inches.

f) A ruled backing sheet is helpful in keeping margins uniform on all pages, particularly if one is inexperienced in typing manuscripts.

    (1) Draw *heavy lines* to indicate the margins.

    (2) Place this sheet between the original copy and the back of the first carbon sheet as a guide.

SPACING AND PARAGRAPHS

616   Observe these rules of spacing:

a) Copy should be double spaced.

b) Triple space between the title and the first line of copy. (See ¶ 615*a*[2].)

c) In general, quoted material of three or more lines, tabulations, and outlines should be single spaced and indented five or more spaces from each margin. If a whole paragraph is quoted, the first word will be double indented ten spaces.

d) All pages (except the first when it contains the title) should have about the same number of lines on each page.

e) A centered subheading should be preceded by three blank lines and followed by one blank line.

f) A side heading displayed on a line by itself should be preceded by two blank lines and followed by one blank line.

g) Begin each new chapter of a long manuscript on a new page.

617   Indent paragraphs five spaces.

PAGING

618   Pages are numbered as follows:

a) The first page is not numbered when it contains the title.

b) All other pages should be numbered consecutively in the upper right corner. Place the number at the right margin, on the seventh line from the top, to leave six blank lines above the page number.

c) Acceptable variations:

    (1) The page number may be centered ½ or 1 inch from the bottom of the page.

    (2) The page number may be typed on line 4 instead of line 7.

    (3) The word "page" may precede the number.

d) Triple space after typing the page number.

RIBBON

619   Use a black record ribbon, so that the copy will be clear and permanent.

FOOTNOTES

620   Arrange footnotes as follows:

a) One line below the last line of the text and starting at the left margin, type a line 2 inches long. This line will separate the copy from the footnotes. Use underscore key. Double space after the line.

b) Single space footnotes, but double space (leave one blank line) between them.

c) Number consecutively with superior (raised) figures. To raise numbers, turn back the cylinder slightly with one hand while typing the number with the free hand.

d) The number preceding a footnote must correspond to the number following the notation to which it refers in the text. Do not space between a word in the text and a superior figure, but separate a superior figure from the first word of a footnote by one letter space.

e) Footnotes must appear on the same page as the notations to which they refer. Plan ahead to provide sufficient space for the footnotes. *Ibid.* refers to the work mentioned in the immediately preceding footnote, but on a different page of that work.

Illustration:

```
    Footnotes are used to identify a person or other
reference mentioned in the report.¹
    A footnote must be separated very clearly from the
body of the report.²
```
_____

```
¹John L. Rowe and Alan C. Lloyd, Gregg Typing, Second
   Edition (New York:  McGraw-Hill Book Company, Inc.,
   1959), page 77.

²Ibid., page 78.
```

ITALICIZED WORDS

621   Underscore words to be italicized in print, such as titles of books and periodicals (see ¶¶ 302, 303) and words accompanied by definitions (see ¶ 297).

SECTION 16

Setting up tables

622   First study the material; then plan the tabulation carefully.

623   In typing money in a column, place a dollar sign before the first figure in the column and before the total. The dollar signs should align in the first space to the left of the longest figure in that column.

624   If all the money in a column is in even amounts (dollars, no cents), no decimals and zeros are needed.

625   If it is necessary to make lines in a table:

a) Ruling is best done with pen and ink, particularly on important work.

b) The underscore may be used for horizontal rules.

c) Use the colon or the apostrophe for vertical lines. If the apostrophe is used, quotation marks may be typed to form double lines.

626 To facilitate the reading of a table, it is wise to use leaders (rows of periods that lead the eye across the page) whenever the items in the first column of the table vary widely in length. Leaders are often used in financial statements between the items and the first column of figures. The shortest line of leaders should have not fewer than three periods. A line of leaders should be preceded and followed by a space. Leaders may be formed by typing periods in solid sequence, without spacing, or by alternately typing periods and spaces. The first method is faster, but the second is neater. If spaces are used, all the periods in all the leader lines must align.

➤ *Tabulation by Mathematical Method*

VERTICAL PLACEMENT

627 Count the number of lines in the table. Include the blank lines to be allowed between the title, columnar headings, and the lines in the table itself.
a) Triple space between the main and columnar headings.
b) Double space between columnar headings and the table.

628 Subtract the number of lines in the table from the total lines available. Typewriters space 6 lines to an inch; so, there are 66 lines on a standard full sheet of paper.

629 Divide by 2. This will give the number of the line on which the typing should begin; it allows for a bottom margin that is, as it should be, slightly wider than the top margin.

HORIZONTAL PLACEMENT

630 Count the longest line in each column. If a column heading is the longest line in its column, consider it the longest line; count it.

631 Total the number of writing spaces needed for all the columns.

632 To that total, add 6 for each between-column blank.
a) Columns should normally be about ½ inch (6 spaces) apart, the normal span of the eye in reading technical copy.
b) Columns can be more or fewer spaces apart. They should be fewer than 6 if the margins resulting from the next step (¶ 633) are less than 1 inch wide.
c) Money columns in financial statements should be only 2 spaces apart.

633 From the center of the paper, backspace half the total (of the columns plus the 6-space blanks) and set the left margin stop at the point to which you backspace. Then, spacing across the paper on the space bar, space through the width of each column and its following blank space, setting tabulator stops for each column.

COLUMNAR HEADINGS

634 A columnar heading must be centered over its column; the important words should be capitalized.

635   A long heading should be broken into two or three lines if possible. Abbreviations are often permissible.

636   In a table with columnar headings that are wider than their columns, it will be necessary to shift the tab stops after the headings are typed, so that the columns are centered below the headings.

637   Before typing the column headings and the first line of the body of a table, study their relationship.

   a) If a line in the heading is shorter than the longest line in that column:
      (1) Subtract the spaces in that line of the heading from the longest line in the column.
      (2) Divide the difference in half and indent the heading accordingly.
   b) If a line in the heading is longer than the longest line in that column:
      (1) Subtract the longest line in the column from the line in the heading.
      (2) Divide the difference in half, to ascertain how far from the start of the heading to indent the column. After typing the heading, reset the tabulator stop accordingly.

COST OF BUSINESS LETTERS

Items	Explanation of Items	Average Cost
Dictator's Time	Average salary, $110 a week	$ .321
Stenographic Cost	Average salary, $78 a week	.730
Nonproductive Labor	Illness, vacations, etc.	.158
Fixed Charges	Rent, light, pensions, etc.	.420
Materials	Paper, carbons, ribbons, etc.	.070
Mailing Costs	Postage, sealing, etc.	.090
Filing Costs	Clerk's time, supplies, etc.	.040
TOTAL		$1.83

Using the Cost of Business Letters table as an example, work the problem as follows:

Vertical placement

Spaces on half sheet of paper 33
Number of lines and spaces in table 14
Spaces available for margins (33 − 14) 19
Line to start on (19 ÷ 2—disregard fractions) 9

Horizontal placement

Longest line in each column: Column 1 19
                               Column 2 29
                               Column 3 12
Total of longest lines 60
Add 6 for each (of the two) between-column blanks 12
Total width of the table 72

Setting margins and tabulator stops

Left margin is found by backspacing half the width of the table from the center of the paper. Half of 72 is 36. Backspace 36 times from the center of the paper. Set margin.

The tabulator stop for column 2 is ascertained by spacing on the space bar once for each stroke in column 1 (19) plus 6 spaces for the blank that is to be between columns 1 and 2. Space 25 (19 + 6) times from the margin stop. Set tabulator stop.

The tabulator stop for column 3 is ascertained by spacing on the space bar once for each stroke in column 2 (29) plus 6 spaces for the blank that is to be between columns 2 and 3. Space 35 (29 + 6) times from the column-2 tabulator stop. Set tabulator stop.

Adjustment for column headings

The heading of column 1 is 14 spaces narrower than its column (19 − 5). Indent 7 spaces (14 ÷ 2) from the left margin stop before typing the heading.

The heading of column 2 is 9 spaces narrower than its column (29 − 20). Indent 4 spaces (9 ÷ 2, disregarding fractions) from the column's tab before typing the heading.

The heading of column 3 is 6 spaces wider than its column (12 − 6). After typing the heading, move the tabulator stop 4 spaces to the right so as to indent the column 3 spaces (6 ÷ 2) from the start of the column heading.

SUMMARY

638 Set margin and tabulator stops before doing any typing.

639 Type the main title on line 9 of a half sheet, centered horizontally and typed in all capitals; then double space to the subheading.

640 Center the subheading, if any, 2 lines below title; then triple space.

641 Type and underscore the three column headings, remembering to indent the first heading 7 spaces from the margin stop, to indent the second heading 4 spaces from column-2 tabulator stop, and to begin the third heading at column-3 tabulator stop. Double space to body of table.

642 Reset the tabulator stop for column 3, so as to indent the column 3 spaces from the start of the column heading. Then type the table.

➤ *Tabulation by Backspace Method*

643 *Vertical placement* (See ¶¶ 627–629.)

644 *Horizontal placement*

    a) Select the key item (longest item) in each column (19–29–12).

    b) Determine the number of spaces (6) to be left between columns.

    c) After clearing out all previous tab stops and the margin stops, backspace from center of paper to center key items 6 spaces apart.

       (1) Backspace three times to center the 6 spaces of each blank area.

       (2) Backspace once for each pair of strokes in the combined key items.

    d) Set the left margin stop at this point (the beginning of the first column).

    e) Space forward once for each stroke in column 1 plus the 6 spaces between columns and set a tab stop at this point (the beginning of the second column).

    f) Repeat step *e* until all tab stops have been set for the columns.

645 *Columnar headings*

If the heading is the longest item in the column, use this as the key item. After setting the tab stop, type the heading and reset the tab stop. (See ¶ 637.)

SECTION 17

Forms of address for official correspondence

646 The following forms of address are correct for government officials, military and naval personnel, church dignitaries, and education officials.

GOVERNMENT OFFICIALS (NATIONAL, STATE, CITY)

Whereas formerly the correct forms of address, salutation, and complimentary closing for use in correspondence with government officials were explicitly prescribed and were very formal, the present tendency is toward simpler, more businesslike forms. The following suggestions are a guide to these forms.

1. The *President of the United States* is usually addressed:

> The President, The White House, Washington 25, D. C.

However, the more informal form is also correct; thus:

> The Honorable (name in full), President of the United States, Washington 25, D.C.

The formal salutations are *Sir:* or *Mr. President:*
The less formal, *My dear Mr. President:*

2. Similarly, the *Chief Justice of the United States* may be addressed either:

> The Chief Justice of the United States, Washington 13, D. C. *or* The Honorable (name in full), Chief Justice of the United States, Washington 13, D. C.

The formal salutations are *Sir:* or *Mr. Chief Justice:*
The less formal, *My dear Mr. Chief Justice:*

3. All other officials, whether Federal, state, or city, are preferably addressed by their personal names preceded by *The Honorable* and followed by the title of their office; for example:

> *Cabinet member:* The Honorable (name in full), Secretary of (name of department, as *Interior*)
> *Senator:* The Honorable (name in full), The United States Senate
> *Governor:* The Honorable (name in full), Governor of (state), (capital of state), (state)
> *Mayor:* The Honorable (name in full), Mayor of (name of city), (city), (state)

4. Salutations: For all officials, *Sir:* is the most formal. *Dear Sir:* is always correct. If the personal name is used, the salutation *My dear Mr.* (last name): is used.

5. The usual complimentary closings may be used.

6. The zone number for all Federal branches except the Supreme Court of the United States is Washington 25. That of the Supreme Court is Washington 13.

MILITARY AND NAVAL PERSONNEL

Addresses. The addresses of both officers and enlisted men of the armed forces should include: (1) full title of rank or rating (as *Major, Sergeant, Ensign*), (2) branch of the service (as *Signal Corps, Ordnance Department*), and (3) some such abbreviation as *U. S. A.* (*United States Army*), *U. S. C. G.* (*United States Coast Guard*), which may follow either the personal name or the branch of the service.

> Major General (name in full), U. S. A.
>   Commanding General, Third Corps Area
> Commander (name in full)
>   Medical Corps, U. S. N. R.
> Sergeant (name in full), U. S. A.
>   First Tank Corps

Salutations. The formal salutation *Dear Sir:* may be used for all ranks or ratings. For personal salutations, the following rules govern.

1. For Army officers, titles are used as follows:

> For generals, lieutenant generals, major generals, and brigadier generals: *My dear General* (last name):
> For colonels and lieutenant colonels: *My dear Colonel* (last name):
> For majors, captains, and first and second lieutenants: *My dear Major* (last name): *My dear Captain* (last name): *My dear Lieutenant* (last name):

2. For warrant officers and all noncommissioned Army officers, the salutation is simply *My dear Mr.* (last name):

3. For Navy officers of the rank of admiral (including vice-admiral and rear admiral), captain, and commander, the salutation is *My dear Admiral* (last name): *My dear Captain* (last name): *My dear Commander* (last name):

4. For all Navy ranks below commander, the saluation is *My dear Mr.* (last name):

CHURCH DIGNITARIES

Roman Catholic

Refer to the *Official Catholic Directory* to find the name and title of any official or dignitary of the Roman Catholic Church. The following outline gives the preferred forms of address and both formal and informal salutations. *Respectfully yours* is the usual complimentary closing for all ranks with the exception of priest, for whom *Sincerely yours* is correct.

> *Cardinal:* His Eminence (given name) Cardinal (surname), (address) Your Eminence:

(*Continued on page 152.*)

Archbishop or Bishop: The Most Reverend (name in full), Archbishop of (place), (or Bishop of [place]). Your Excellency:

Monsignor: The Right Reverend Monsignor (name in full), (address). My dear Monsignor:

Priest: The Reverend (name in full), (address). Reverend Father: (*formal*); Dear Father (last name): (*informal*).

Mother Superior: The Reverend Mother (name), (address). Reverend Mother: (*formal*); or My dear Mother Superior: (*informal*).

Sister: Sister (name): My dear Sister: or Dear Sister (name):

Protestant clergy

Protestant Episcopal Bishop: The Right Reverend (name in full), Bishop of (place), (city), (state). Right Reverend and Dear Sir: (*formal*), or My dear Bishop (last name): (*informal*).

Protestant Episcopal Dean: The Very Reverend (name in full), Dean of (place), (address). My dear Dean:

Methodist Episcopal Bishop: Bishop (name in full), Bishop of (place), (city), (state). My dear Bishop (last name):

Other Clergymen: The Reverend (name in full), (address). Dear Mr. (last name):

With a Doctor's degree: Dr. (name in full), (address). Dear Doctor (last name):

Jewish Rabbi

Rabbi (name in full), (address). My dear Rabbi: (*formal*); or My dear Rabbi (last name): (*informal*).

EDUCATION OFFICIALS

President of a College or University: Dr. (name in full), President of (name of college), (address). Dear Doctor (last name):
or

President (name in full), (name of college), (address). Dear President (last name):

Professor: Professor (name in full), Department of (name of department), (name of college), (address). Dear Professor (last name):
or

Dr. (name in full), Professor of (subject), (name of college), (address). Dear Doctor (last name):

Superintendent of Schools: Mr. (or Dr.) (name in full), Superintendent of (name of city) Schools, (address). Dear Mr. (or Doctor) (last name):

Member of Board of Education: Mr. (or Mrs. or Miss) (name in full), Member, (name of city) Board of Education, (address). Dear Mr. (or Mrs. or Miss) (last name):

Principal: Mr. (name in full), Principal, (name of school), (address). Dear Mr. (last name):

Teacher: Mr. (or Mrs. or Miss) (name in full), (name of school), (address). Dear Mr. (or Mrs. or Miss) (last name):

The formal salutation *Dear Sir:* or *Dear Madam:* may be used for all these officials.

SECTION 18

A brief glossary of grammatical terms

Abstract noun. (See *Noun.*)

Adjective. One of the eight parts of speech; a word used to modify a noun or a pronoun; as *indelible* ink.

   Clause. (*See Clause.*)

   Comparison of. (See *Comparison.*)

   Predicate. (See *Complement.*)

Adverb. One of the eight parts of speech; a word used to modify a verb, an adjective, or another adverb. An adverb answers the questions when? where? in what amount? to what degree?

> He signed the note *slowly.* (Modifies verb *signed.*)
> We moved to a *rapidly* growing suburb. (Modifies adjective *growing.*)
> She agreed *most* reluctantly. (Modifies adverb *reluctantly.*)

   Clause. (See *Clause.*)

   Conjunctive. An adverb that connects the main clauses of a compound sentence; as *however, therefore, nevertheless, hence, moreover, otherwise, consequently.* Also known as *adverbial connective.*

   Relative. An adverb that introduces a subordinate clause and serves both as an adverb and a connecting word; as *after, before, how, since, till, when, where, while.*

Antecedent. A word or words to which a pronoun refers.

> He is the *person who* dictated the letter.
> Fill your *pen* before *it* becomes dry.

Appositive. A noun or a group of words that, set beside another noun, denotes the same person or thing.

> Mr. Mead, *the purchasing agent,* called.

Article. Classed as an adjective. The *definite* article is *the;* the *indefinite, a* or *an.*

Auxiliary. (See *Verb.*)

Case. The form of a noun or of a pronoun that indicates its relation to other words in the sentence. There are three cases—*nominative, objective,* and *possessive. Nouns* have the same form in the nominative and objective cases, but a special ending for the possessive. The forms for *pronouns* are:

Nominative	Objective	Possessive
I, we	me, us	my, mine, our, ours
you	you	your, yours
he, she, it	him, her, it	his, hers, its
they	them	their, theirs
who	whom	whose

(Continued on page 154.)

Nominative. Used for the subject or the complement of a verb.

>*He* sings well. (Subject.)   It is *I*. (Complement.)

Objective. Used for: (1) the direct object of a transitive verb, (2) the object of a preposition, (3) the subject of an infinitive, (4) the complement of an infinitive.

>Tom hit *him*. (Direct object of *hit*.)
>John beckoned to *me*. (Direct object of preposition *to*.)
>The president encouraged *him* to run for office. (Subject of infinitive *to run*.)
>He believed me to be *her*. (Complement of infinitive *to be*.)

Possessive. Used to show ownership. See ¶¶ 492–503 for the formation of the possessives of nouns.

Clause. A group of related words within a sentence, containing a subject and a predicate.

A *main* (or *independent* or *principal*) clause states a complete thought within itself. A *subordinate* (*dependent*) clause is not complete within itself and cannot stand alone.

>I will go (main clause) if the occasion demands my presence (subordinate clause).

Co-ordinate. Clauses of the same rank. They may be principal or subordinate clauses.

>*The truck left an hour ago,* and *our messenger is not due.* (Principal.)
>*When the wind blows* and *when snow piles high,* home fires are welcome. (Subordinate.)

Restrictive. A clause that limits, defines, or identifies the noun of the main clause and that could not be omitted without changing the meaning of the main clause. Restrictive clauses are *not* set off by commas.

>The magazine *that came yesterday* contains some beautiful illustrations.

Nonrestrictive. A clause that adds descriptive information about the noun of the main clause and that could be omitted without changing the meaning of the main clause. Such clauses are separated from the main clause by commas.

>Their warehouse, *which is also their shipping department,* is on Third Street.

An *adjective clause* is a subordinate clause that modifies a noun or a pronoun in the main clause. Adjective clauses are joined to the main clause by relative pronouns (*which, that, who, whose, whom*).

>The charge, *which includes painting,* seems reasonable. (Modifies *charge*.)
>The plan *that was recommended* did not prove practicable. (Modifies *plan*.)

An *adverb clause* is a subordinate clause used as an adverb. Adverb clauses indicate place, time, manner, cause, purpose, condition, result, reason, contrast.

>Your order will be filled *as soon as stock is received*. (Time).
>I am advised to move to a locality *where the climate is dry*. (Place.)
>She worked *as though her life depended on it*. (Manner.)
>Please write me at once *if you have any suggestions*. (Condition.)
>*Because our plant is closed,* we cannot accept the order. (Reason.)
>We should have the data Monday, *so that the report may be completed*. (Result.)
>The material last received was too thin, *whereas this is too thick*. (Contrast.)

(*Continued on page 155.*)

Noun. A subordinate clause used as a noun.

> *That the plan was a failure* cannot be denied.

Elliptical. Clauses from which subject and predicate have been omitted. (See ¶ 610 *d.*)

Collective noun. (See *Noun.*)

Common noun. (See *Noun.*)

Comparison. The change in the form of an adjective or of an adverb to indicate degrees in quality, quantity, or manner. There are three degrees:

> *Positive,* the simple form; as *old, beautiful* (adjectives); *near, quietly* (adverbs).

> *Comparative,* which indicates a higher or lower degree of quality or manner than is expressed by the positive degree. It is used when two objects or manners are compared. It is regularly formed by adding *er* to the positive degree (*older, nearer*). In longer words, it is formed by adding *more* or *less* to the positive (*more beautiful, less beautiful; more quietly, less quietly*).

> *Superlative,* which denotes the highest or lowest degree of quality or manner and is used when more than two objects or manners are compared. It is regularly formed by adding *est* to the positive degree (*oldest, nearest*). In longer words, it is formed by adding *most* or *least* (*most beautiful, least beautiful; most quietly, least quietly*).

Complement. A general term used to denote a word or a word group used to complete the sense of the verb. It may be an object, a predicate noun, or a predicate adjective.

An *object* follows a transitive verb (see *Verb*).

> He mailed the *letter.*

A *predicate noun* follows a linking verb. It explains the subject and is identical with it. (Also called *predicate complement, subject complement,* and *predicate nominative.*)

> Miss Stewart is our *office manager.* (*Office manager* refers to *Miss Stewart.*)

A *predicate adjective* completes the sense of a verb. (Also called a *predicate complement.*)

> The charge is *excessive.*

Complex sentence. (See *Sentence.*)

Compound sentence. (See *Sentence.*)

Conjunction. One of the eight parts of speech; used to connect words, phrases, or clauses.

> *Co-ordinate conjunction.* Used to connect words, phrases, or clauses of equal rank. The chief co-ordinate conjunctions are *and, or, but, for, nor, either . . . or, neither . . . nor.*

> *Subordinate conjunction.* Used to join subordinate clauses to main clauses. A few common ones are *when, where, after, before, if, whether, since, though.*

> *Correlative conjunctions.* Regularly used in pairs; as *not only . . . but also, either . . . or.* (See ¶ 609 *b.*) Correlatives are a type of co-ordinating conjunctions.

Conjunctive adverb. Also known as *adverbial connective.* (See *Adverb.*)

Connective. A word that joins words, clauses, or sentences. The chief connectives are conjunctions, prepositions, and relative pronouns.

Consonant. The letters *b, c, d, f, g, h, j, k, l, m, n, p, q, r, s, t, v, x, z. W,* as in *work,* and *y,* as in *youth,* are also consonants. (See also *Vowels.*)

Contraction. A shortened form of a word in which an apostrophe indicates the omitted letters; as *don't* for *do not,* and *o'clock* for *of the clock.*

Co-ordinate conjunction. (See *Conjunction.*)

Dangling modifier. A modifier that is attached to no word in a sentence or to the wrong word (See ¶ 610.)

Declarative sentence. (See *Sentence.*)

Demonstrative pronoun. (See *Pronoun.*)

Direct address. A construction in which a speaker or a writer addresses another person directly.

> *Mr. Stewart,* what is your opinion?

Direct object. (See *Object.*)

Direct quotation. (See *Quotation.*)

Exclamatory sentence. (See *Sentence.*)

Gender. The modification of a noun or pronoun to denote the sex of the object named; as *man, woman; he, she, it.*

Gerund. A verb form ending in *ing* and used as a *noun.* Do not confuse with present participle. (See *Participle.*)

> *Selling* is fun. (Subject of sentence.)
> I enjoy *selling.* (Direct object of *enjoy.*)
> She is experienced in *selling.* (Object of preposition *in.*)

Dangling. A gerund that is attached to no word in a sentence or to the wrong word. (See ¶ 610 *c.*)

Idiom. An expression that cannot be explained by ordinary rules of grammar, but that has come to be considered good usage despite this fact; as *hard put to it,* meaning "in great extremity." The transcriber encounters most often prepositional idioms (see ¶ 604) and idiomatic possessives (see ¶ 507.)

Imperative sentence. (See *Sentence.*)

Indefinite pronoun. (See *Pronoun.*)

Independent clause. (See *Clause.*)

Indirect object. (See *Object.*)

Indirect question. (See *Question.*)

Indirect quotation. (See *Quotation.*)

Infinitive. The form of the verb usually introduced by *to.* (*To* is known as the *sign of the infinitive.*) There are two forms of infinitive: the *present,* or simple, form (*to see*); and the *perfect,* which consists of *to have* plus the past participle of the verb (*to have seen*). After certain verbs *to* is omitted: *can, could, may, dare, make, help, might, must, need.*

> It would help us (to) finish the job.

An infinitive may be used as a noun, an adjective, or an adverb. It can have a subject, take an object, and be modified by an adverb, like any verb.

> Noun: *To do her a favor* is a pleasure. (Subject.)
> She asked *to see the book.* (Object.)
> He is *to see him at once.* (Predicate complement.)

(*Continued on page 157.*)

> Adjective: I still have two more letters *to transcribe.* (Modifies *letters.*)
> Adverb: He resigned *to take another position.* (Modifies *resigned.*)

Infinitive phrase. (See *Phrase.*)

Intensive pronoun. (See *Pronoun.*)

Interjection. One of the eight parts of speech; a word showing emotion; usually without grammatical connection.

> *Oh,* so that's it.   *Hooray!* We win.

Interrogative pronoun. (See *Pronoun.*)

Interrogative sentence. (See *Sentence.*)

Mode. (See *Mood.*)

Modifier. A word, phrase, or clause that qualifies, limits, or restricts the meaning of a word. Adjectives and adjective phrases and clauses modify nouns; adverbs and adverbial phrases and clauses modify verbs, adjectives, or other adverbs.

> Adjectives: an *old* man (an adjective), a man *of olden days* (an adjective phrase), a man *who was too old to attend* (an adjective clause).
> Adverb: Speak *clearly* (an adverb). Speak *in a clear voice* (an adverbial phrase). Call *when you are ready* (an adverbial clause).

> *Dangling.* (See *Dangling modifier.*)

Mood (Mode). The form of the verb that shows the manner of the action. There are three moods: *indicative, imperative,* and *subjunctive.*

The *indicative* states a fact or asks a question.

> The safe is open.   Is the safe open?

The *imperative* expresses a command or makes a request.

> Answer that bell.   Please transcribe this letter at once.

The *subjunctive* expresses a doubt, a condition contrary to fact, a wish, a concession.

> I wish I *were* going to the convention.
> If I *had* her ability, I would seize the opportunity.
> If we *should* be late, don't wait for us.

Nominative form. (See *Case.*)

Nonrestrictive clause, phrase. (See *Clause; Phrase.*)

Noun. One of the eight parts of speech; the name of a person, place, or thing; as *boy, mountain, box.*

Abstract. The name of a quality or of a general idea; as *courage, freedom.*

Collective. A noun that represents a group of persons, animals, or things; as *audience, company, flock.*

Common. The name of any one of a class of persons or things; as *child, house.*

Predicate. (See *Complement.*)

Proper. The name of a particular person, place, or thing; as *Henry, San Diego, Library of Congress.* Proper nouns are capitalized.

Number. The change in the form of a noun, pronoun, or verb in order to designate whether one person or thing (singular) or more than one (plural) is meant.

> Noun: girl, girls.   Pronoun: she, they.   Verb: He *sings,* they *sing.*

Object. The person or thing that receives the action of the verb. An object may be a word, a phrase, or a clause.

> I bought a *radio.* (Word.)
> She likes *to skate.* (Infinitive phrase.)
> I did not realize *that it was so late.* (Clause.)

Direct. The person or thing that is directly affected by the action of the verb. (The object in each of the sentences illustrating "Object" above is a *direct* object.)

Indirect. The person or thing indirectly affected by the action of the verb. The indirect object can usually be made the object of the preposition *to* or *for.*

> He gave (to) *me* the book.

Ordinal number. The form of a number used to show the order or succession in which names, objects, and so on are considered; as *first, second, twelfth.* Ordinals are adjectives.

Parallel structure. (See ¶ 609.)

Participial phrase. (See *Phrase.*)

Participle. A word that is both a verb and an adjective. There are three forms:

Present. Ends in *ing;* as *making, advertising.*

Past. Ends in *ed, d, t, en, n;* or may be an entirely different word from the present form; as *heated, heard, lost, seen, sung.* The past participle is the third principal part listed after each verb in the dictionary.

Perfect. Consists of *having* plus the past participle; as *having heated, having lost.*

Because a participle is an adjective, it modifies a noun.

> The *leaking* pipe caused trouble.
> *Saddened* by his failure, he lost interest in his work.
> *Having cleaned* her desk, she set to work.

Also, because a participle is a verb, it may take an object and be modified by an adverb.

> *Waving his hand,* he drove quickly away. (Object: *hand.*)
> *Speaking quickly,* she described the project in detail. (*Quickly* modifies *speaking.*)

Dangling. A participial phrase attached to no word in a sentence or to the wrong word. (See ¶ 610 *a.*)

Parts of speech. The eight classes into which words are grouped according to their uses in a sentence; namely, verb, noun, pronoun, adjective, adverb, conjunction, preposition, interjection.

Person. The characteristic of a word that indicates whether a person is speaking (*first person*), is spoken to (*second person*), or is spoken about (*third person*). Only personal pronouns and verbs change their forms to show person.

> First person: *I* prefer this book. *We* prefer this book.
> Second person: *You* prefer this book.
> Third person: *He prefers* this book. *They prefer* this book.

Personal pronoun. (See *Pronoun.*)

Phrase. A group of two or more words, not having a subject and a predicate, used as a single part of speech.

> *Gerund phrase.* A gerund plus its object and modifiers. It is used as a noun.
>
>> *Loading a truck beyond its capacity* weakens the motor.
>
> *Infinitive phrase.* An infinitive plus its subject, object, and modifiers; may be used as a noun, an adjective, or an adverb. An infinitive phrase that is attached to no word in a sentence or to the wrong word is called a *dangling* infinitive. (See ¶ 610 *b.*)
>
>> *To pass this subject* requires conscientious study. (As a noun.)
>> We still have more checking *to do.* (An adjective modifying *checking.*)
>> He resigned *to enlist.* (An adverb modifying *resigned.*)
>
> *Nonrestrictive phrase.* A phrase that can be omitted without changing the meaning of the sentence.
>
>> Emma, *wishing to improve her typewriting skill,* registered for a course.
>
> *Participial.* A participle (which see) and its object and modifiers; used as an adjective.
>
>> We heard the rain *splashing on the window.*
>> The old man, *confused by the bright lights,* stepped in the path of the car.
>> I can now relax, *having finished the assignment.*
>
> *Prepositional.* A preposition and its object; may be used as an adjective or an adverb.
>
>> The package *on the large desk* is ready to be sent. (Adjective.)
>> He has gone *to Cleveland.* (Adverb.)
>
> *Restrictive.* A phrase that limits, defines, or identifies something; cannot be omitted without changing the meaning of the main clause.
>
>> The chapter *explaining the law* appears at the end of the book.

Predicate. That part of a sentence that makes a statement about the subject.

> Sales *are increasing.*
>
> *Compound.* Two or more simple predicates joined usually by a conjunction.
>
>> The tide *rises and falls.*
>
> *Complete.* The simple predicate plus modifiers.
>
>> Our stock has been decreasing ever since January 1. (Simple predicate: *has been decreasing;* complete predicate: *has been decreasing ever since January 1.*)

Predicate adjective, complement, nominative, noun, object. (See *Complement.*)

Prefix. A letter, syllable, or word joined at the beginning of a word to change its meaning; as *a*float, *re*upholster, *under*nourished.

Preposition. One of the eight parts of speech; used to show the relation of a noun or pronoun to some other word in the sentence. The noun or pronoun following a preposition is in the objective case.

> Come with *me.*

Prepositional phrase. (See *Phrase.*)

Principal clause. (See *Clause.*)

Principal parts. The forms of a verb from which other forms are derived. They are *present infinitive, past tense,* and *past participle. Save, saved, saved; flee, fled, fled; choose, chose, chosen.*

Pronoun. One of the eight parts of speech; used in place of a noun; as *I, he, it.*

    Demonstrative. This, that, these, those.

    Indefinite. Each, either, any, anyone, someone, everyone, few, all, etc.

    Intensive. Myself, yourself, etc.

    Interrogative. Who, which, what, etc.

    Personal. I, you, he, she, it, we, they.

    Relative. Who, whose, whom, which, that, and compounds with *ever,* as *whoever.*

Proper noun. (See *Noun.*)

Possessive. (See *Case.*)

Question. Direct. A question in its original form, as put by one person to another.

    His next remark was, "What is your opinion?"

    Indirect. A statement of the substance of a question without the use of the exact words of the speaker.

    He asked me what my opinion was.

Quotation. Direct. A quotation of words exactly as spoken or written.

    She said, "I plan to take a ten o'clock train."

    Indirect. A statement of the substance of a quotation without using the exact words.

    He said that *he would take a ten o'clock train.*

Relative pronoun. (See *Pronoun.*)

Restrictive clause, phrase. (See *Clause; Phrase.*)

Sentence. A group of words representing a complete thought and containing a subject and a verb (predicate) with their modifiers.

    Simple. A sentence containing one main clause and no subordinate clauses.

    I have no unfiled correspondence.

    Compound. A sentence consisting of two or more independent clauses.

    Our Boston office has been closed, and our Dallas office has been moved.

    Complex. A sentence containing one independent clause and one or more dependent clauses.

    We will make an exception to our rule if conditions warrant.

    Declarative. A sentence that makes a statement.

    All the newspapers were sold.

    Interrogative. A sentence that asks a question.

    When does the conference begin?

    Exclamatory. A sentence that expresses strong feeling.

    What a tragic thing!

(Continued on page 161.)

Imperative. A sentence that expresses a command.

> Send a wire.

Subject. A word or a group of words naming the person, place, or thing about which something is said.

> *The book* was printed in Chicago.
> *That the work will be completed by the first of the month* is doubtful.

Compound. A subject consisting of two or more simple subjects joined by conjunctions.

> *Vermont and New Hampshire* are New England states.

Subjunctive mood. (See *Mood.*)
Subordinate clause. (See *Clause.*)
Subordinate conjunction. (See *Conjunction.*)
Suffix. A letter, syllable, or word added to the end of a word to modify its meaning; as friend*ly*, count*less*, receiver*ship*, lone*some*, thank*ful*.
Superlative degree. (See *Comparison.*)
Syllable. A single letter or a group of letters taken together to form one sound.
Tense. Changes in the form of a verb to show the time of the action. The three *simple,* or *primary,* tenses correspond to the three time divisions. They are *present* (I *think*), *past* (I *thought*), and *future* (I *shall think*).

The three *compound,* or *secondary,* tenses represent the degree of completeness of an action. They are *present perfect* (I *have thought*), *past perfect* (I *had thought*), and *future perfect* (I *shall have thought*).

Agreement. The harmonizing of the verb of the main clause and that of a subordinate clause. (See ¶ 581 for illustrative sentences.)

Verb. One of the eight parts of speech; a word used to express action or state of being. (See also *Mood.*)

> The bell *rang.* (Action.)   The book *is* thick. (State of being.)

Auxiliary. A verb that helps in the formation of the particular form of another verb. The chief auxiliaries are *be, can, could, do, have, may, might, must, ought, shall, should, will, would.*

Finite. A verb that is used as the predicate of a sentence (I *write*), as distinguished from infinitives, gerunds, and participles, which cannot be so used (I like *to write*).

Intransitive. A verb that does not require an object to complete its meaning.

> The clock *stopped* at ten-thirty.

Linking. A verb that has little meaning of its own but is used chiefly to connect a subject with a predicate adjective or noun. The various forms of *to be* are the most commonly used linking verbs. *Become, look, seem, turn* are often linking verbs.

> He *became* a mining engineer.

Principal parts. (See *Principal parts.*)

Transitive. A verb that requires an object to complete its meaning. (See also *Object.*)

> The clerk *filed* the letter.

Verbal. A word that partakes of the nature of a verb plus a noun or a verb plus an adjective. (See *Gerund, Infinitive, Participle.*)

Voice. The distinction in the form of a verb that indicates whether the subject acts or is acted upon.

> *Active.* A verb is in the active voice when its subject is the doer of the act.
>
> > He *slammed* the door.
>
> *Passive.* A verb is in the passive voice when its subject is acted upon.
>
> > The door *was slammed* by him.

Vowel. The letters *a, e, i, o,* and *u. W* (as in *awl*) and *y* (as in *cry*) are sometimes vowels. (See also *Consonant.*)

SECTION 19

Reference books for the stenographer and typist

Certain basic reference books are a "must" in almost any business office. In addition, each type of business has its own reference sources. The public library also is a good source of information.

DICTIONARIES AND WORD BOOKS

Webster's New International Dictionary of the English Language, Second Edition (the unabridged form). OR: *Webster's New Collegiate Dictionary* (the desk-sized form). Springfield, Mass., G. & C. Merriam Company.

Webster's New World Dictionary of the American Language, College Edition. Cleveland, The World Publishing Company.

Funk & Wagnalls' New Standard Dictionary of the English Language (the unabridged form). OR: *Funk & Wagnalls' New College Standard Dictionary* (the desk-sized form). New York, Funk & Wagnalls Company.

Webster's Dictionary of Synonyms.

Technical dictionaries according to type of business (as legal, medical, financial, chemical, aeronautical dictionaries).

Roget's Thesaurus. New Edition. New York, Thomas Y. Crowell Company. (How to find the *word* to fit an *idea.*)

Leslie: *20,000 Words,* Fourth Edition. New York, McGraw-Hill Book Company, Inc. (A pocket-sized book for checking spelling and word division.)

ENGLISH GRAMMARS AND STYLE BOOKS

Woolley, Scott, and Bracher: *College Handbook of Composition,* Sixth Edition. Boston, D. C. Heath and Company.

Stewart, Hutchinson, Lanham, and Zimmer: *Business English and Communication,* Second Edition. New York, McGraw-Hill Book Company, Inc. (A complete course in business English and business writing.)

Mayo: *Communications Handbook for Secretaries.* New York, McGraw-Hill Book Company, Inc. (A guide to effective speaking and writing.)

Perrin: *Writer's Guide and Index to English,* Third Edition. Chicago, Scott, Foresman and Company. (Part One treats general topics of English; Part Two, details of grammar arranged alphabetically.)

A Manual of Style, 11th Edition. Chicago, The University of Chicago Press. (A standard handbook for anyone who prepares typewritten copy for the printer.)

U.S. Government Printing Office: *Style Manual.* Washington 25, D.C., Superintendent of Documents. (Typographical rules followed in Government printing.)

BOOKS OF FACTS, BOOKS OF QUOTATIONS, WHO'S WHO'S, ETIQUETTE

The World Almanac and Book of Facts. New York, The New York World–Telegram and The Sun. (An annual; statistics on a wide variety of topics.)

Columbia Encyclopedia. New York, Columbia University Press. (One volume.)

Bartlett's Familiar Quotations, 13th Edition. Boston, Little, Brown and Company.

Post: *Etiquette.* New York, Funk & Wagnalls.

Amy Vanderbilt's Complete Book of Etiquette. Garden City, New York, Doubleday & Company.

Carney: *Etiquette in Business.* New York, McGraw-Hill Book Company, Inc.

The Cumulative Book Index. New York, The H. W. Wilson Company. (Lists of books published in the United States.)

Readers' Guide to Periodical Literature. New York, The H. W. Wilson Company. (For locating magazine articles.)

Who's Who in America. Chicago, A. N. Marquis Company. (Similar biographical dictionaries covering persons in various fields: *Who's Who in Commerce and Industry, Who's Who in Engineering, Who's Who in Railroading, Who's Who of American Women,* etc.)

DIRECTORIES

Local city directories; lists of city officials.

Local telephone directories (both alphabetic and classified).

The Social Register (for individual cities).

Business, industrial, and professional directories according to the type of business; for example, *Rand McNally Bankers Directory; The Martindale-Hubbell Law Directory; Kelly's Directory of Merchants, Manufacturers, and Shippers of the World; Ayer's Directory of Newspapers and Periodicals.*

Register of Directors and Executives. New York, Standard & Poor's Corp.

Congressional Directory. Washington 25, D.C., Government Printing Office.

GEOGRAPHIC AND TRAVEL INFORMATION

Webster's Geographical Dictionary. Springfield, Mass., G & C. Merriam Company.

The Postal Manual. Directory of Post Offices. Directory of International Mail. Washington 25, D.C., United States Printing Office.

Rand McNally Commercial Atlas and Marketing Guide. Chicago, Rand McNally & Company.

Road maps and travel information service of various automobile associations, oil companies, and map publishers.

Local city map.

Hotel Red Book. New York, American Hotel Association.

FINANCIAL AND SHIPPING INFORMATION

Dun & Bradstreet's Ratings and Reports. New York, Dun & Bradstreet. (By subscription only.)

Moody's Manuals. New York, Moody's Investors Service.

Bullinger's Postal and Shippers Guide. New York, Bullinger's Monitor Guide, Inc.

Exporters' Encyclopedia. New York, Thomas Ashwell & Company, Inc.

SECRETARIAL HANDBOOKS

Bredow: *Handbook for the Medical Secretary,* Fourth Edition. New York, McGraw-Hill Book Company, Inc.

Hutchinson: *Standard Handbook for Secretaries,* Seventh Edition. New York, McGraw-Hill Book Company, Inc. (Detailed information on a wide variety of secretarial procedures.)

Lee, Dickinson, and Brower: *Secretarial Practice for Colleges.* New York, McGraw-Hill Book Company, Inc.

Leslie and Coffin: *Handbook for the Legal Secretary.* New York, McGraw-Hill Book Company, Inc.

TYPEWRITING

Lloyd, Rowe, and Winger: *Gregg Typewriting for Colleges.* New York, McGraw-Hill Book Company, Inc.

Rowe and Lloyd: *Gregg Typing,* Second Edition. New York, McGraw-Hill Book Company, Inc.

Thompson: *Tabulation Typing.* New York, McGraw-Hill Book Company, Inc.

EXERCISES

Important Note: Unless this book is your own property, do not write answers to the exercises on the pages of this book. Instead, write answers in a notebook or on separate sheets of paper.

EXERCISE 1.   *Using the dictionary*

This exercise is designed to give you practice in using the dictionary, the most important reference book for the stenographer and the typist. The exercise is based on material in the Merriam *Webster's New Collegiate Dictionary.*

1. What marks are used to indicate: (*a*) syllables and (*b*) hyphenation of compound words?
2. Give the preferred spellings of *goodwill, jag,* and *coordinate.*
3. Give the preferred pronunciation of *predecessor, hospitable,* and *puerile.*
4. The change of accent from one syllable to another changes the meaning of many words. Give the changes in pronunciation and meaning for *content, perfect,* and *record.*
5. What parts of speech are *esoteric* and *after?*
6. Give the principal parts of the verbs *identify, spring,* and *lend.*
7. Give the possessive and objective cases of *he, it,* and *who.*
8. Give the plurals of *vacancy, basis, genius, hanger-on,* and *deer.*
9. Give the comparative and superlative forms of *lengthy, well,* and *ill.*
10. Which of the following are hyphenated, are one word, are two words: *payoff, enroute, manhour, inasmuchas?*
11. Classify *ruction, yegg,* and *bamboozle* as to "usage labels."
12. Give a synonym for *odium, sentiment,* and *churlish.*
13. What do the foreign phrases *ipso facto, vis-à-vis, bona fide* mean?
14. Give the meanings of the abbreviations *op. cit., cwt., CIA, B/L.*
15. How do you pronounce *Vallejo?* Is *Dayton* in *Ohio* or *Tennessee?*

EXERCISE 2. *The letter*

This exercise covers "Details That Mark the Acceptable Letter," ¶¶ 59–175. Each of the eight groups contains five items. In each group, two of the five items are correctly written. On your answer sheet list the numbers 1 to 8, and write the two letters that correspond to the two correctly written items in each numbered group. Be prepared to correct the errors in the other items.

Writing of dates

1. (*a*) Your order of November 10th has been shipped.
   (*b*) That advertisement was in the June, 1960, issue of the magazine.
   (*c*) By the first of March, we expect to have the survey completed.
   (*d*) This shipment should reach you not later than the 15 of May.
   (*e*) Our records indicate that we paid this bill on Dec. 28, '60.

Inside address, salutation, and Attention and Subject lines

2. (*a*) Mr. George R. McDonald
       Manager, Credit Department
       The City of Paris
       Sutter and Powell Streets
       Chicago 12, Illinois

       Dear Mr. McDonald:

   (*b*) Mr. R. J. Cahn
       Editor, The Northwest Review
       1275 McArthur Boulevard
       Seattle, 9 Washington

       Dear Mr. Cahn:

   (*c*) George R. Brackett
       4907 W. Higgins Ave.
       San Francisco 9, Calif.

       Dear Mr. Brackett:

   (*d*) Farley Cement Company
       2040 Chumasero Drive
       Great Falls, Montana

       Attention Purchasing Agent
       Gentlemen:

   (*e*) Mr. Albert R. Bryant Jr.
       Manager Hilton & Culver, Inc.
       One Sansome Street
       Saint Paul 9, Minnesota

       Dear Mr. Bryant:

3. (*a*) The Childrens Store
       Lincoln & Fifth
       Cleveland 4, Ohio

       Subject: Credit Slip No. 89
       Gentlemen:

   (*b*) Mr. Elmer R. Hill, Treasurer
       Crowley-McCarthy, Inc.
       794 West Clay Street
       Duluth 18, Minnesota

       Dear Mr. Hill:

   (*c*) Messrs Hurd & Hargis
       2010 Montgomery Street
       City

       Gentlemen:

(d) Mr. William R. Collingwood
Manager, Atlas Company, Ltd.
289 Union Street
St. Louis 14, Missouri

Dear Mr. Collingwood:

(e) Mrs. Donald C. Brady
892 Seventh Avenue, W.
Tuscon, Arizona

My Dear Mrs. Brady:

4. (a) Dr. Preston R. Paul
2890 9th Avenue
Glendale 10, California

Dear Dr. Paul:

(b) Preston Development Company
4900 West 29th Street
San Diego 18, California

Attention of Mr. Dowd

Dear Sir:

(c) Mr. Oscar T. Mead, Pres.
Los Angeles
California

Dear Mr. Mead:

(d) Mr. John T. McBride
Merchandising Director
Longstreet & Cullen
1020 Stockton Street
Nashville 9, Tennessee

Dear Mr. McBride:

Invoice No. 978

(e) Businessmen's Association
2057 O'Farrell Street
Syracuse 12, New York

Gentlemen:

Complimentary closing and signature

5. (a) If the firm name is part of the signature, type it four spaces below the complimentary closing.
(b) The dictator's name may be typed in full in the identification data.
(c) Allow at least six spaces for the handwritten signature.
(d) If the dictator's title is a long one, place it on the line below his typed signature.
(e) In the identification data, the transcriber's initials precede the dictator's.

6. (a) A "cc" notation indicates that a file carbon copy has been made.
(b) Only the first word of a complimentary closing is capitalized.
(c) If the dictator's name is typed in the signature line, it is not necessary to use his initials in the identification data.
(d) The identification data are typed below an enclosure notation.
(e) The title *Mr.* is sometimes typed in the signature line.

7. (a) If a letter is to be sent by registered mail, this information could be typed below the identification data.
(b) If a letter contains a postscript, place the identification data two spaces below the postscript.
(c) *Miss* should be placed in parentheses in an unmarried woman's typed signature.
(d) The notation "bcc Mr. Nee" indicates that a carbon copy is to be sent to Mr. Nee, but this notation appears only on the file carbon copy.
(e) The identification data are never written on the same line as the typed title of the signer.

Two-page letter, letter styles, and envelopes

8. (a) An Attention notice is placed in the lower left corner of an envelope.
(b) Never carry over fewer than six lines to the second page, and start the second page 2 inches from the top.
(c) In the full-blocked letter style, the date may be centered or it may end even with the right margin.
(d) In addressing a small business envelope, start the address on the eleventh line and five or six spaces to the right of center.
(e) The heading of the second page of a two-page letter includes the name of the addressee, the page number, and the date.

EXERCISE 3.   *Punctuation*

This exercise covers. "Punctuation Pointers," ¶¶ 183–348. Each of the fourteen groups in this exercise contains five sentences. Two of the five are correctly punctuated. On your answer sheet write the two letters that correspond to the correctly written sentences in each group. Be prepared to correct the errors in the other sentences.

1. (a) We can reduce automobile insurance rates, if we will reduce the number of automobile accidents.
   (b) We try to render a little extra service, such as checking your tires and washing your windows.
   (c) Our book, "Estimating Costs" was mailed yesterday, you should receive it by Friday.
   (d) Mr. R. L. Lewis, Jr., is a director of that company.
   (e) The report is not complete no matter what Mr. Brown says.

2. (a) Please send me copies of the following booklets; Your Budget, Your Food Dollar and Your Clothing Dollar.
   (b) The manager said that, "The volume of business done by the California office has doubled in the last year."
   (c) Two years ago, Mr. Johns, the meeting was held in Chicago; last year in New York.
   (d) We will take care of all the details—transportation, reservations, sight-seeing tours—without extra cost to you.
   (e) The advertisement read: "This means that as a stenographer you are first-line material for one of these jobs . . . for never before has the demand been so great for rapid stenographers. . . ."

3. (a) If you would like a confirming order for this shipment, please let us know and we shall be glad to send it.
   (b) In my letter to the Green Company, I said: "This will confirm our telegram which read, "Goods damaged as you did not mark 'Fragile' on the package."
   (c) I know that as soon as your customers learn what this cleaner can do, you will have a great many calls for it.
   (d) Mark the orders for the following companies "Rush": Lewis & Lee; The Roy Company, Inc.; Davis Company; and Lawton Stores, Ltd.
   (e) "We have the confirmation", he said, "on order No. 9874."

4. (a) Call the stenographic pool, ask for Miss Burns.
   (b) Letterheads, envelopes, carbon paper, etc. are in the top drawer.
   (c) The new rules, which, we regret to say, have affected the morale of our workers, will be discussed at our meeting on Monday.
   (d) The John L. Norris Company, Inc., has an excellent credit rating.
   (e) The copy of the report, and the agenda will be duplicated today, and will be mailed to you tomorrow.

5. (a) Dependability, courtesy, honesty, and punctuality, these were the personal traits he stressed.
   (b) Have you heard the proverb that a penny saved is a penny earned?
   (c) Your failure however, to send us a check for the shipment you received last month, causes us to wonder, Mr. Brown, if you were dissatisfied with the goods.
   (d) "California has tripled its population in recent years, and the 'Westward Movement' is still going on," he said.
   (e) This piece is as strong as, if not stronger, than that one.

6. (a) Your shipment of July 14 arrived yesterday; but, since the merchandise is defective, we are returning it to you today.
   (b) How can we increase our production? our sales? our profits?
   (c) The word strictly for example, is often misspelled.
   (d) The objections came from the clerks, and the typists, and the manager.
   (e) May we have a copy of your catalogue?

7. (a) Our estimate includes: the cost of lumber, insulating material, and paint, as well as the labor cost.
    (b) All donations, however small they may be, will be appreciated.
    (c) That store certainly follows the policy of *caveat emptor* (let the buyer beware.)
    (d) It is a pleasure to work here as you had told me it would be.
    (e) He was careful in his work, saw that it was completed on schedule, and co-operated with his co-workers.

8. (a) There is a firm in Portland, Oregon that manufactures a large, plastic container of that type.
    (b) What famous address starts "Four score and seven years ago, etc."?
    (c) Answers to our questionnaire have already been received from dealers in Reno, Nevada, Cincinnati, Ohio, Miami, Florida, and Dallas, Texas.
    (d) What are the various meanings of "capital"?
    (e) Please file this application with our personnel director, answering the questions to the best of your ability.

9. (a) Mr. Wilson asked him when he was leaving for New York?
    (b) The company had a good product to sell; furthermore the product was reasonably priced.
    (c) Mr. Beach himself made that mistake.
    (d) Mr. Ray is chairman—or is he vice-chairman?—of that committee.
    (e) The Lane Company in Pittsburgh, California sent the pamphlet entitled, "Check Your Equipment Now"!

10. (a) Was it Assemblymen Ladd (San Francisco) or Hall (Los Angeles)?
    (b) We hope the shipment arrived in time for your scheduled sale and we look forward to serving you again in the near future.
    (c) Records made of this material are not only durable, but also provide excellent reproductions.
    (d) If our idea appeals to you, and you want to give it a trial; our representative will be glad to call on you.
    (e) Use a 5-inch line (60 spaces, elite; 50 spaces, pica) for this memo.

11. (a) I heard him say: "You received our letter of May 2 didn't you?"
    (b) We hope that the adjustment made on your recent order was entirely satisfactory, and that our business relations will continue to be as pleasant in the future as they have been in the past.
    (c) All the businessmen in this community, who are honest and sincere in their dealings, have warned us against this company.
    (d) This is the important point: the conclusions have been arrived at after careful study and deliberation.
    (e) You should read the article entitled "Dressing for the Interview."

12. (a) John finished the report yesterday (Wednesday); a copy will be sent to you soon.
    (b) I think this policy would give me the protection I need, but at the same time would not cost too much.
    (c) The owner was so pleased with the work done by his employees, that he gave them a bonus.
    (d) I do know this, however, advertising in your paper brings results.
    (e) We have been able to do this because of the modern equipment that we recently purchased.

13. (a) We placed the first advertisement in the April 15, 1950 issue of your paper.
    (b) Please write us as soon as possible, as we must make a decision this week.
    (c) One branch office is located in San Francisco; another in Houston.
    (d) To sell your product effectively you must stand behind it.
    (e) You can be in Chicago tomorrow if you go by plane.

14. (a) I believe Butler & Son, Inc. has an office in San Francisco.
    (b) Please recheck the following invoices: Nos. 889, 918, 947, and 988.
    (c) The less engine friction, the less wear and tear on your car.
    (d) The office manager said, that the rule would not be rescinded.
    (e) I, myself, did not receive official notice until yesterday.

EXERCISE 4.   *Punctuation*

This exercise covers "Punctuation Pointers," ¶¶ 183–348. Punctuate the following sentences.

1. Obviously upset by the criticism he refused to discuss the matter
2. The manager who is an expert in this field will lead the discussion
3. Have you read the article entitled How to Increase Your Vocabulary
4. The apartment is now available however and if you are still interested I should like to hear from you
5. In the Chicago office for example this plan saved the company thousands no it was nearer tens of thousands of dollars a year
6. Please tell him that when the shipment arrives I shall call him
7. However as we have the same interests at stake we can co-operate fully
8. The foreman spoke as though he were angry
9. His intinerary provides for stopovers in Seattle Washington St Paul Minnesota and Chicago Illinois
10. Please get these items from the drawer marked Stationery 3 letterheads 3 sheets of yellow paper and a piece of carbon paper
11. The operating costs as he probably told you are too high
12. Failing to heed the red light the driver by his carelessness caused a serious accident
13. We recently opened an account in the name of George R Ralston who formerly had an account with your company
14. Our estimates are based on expert knowledge not on guesswork
15. The personality traits however that he was most interested in were initiative loyalty and dependability
16. I thought that as a civic leader you might be interested in this idea
17. We must insist that you take care of this matter by the first of next month otherwise we shall be forced to take legal action
18. If you would like to receive our booklet regularly please let us know and we shall be glad to send it
19. Other items Mr Dowd should be included if we decide to do this
20. His work is closely connected with but not dependent on Mr. Clark's research project
21. The roads were slippery hence we proceeded with caution
22. Mr Lee our president will arrive on Friday May 18 in your city
23. She asked Did you say the check was marked Insufficient Funds
24. Mr Lewis called in Roy and questioned him about the transaction
25. We are glad to say that in spite of the great increase in the cost of materials we find it possible to continue our present low prices without any sacrifice of quality
26. That machine is an electric this one a manual
27. The bill of lading was marked Weigh again at destination
28. The negotiators however will consider three important issues that is health insurance pensions and working conditions
29. Your estimates must be accurate no builder as you well know can afford to make the mistake of bidding too low
30. I think the proposed change will save time labor and material
31. With our system you will not have to ask yourself Have I allowed enough for overhead expenses
32. As I told you Mr Mann said that the shipment had arrived
33. Ours is a simple quick economical method of estimating costs
34. This little booklet Know Your Stocks contains many important facts and much useful information
35. The exasperated supervisor cried Fire him

EXERCISE 5.   *Capitalization*

This exercise covers "When to Capitalize," ¶¶ 349–384. Copy the following sentences, capitalizing all the words that should be capitalized.

1. there was a strong south wind blowing as we left england to cross the channel to france.
2. i know, senator, that he was questioned by the securities and exchange commission; and the commission exonerated him of all wrongdoing.
3. his father is running for mayor; supervisor-elect carr is his uncle.
4. mr. mayo, general manager of our company, was in the east last spring.
5. the secretary's minutes were approved as read.
6. he is an editor for the associated press; his son works for the government.
7. i should like a copy of "making your home attractive with glass."
8. this booklet summarizes the results of a survey made by the bureau of mines of the department of the interior.
9. murray's has closed that department in its main store but is enlarging it in its fifth avenue store.
10. at the meeting in atlantic city, he advocated federal as well as state aid for education.
11. orders came from every state in the union, as well as from canada.
12. our vice-president said that his minister called the law injurious.
13. winston churchill, former prime minister of great britain, is also a well-known author.
14. booker t. washington was a famous american negro educator.
15. for additional information, see chart 18, on page 138, in chapter VI.
16. we shall be glad to send our brochure, "coast-to-coast radio advertising."
17. canada is a member of the commonwealth.
18. it was mr. paul r. leslie, vice-president of standard products, inc., who spoke.
19. a congressman introduced a bill to raise the salaries of federal employees.
20. the navy refused to comment on the report issued by ex-governor ellis.

EXERCISE 6.   *Numbers*

This exercise covers "How to Write Numbers," ¶¶ 385–428. On your answer sheet rewrite any numbers that are incorrectly written in the following sentences.

1. Traveling by air, in four weeks' time, I visited dealers in 22 states.
2. The interest rate is six per cent, and your first payment of $60.00 is due in thirty days.
3. The Morris Company celebrated their 25th year in business last week, and I have been their representative for over 20 years.
4. This rug measures six by eight feet; the sale price is $98.00.
5. 600 people attended the meeting, which began at 8 o'clock.
6. As our terms are 3% thirty days, net sixty days, we are returning your sixty-day note for correction.
7. If you are over 45 years old, that company will not hire you.
8. The damage amounted to $3,789.40; insurance covered almost ½ the loss.
9. The container is 5 3/8 inches by 7½ inches and weighs 3 pounds 4 ounces.
10. In 1960, 204 clerks were employed by that company; and their salaries ranged from $200–450 a month.
11. The full report is on pages 618–645 in Chapter 5; and additional comments are on pages 688, 690, and 698.
12. Order sixteen number 387 model in size fourteen.
13. As you will see on page 1,303, discounts range from five to 20 per cent.
14. The report shows that in 1950 the company had five salesmen; in 1955, 25; in 1960, 70.
15. Your order for 6 15-foot strips, at 65¢ a foot, has been received.

16. Mr. George will take the plane that leaves at 7:35 p.m.
17. The fire was discovered at ten a.m.; damage was estimated at eighty-nine dollars.
18. Under this plan, we have reduced absences from work by 50% in the last 2 or 3 months.
19. The closing quotation was 97¼, down one and one-eighth points.
20. Data for 1955–1960 indicated a decrease of 8% in the last 5 years.
21. This office is open from 9 to 5, Monday through Friday.
22. Renew your subscription now by mailing us your check for $6.00 today.
23. The order for 20 chairs, 12 desks, and seven filing cabinets was sent today.
24. A full description of this model is given on page nine of our catalogue.
25. Our terms are 3 per cent 10 days, 1 per cent 30 days, net 60 days.

EXERCISE 7.   *Spelling—plurals*

This exercise covers "The Formation of Plurals," ¶¶ 468–491. On your answer sheet write the plural form of each of the following.

1. representative	7. trio	13. child	19. mi.
2. box	8. veto	14. editor in chief	20. f.
3. process	9. zero	15. runner-up	21. C. P. A.
4. chassis	10. chief	16. take-off	22. 1900
5. century	11. leaf	17. armful	23. wheat
6. valley	12. businessman	18. No.	24. economics

EXERCISE 8.   *Spelling—possessives*

This exercise covers "The Formation of Possessives," ¶¶ 492–509. Copy the following phrases and indicate the possessive forms wherever they are needed.

1. the individual citizen rights
2. Mr. Forbes remark
3. the taxpayer meeting
4. sale of men and boy coats
5. its dimensions
6. everyone education
7. somebody else notebook
8. Meier & Frank store
9. Bureau of Mines regulations
10. the payee and the payer notes
11. Mr. Lee, the manager, report
12. The theory is Mr. Hills.
13. three year experience
14. the auditor completing the work
15. Roy. R. Dowd, Sr., position
16. Can we depend on you attending?
17. the bridge towers
18. the Drs. diagnoses

EXERCISE 9.   *Compound words*

This exercise covers "One Word, Two Words, or Hyphenated?" ¶¶ 510–533. On your answer sheet rewrite any of the following sentences in which the hyphen is not correctly used. (Some of the sentences are correct.)

1. Sometime ago, some one suggested that we use TV advertising.
2. Your coworker signed the two-year-service contract.
3. The data on over-head costs are up-to-date in every respect.
4. The cheaply-constructed house suffered severe damage in the earthquake.
5. It was a waste of time to ask him; he side-stepped the issue.
6. Our low-priced-trial subscription maybe of interest to you.
7. I thought it was mailed at a postoffice in Oakland, but it was post marked "San Francisco."
8. We should like to receive payment of your long-over-due bill.
9. All non-essential information has been eliminated; sixty two errors were found; the enclosed résumé is self-explanatory.
10. We are almost grateful for your contribution and cooperation.

11. Re-mark these overtime slips so that the numbers can be easily read.
12. Vice-President Ryan and Senator-elect Lee will arrive sometime in mid-June.
13. That friendly-looking saleswoman said the smallest sized book was sold.
14. The figures on long-and-short-term loans came from the semi-annual report of a company well-known in that field.
15. The company is already to start its sales campaign some time next week.
16. Secretary Treasurer Dowd does not in anyway approve of the make-up of the report.
17. This list is designed for everyday use on your shopping tours.
18. The carefully-thought-out campaign has all ready produced results.
19. He claims that all the girls in that bookstore are under-paid.
20. I am here from eight to five everyday except Sunday.
21. Lynn left because she secured a better paying job with the Linton Company.
22. When I called Miss Leslie today, I found that she is working part-time.
23. The cost is low for any one of the plans outlined in the enclosed booklet.
24. Our shop is well-equipped to do excellent repair work or high-grade paint jobs.
25. They claim that they have the lowest-priced models on the market.

EXERCISE 10.   *Subject and verb, and verb problems*

This exercise covers "Subject and Verb" and "Verb Problems," ¶¶ 555–582. On your answer sheet write your choice of the verb that would be correct in each of the following sentences.

1. In the folder marked "In" (is, are) the letter and the invoice.
2. A block and tackle (is, are) needed to move that machine.
3. A majority of the stockholders (want, wants) a change of management, but the Board (is, are) opposed to this action.
4. Mary (lie, lay) awake for hours last night worrying about that error.
5. This letter, along with those invoices, (has, have) to be retyped; not one of the invoices (are, is) correct.
6. We (shall, will) be glad to talk with your agent.
7. As I promised you yesterday, I (shall, will) (take, bring) the report to Mr. Perry today.
8. Our stock of curtains and draperies (are, is) described on page 9.
9. I think 5 gallons (is, are) enough, but he (don't, doesn't) agree with me.
10. The number of orders for that item (have, has) increased greatly; a number of them (have, has) come from Canada.
11. On Mr. Swan's desk (is, are) the reports you want, and the sales memoranda (are, is) in that file drawer.
12. (May, Can) I borrow the book that is (laying, lying) on your desk?
13. Many a store and factory (are, is) installing this equipment.
14. We (shall, will) not do her work for her!
15. The Griffin Corporation (has, have) expanded their services, and they will have their representative call next week.
16. If Robert (was, were) here, he could do that job.
17. I (shall, will) be glad to send you samples of these materials.
18. He is one of the salesmen who (was, were) given a bonus and the only one of the salesmen who (was, were) promoted.
19. Neither the manager nor the salesmen (is, are) enthusiastic about this change.
20. To be successful, you must (sit, set) a goal toward which to work; and you cannot "(sit, set) down" on the job if you want to achieve that goal.
21. Don't worry about it, for I (shall, will) be more careful next time.
22. To Mrs. Burke (have, has) fallen the responsibilities of this project.
23. I (should, would) like to have a copy of your booklet.

24. Neither the clerks nor Mrs. Jacks (like, likes) the new arrangement.
25. None of the lists (have, has) been revised, and no one in this office (want, wants) the job.
26. Is it Kelly's or Frederick's that (stock, stocks) that model?
27. Among the many companies who submitted bids for this project (was, were) Davis & Mercer, Inc.
28. I am determined she (shall, will) not be my assistant.
29. I wish I (was, were) able to take dictation at a faster rate.
30. The Board of Supervisors (has, have) approved that motion; the Board, however, (was, were) divided on the salary proposals.
31. They (would, should) like to have you call.
32. Attached to this letter (are, is) two copies of the original agreement.
33. There (is, are) a memorandum on that transaction in the file.
34. We (shall, will) pay our overdue account by the 10th of the month.
35. She is one of the stenographers who always (follows, follow) directions.

EXERCISE 11.   *Pronouns*

This exercise covers "Pronouns," ¶¶ 583–594. On your answer sheet write your choice of the pronoun that would be correct in each of the following sentences.

1. That was (she, her) (who, whom) you met in the elevator this morning.
2. Have you decided (who, whom) is to supervise this job, Dan or (me, I)?
3. (Its, It's) (us, we) who did that work, not (she, her).
4. (Whomever, Whoever) made the error is the one (who, whom) should be fired.
5. Mr. Alden, (who, whom) you know, and (I, me) are going east.
6. If you see Mr. Lester or Mr. Davis, call (their, his) attention to this oversight.
7. Can you take dictation as rapidly as (she, her)?
8. It could have been (they, them) (who, whom) gave us that information.
9. He asked Miss Davies and (I, me) to type the report.
10. He is the man (that, who) wrote the report (that, which) was rejected.
11. She is the stenographer (who, whom) you want.
12. They took the callers to be (we, us).
13. If I were (her, she), I would accept the position.
14. Just between you and (I, me), everyone was co-operative except Miss Fox and (her, she).
15. Mrs. Kane and (we, us) girls are going to buy the wedding gift.
16. We have questioned all the people (who, whom) we have reason to believe were involved in the transaction.
17. (Who, Whom) do you think we should send on this trip?
18. What made you think it was (I, me)?
19. (Who, Whom) would like to ride with Mr. Dowd and (me, I)?
20. The extra typists, Miss Dorn and (she, her), will help you.
21. He wanted to know (who, whom) the salesman was.
22. The manager was thought to be (him, he).
23. That job will be done by the new typists, Muriel and (she, her).
24. Mr. Turner told Nancy and (I, me) to prepare a new work schedule.
25. He is the man (who, whom), they say, will get the promotion.
26. Anyone (who, whom) you recommend will be a well-trained person.
27. The new typist was thought to be (I, me).
28. It is (we, us) who must re-examine our sales policy.
29. Everyone except (she, her) was pleased about his appointment.
30. You can delegate that authority to (whomever, whoever) you wish.

EXERCISE 12. *Adjectives, adverbs, and prepositions*

This exercise covers "Adjectives and Adverbs" and "Prepositions," ¶¶ 595–608. On your answer sheet write your choice of the word that would be correct in each of the following sentences.

1. It will (take only, only take) two days more to finish this job.
2. I (remember, remember of) your telling me that their sale (of, on) coats was (sure, surely) a good one.
3. The mechanism sounds (queer, queerly) to me.
4. Which piece of cardboard is the (most, most nearly) square?
5. Miss Nee transcribes very (rapid, rapidly), and she is more efficient than (any, any other) girl in the office.
6. Of the two letter styles, this is the (less, least) attractive.
7. Where did Robert (go to, go)?
8. You will have to step (upon, up on) the desk to reach that shade.
9. We are (very, very much) displeased with the terms of this contract.
10. You will work (easier, more easily) if your desk is well organized.
11. This automobile (sure, surely) runs (smooth, smoothly).
12. Which of the two dresses would be the (most, more) practical?
13. She (hadn't, had) scarcely finished the job when Mr. Mell called.
14. I am (real, really) sorry I was rude, but I do not feel (well, good).
15. You did (good, well) in the speech test, but you should make an effort to speak more (distinct, distinctly).
16. He dictates (quite, rather) rapidly, and he is always (real, very) pleasant.
17. As he told me, they (sell only, only sell) to the local jobbers.
18. This is a (real, really) difficult situation.
19. Ellen is (sure, surely) an accurate typist.
20. I (can't, can) hardly believe that he told her she did very (good, well) for an inexperienced worker.
21. It is a pleasure to work in a (real, really) quiet office again.
22. He should (pay, pay up) his past-due account at once.
23. She feels (bad, badly) about her rudeness.
24. This offer is (only good, good only) until June 30.
25. Mr. Philips is (sure, surely) qualified to give you expert advice.
26. His was the (most, most nearly) unique design submitted in the contest.
27. Which is the (cheaper, cheapest) of these three chairs?
28. She writes (bad, badly) with her injured hand.
29. A couple (men, of men) called while you were out.
30. Our list of subscribers now (almost numbers, numbers almost) 300,000.

EXERCISE 13. *Words often confused*

This exercise covers "Words Often Confused," ¶ 611. On your answer sheet write your choice of the words that would be correct in each of the following sentences.

1. This advertising has had an (adverse, averse) (affect, effect) on our present business, and it may (affect, effect) our future business.
2. Our (advice, advise) is to (advice, advise) you to (accept, except) a one-year (guarantee, guaranty) on this machine.
3. You and your (assistance, assistants) will find your (complementary, complimentary) copy of our handbook very helpful, we are sure.
4. The proposed (cite, site) of the plant has (access, excess) to the sea.

5. On what (basis, bases) do you (choose, chose) to (precede, proceed) in (affecting, effecting) the desired outcome in this (instance, instants)?

6. He is an (eminent, imminent) man in this field, and his (advice, advise) will be of (practical, practicable) value in this survey.

7. The (council, counsel, consul) voted to rescind the ruling and (cited, sighted) (precedence, precedents) supporting the action.

8. We are (confidant, confident) that there is more call for your product now (than, then) there was (than, then).

9. Use this (device, devise) to produce the desired (affect, effect).

10. His (adherence, adherents) to high (principals, principles) has been evident throughout his career as a (legislator, legislature).

11. How much (further, farther) away is the proposed (cite, site)?

12. Action in this (instance, instants) (preceded, proceeded) consultations.

13. Operating solely in Oregon, the company will (lose, loose) (its, it's) license if it does not (ascent, assent) to the (prescribed, proscribed) rules set forth in the (statue, statute) governing (intrastate, interstate) transportation.

14. All (perspective, prospective) workers should apply to our (personal, personnel) director.

15. If you will return the defective desk, you will be (aloud, allowed) full credit (therefor, therefore).

16. The samples of (stationary, stationery) are (quiet, quite) unacceptable.

17. Before we (precede, proceed) with our plans for the campaign, what is the (principle, principal) problem involved?

18. My (advice, advise) is to change the (ad, add) at once.

19. He (disproved, disapproved) of the (ordnance, ordinance) on all-night parking and has promised to (canvass, canvas) the (residence, residents) of the neighborhood.

20. Thank you for the (complementary, complimentary) copy of the (currant, current) issue of your magazine.

21. The company needs additional (capital, capitol) now.

22. He (choose, chose) a reliable contractor and specified high-grade materials.

23. He was recently (indicted, indited) for the embezzlement of company funds.

24. The lease specifies that the (lesser, lessor) is liable for such repairs.

25. Careful planning (preceded, proceeded) the actual launching of the campaign.

EXERCISE 14. *Words and phrases often misused*

This exercise covers "Words and Phrases Often Misused," ¶ 612. It also will be necessary to refer to ¶¶ 582, 603, and 608. On your answer sheet write your choice of the word or phrase that would be correct in each of the following sentences.

1. (All, All of) us (have got, have) electric typewriters now.

2. Try (and, to) call him; he may (of, have) forgotten the appointment.

3. After having (a, an) opportunity of looking at her work, can you honestly say you think she types (good, well)?

4. The reason you are not succeeding as a stenographer is (because, that) you do not have an adequate vocabulary.

5. The notebook that was (laying, lying) there yesterday is the kind (of, of a) notebook I always use.

6. He must (of, have) forgotten the appointment, for I know he is (very, very much) interested in Mr. Allen's proposal.

7. She made friends (due to, because of) her pleasing personality.

8. She is (quite, very) efficient, but Rae is more pleasant than (she, her).

9. (Both, Both of) the samples of bond paper are satisfactory, but this is (awfully, very) poor carbon paper.

10. I shall (take, bring) the machine to Mr. Perry, but I doubt (if, whether) he will be able to (fix, repair) it.

11. Miss Jensen was (somewhat, kind of) disappointed with the results of the survey; you (couldn't, could) hardly expect her to be pleased.

12. I (remember, remember of) his saying he might (of, have) mislaid it.

13. It looks (as if, like) this ribbon is worn out.

14. I do not know (as, that) I agree with you, but (all, all of) us should co-operate with (each other, one another) at this time.

15. Try (and, to) do this job (like, as) you were told to do it!

16. These containers are different (than, from) the sample you sent me.

17. (That there, That) style is not (so, as) attractive (so, as) this one.

18. The two men are (both alike, alike) in some respects, but Mr. Hall is (sort of, rather) shy.

19. I could (have, of) finished this work tonight if that memorandum had not been (accidently, accidentally) destroyed.

20. The prices are higher now (then, than) they were (then, than).

21. Come in (to, and) see me (at about, about) two o'clock.

22. The paper was (laying, lying) on the floor (in back of, behind) her desk.

23. (Because of, Due to) high winds, the plane did not leave on time.

24. You (want to, should) be more punctual.

25. There are a few of (those, that) kind (inside of, inside) that cabinet.

26. Each writer (claims, asserts) he is an expert in this field.

27. He does not know yet (if, whether) he will get the job.

28. It will be (alright, all right) to cross it (off, off of) the list.

29. This job is (most, almost) completed, and I am (sure, surely) glad.

30. His failure was (due to, because of) unfortunate or poor investments.

31. He was neither efficient (nor, or) pleasant.

32. Is there any doubt (whether, that) the transaction was illegal?

33. Mr. Lahr's appointment was (due to, because of) his technical knowledge.

34. The company is not (so dependable, as dependable) as we thought.

35. Come in (and, to) see our stoves before you buy one (anywhere, anywheres) else.

INDEX

Numbers refer to *paragraph* numbers of the text except for a few cases in which *page* precedes the numbers.